CW01432456

ALL IN

MARY EARPS

ALL IN

**FOOTBALL, LIFE AND LEARNING
TO BE UNAPOLOGETICALLY ME**

LEAP

First published in the UK in 2025 by LEAP
An imprint of Bonnier Books UK
5th Floor, HYLO, 105 Bunhill Row,
London, EC1Y 8LZ

The right of Mary Earps to be identified as Author of this work
has been asserted by her in accordance with the Copyright, Designs and
Patents Act, 1988.

A CIP catalogue record for this book is available from the British Library.

Hardback ISBN: 9781806171279

Also available as an ebook and an audiobook

1 3 5 7 9 10 8 6 4 2

Design and Typeset by Envy Design Ltd
Printed and bound by CPI (UK) Ltd, Croydon CR0 4YY

MIX
Paper | Supporting
responsible forestry
FSC
www.fsc.org   FSC® C013604

The authorised representative in the EEA is Bonnier Books UK (Ireland) Limited.
Registered office address:
Block B, The Crescent Building
Northwood, Santry
Dublin 9, D09 C6X8
Ireland
compliance@bonnierbooks.ie

www.bonnierbooks.co.uk

ACCOLADES

Sports Honours and Awards

FIFA FIFPRO Women's World 11, 2023 & 2024

Women's FA Cup, Manchester United, 2023-24

EA Sports FC Team of the Year, 2023

Ballon d'Or Féminin, 5th ranking & highest ever for a goalkeeper, 2023

IFFHS Women's World Best Goalkeeper, 2023

IFFHS Women's World Team of the Year, 2023

FIFA Women's World Cup Golden Glove, 2023

Women's Finalissima, England, 2023

Arnold Clark Cup, England, 2023

FIFA Women's World Cup runner-up, England, 2023

Women's Super League Golden Glove, 2023

Women's FA Cup runner-up, Manchester United, 2022-23

The Best FIFA Women's Goalkeeper, 2022 & 2023

PFA WSL Team of the Year, 2022-23

England Women's Player of the Year, 2022-23

Arnold Clark Cup, England, 2022

UEFA Women's Euros, England, 2022

UEFA Women's Championship Team of the Tournament, 2022

Freedom of the City of London, 2022

SheBelieves Cup, England, 2019

Frauen-Bundesliga, VfL Wolfsburg, 2018

DFB-Pokal, VfL Wolfsburg, 2018

PFA WSL Team of the Year, 2016-17

World University Games, Gold, Loughborough, 2013

Premier League Cup runner-up, Nottingham Forest, 2010-11

Cultural Honours and Awards

Guinness World Records, most wins The Best FIFA Women's Goalkeeper, 2025

MBE, 2024

First female professional football player honoured with a wax figure in Madame Tussauds, London, 2024

World Football Summit Gamechanger Award by GREAT 2024

Women's Football Awards, World Cup Hero, 2023

BBC Sports Personality of the Year, 2023

BBC Women's Footballer of the Year, 2023

Sunday Times Sportswoman of the Year, 2023

Northwest Football Awards, Bill Seymour Impact Award, 2023

Vogue Forces for Change Honouree, 2023

GQ Men of the Year Honouree, 2023

Honorary doctorate, Loughborough University, 2023

For my loved ones and anyone who has ever been in my corner: you have given me the strength to be unapologetically myself. And for all those who are still finding the strength to be themselves.

CONTENTS

PREFACE

There is a sweet spot that enables you to decide where you go next in life and the height of success that you scale.

I have been fascinated by it since I was young; hungry for insights into how the best became the best, compelled by stories of people who understood their bodies and minds with enough intricacy to push them beyond their apparent limits, to reach through the pain and get to that sweet spot in order to set something free: a new opportunity, their next achievement, happiness.

I learned that it comes from knowing yourself.

Like anyone, it took me time to work out who I was – as a person, as an athlete, as a goalkeeper.

But of course the signs were there all along: a loud, unafraid child; a hard-working and competitive teenager; a committed and ambitious young player; then a person determined to live life and seize every one of the chances I earned for myself with conviction.

Each time I had the opportunity to push forwards or stand still and stay comfortable I would ask, what's the worst that could happen? I could fail (not that I liked to fail or to stay comfortable). At least I could look myself in the mirror afterwards and say that I tried.

And the best that can happen? You can change your life. You can max out on who you're meant to be. You can reach the things that you dreamed of for yourself – and those that you never even dared to imagine.

The path to get to that point was un-straightforward. It was hard, and at times it was ugly. It tested me frequently and, at its most emotionally challenging, I almost lost myself along the way.

There were dear ones who supported me. Others, though, would have let me fade away. But I could not accept that for myself. My mentality would not allow it. I had more to do, more to achieve, more to learn.

And so, to this book. To my own lessons.

I didn't want to tell my story until I could tell all of it, unapologetically. Well, all of it this far because there is plenty more of me to come.

I would never give a half-hearted account of my life because that's not how I was made, and it's not ever how I've been able to do things. I would rather not do something than be unable to do it fully.

When I commit to something, I do it with my whole heart. I go all in.

So, that is what I've done in these pages. I've given all of myself, all of my journey and all that I have learned along the way.

I have, as you will read, long trusted in gut feelings and now, in the months after retiring from England's Lionesses, it feels like the right time to do that, to take stock of the magnitude of everything that's happened in the past few years of my life, its impact and how I got there and to share more of me for the first time.

I have had to learn to be open and vulnerable. I found entering the spotlight daunting but it is because of all those who were there supporting me that I came to realise the extent of what I could do with it, and that my journey could act as a guide for others.

In writing, therefore, my intention has been to do so with purpose and in appreciation of the love and support that I have felt from so many out there – you've been a big part of my life and helped to change it. In return, I hope I can inspire and help you to make changes you want to make in yours, however big or small those may be.

As I assembled my stories and all that I have learned and can pay forwards from them, it sharpened in my mind how much high-performance sport, and being a woman in that arena, has to teach us.

For those who love the beautiful game in the all-encompassing way that I do, I know you will read with interest my experiences within it, right from my very first penalty save to playing the Euros and World Cup and being named best in the world. But for those who've never picked up a football or saved a goal or perhaps even watched a match, I think you will find takeaways from this life I've lived in sport. It might be from the difficulties and then acceptance that I found in not fitting in – and the position I chose, in goal, that reinforced that by literally marking me out in a box – or from being part of the teams that I've had and still have the honour to play with; from the principles that guided me and never left me through each stage of life and the game; through the resilience to find what worked for me and not change it on the way to or at the top; or from the battles, personal and professional, that I fought to advocate for change.

Once I earned the right to a platform where my voice could be heard, my greatest ambition has been to leave goalkeeping and the game in a better place for those who follow, and then the players that follow them, for generations of young keepers and of girls and women who pull on the shirt or wonder if they can.

I hope that as you read some of what is in these pages it helps you to discover a better place or change your own environment too.

Being a great goalkeeper requires many things, but there are three above all else: preparation, intuition and the conviction to go all in when your moment comes. I hope my story can serve as a playbook for harnessing those powerful forces in your life too.

PROLOGUE

The noise inside Sydney's Olympic stadium was loud – thunderously loud – but I couldn't hear the whistles or screams, the feverish cheers or the goading boos carrying through the stands. I didn't notice the feel of the cool August air on my skin. I didn't feel dread at the pressure of facing a penalty while England were 1-0 down in a World Cup final.

In fact, I loved the pressure. My best performances arrived under pressure.

It was the 68th minute of the biggest match of my life, and our rivals, Spain, had been awarded a penalty.

This wasn't a moment to be in my feelings. I couldn't stop to reflect on how it felt to stand in goal, on football's grandest stage. It wasn't the time to pause and think about the journey that had led me there, to that Sunday night in the summer of 2023. I could do that afterwards.

This was only about readiness, about years of preparation

and executing it now, in the moment that mattered most. I had worked out of my skin my entire life to be ready to stand in that net as Jenni Hermoso walked up to the penalty spot to take her shot.

Earlier that afternoon, the same crowds of England fans who now filled the stands had gathered outside our hotel, overlooking Sydney's iconic harbour. As we boarded the team bus to the final, I'd taken out my headphones for a few seconds, smiling and pausing just to remember what it sounded like as I let their excitement reverberate through me, soaking in the buzz.

On our stadium visit the day before I had stopped too, to smell the grass that we were about to play on. If this was the one and only World Cup final I played then I didn't want to miss a single detail nor waste a second, because the next moment was never guaranteed, in any life, certainly not football. I knew how easily it could all be taken away from me. After all, it had been, not long ago.

As we walked out into that clear night, I allowed myself to feel my teammates' presence beside me, as we stood, arms interlaced around one another's shoulders, the occasion passing between us like an energetic charge as we sang the words of the national anthem. No honour could touch that. Representing England was my favourite thing ever.

From kick-off, Spain dominated with their possession, creating chances while we chased shadows. To be trailing so early was gutting. We hadn't lost hope, though. It would be hard, but they were beatable, I was sure of it.

I worked to rally and motivate the girls, stretching my body, mind and voice, relying on every extra repetition I'd put in after training since the day I'd first touched a ball. The consistency now lived intuitively within me.

I didn't see what happened before the whistle blew in the 68th minute, the backs of tangled bodies were turned towards me, England's blue shirts and Spain's red colliding to block my view of the ball on the other side.

Whatever it was, it had been called into review and I saw the referee's body language, her mouth and her hand, indicating a handball before I heard the sound of her voice accompany it over the tannoy.

THE PENALTY

I tried to assess which one of their players was taking it. Caldentey or Hermoso? I didn't have a preference, but it changed where I was going to dive.

Hermoso walked up to the ball. I felt good about it, like I could save anything that came towards me.

I put my hands on my knees, studied her body shape, trying to read the cues, and looked her dead in the eyes.

I'd done my research. I knew every penalty she'd taken for club and country, so I knew she was a left-footer, that she liked a slow run-up and would look at me for a little bit before putting it the opposite way.

I'd developed an entirely new penalty technique for exactly that type of player. Guessing a side and diving at the right height wasn't enough here; it was about timing, weight distribution and patience. And it was sensationally difficult.

The whistle blew. Like a movie racing along at triple speed, I had seconds to implement in my mind what I would do next with my body. Did she know that I knew? Would she go to my left as she always did or was she going to flip it the other way?

Timing was everything. I moved my right foot so it looked like I was going to dive to my right, then pushed to my left to make her believe I was going the other way. She had to see the push at exactly the right instant, when she'd already committed to where she was kicking the ball. I went left. I grabbed it with both hands and rolled my body over it, bringing the ball tight into my chest, like I would never let it go, then rising straight back up again in one single fluid motion.

THE SAVE

Saving a penalty is one thing, keeping hold of it is another. I loved the feel of saving and holding a football in my hands.

'Fucking, yes!' I screamed.

I'm happy.

I've saved a penalty in a World Cup final. I could see the elation. I could see the momentum change in the shifts in the bodies, the contorting faces, the fists punching the air, in my teammates and in the fans.

All I knew was that there was no time or energy for anything but the game. We had 20 minutes left and we needed a goal. We had fire and resilience in spades. *I* had fire and resilience in spades.

We played on.

Little did I know that as the save played out on TV and made its way around the globe there was another shift taking place. A shift in my own life.

In my hotel room the next morning I woke to a world that I didn't recognise, but where millions recognised me. Where goalkeeping, the job that I loved, and my goalkeeping, mattered.

It was something I had dreamed of for as long as I could remember.

For the longest time, no one saw it. Now, though, they talked about the save – my mentality, the passion, my composure – in superlatives.

But the story of the person, who I was as Mary the goalkeeper, was not about that one save – it couldn't be. It wasn't an isolated moment. It was the outcome of the same work I had always done in my relentless pursuit to become the world's number one. I'd fought tooth and nail to get there, to be in goal that day.

The story of the save was about everything that came before.

PART ONE

PREPARATION

ONE

EVERYTHING TO COMPLETION

This isn't my first book. As a girl, I wrote the same story over and over again. I even drew the same picture on the front cover of my stapled, folded-over pages each time.

Mary Earps was playing in a World Cup final; she was in goal for England and her save could win them the trophy.

At ten years old I was a little too tall for the plastic chair I sat on at the kids' table in the bay window of our home, looking out over the hedges and driveway that fed into the Nottingham street I grew up on.

I was just little enough, though, to dream big.

Every school holiday, I'd gather the white sheets of A4 from my parents' printer, set out my pencils and crayons and draw the frame of a goal on the first piece. I'd drag my pencil across the page, sketching a crossbar then posts, two triangles receding backwards into the whiteness and a line connecting them at the bottom. Then I'd cross-hatch the space in-between to complete a net that I always intended to be three-dimensional but never was.

Heading into the net was a football with *whoosh* lines bursting off the irregular circle and propelling it in like a comet. I imagined myself in there, then I imagined the words of my story.

In my family, we called that room where I sat writing out my World Cup dreams the red room, on account of the terracotta carpet that Mum and Dad put down soon after they'd moved in. It had a TV, stacks of toys, a piano where I used to practise, and later a miniature pool table and games console where my brother Joel, my little sister Annabelle and I would spend the rare moments of our childhood that weren't taken up with playing outside, performing in a dance show, or on a pitch or at the leisure centre doing every activity going.

It's probably just as well that I was always kept occupied because Mum says I never sat still. She claims I was fiercely independent from the get-go, even as a baby.

I'd arrived a day earlier than my due date, on 7th March, 1993, after putting her through a 19-hour labour, which Dad, a Liverpudlian and Liverpool fan who'd once trialled there as a boy, notably remembers for taking place during a six-goal FA Cup thriller between Manchester City and Spurs.

Mum says that at eight pounds and eight ounces I was the most difficult of her three births. Joel was born a year and eight months after me, and Annabelle was six years younger. Once I'd arrived, she would push me around in my buggy and people would comment on my smile and happy disposition. And my chubby wrists.

I was up and walking at 11 months, and my curious nature coupled with my inability to sit still meant accidents were frequent. I'd single-mindedly climb the furniture, scrambling over the ottoman my parents put in front of the TV and video player in the red room to keep me from fiddling with the controls, or I'd launch myself off a sofa while they sat just two feet away, then I'd carry on undeterred as I hit my head on the corner of the TV cabinet.

If I fell over or hurt myself, I didn't cry. Instead, I'd dust myself down and carry on running.

It was far more usual for me to be found laughing. In fact, the only family memory we have of me crying in public was during the nursery Christmas play, when at four years of age I had been handed the odd task of getting stuck in a prop cardboard chimney. I wasn't playing Santa himself, but somehow that was what was expected of me. When my big moment arrived, I distinctly remember the excitement of taking my turn on stage being replaced by a feeling of *I don't want to do this*.

So, I didn't.

I stood to the side, looked out at the parents and teachers and refused to move, as my face crumbled with embarrassment. A staff member eventually managed to coax me to give an unenthusiastic performance, and right then I knew what it felt like to have to do something someone else demanded of me and what it felt like to do what *I* wanted to do.

I knew what I liked as a child, and that was anything messy. I liked painting using my hands and feet, or baking in our kitchen or at friends' houses. Wherever I was I'd gleefully distribute flour everywhere as I got to work. I didn't see danger, which is why I freely flung myself off things. When we went to the park I was all over the play equipment, and as soon as I was big enough – or probably not quite – I was straight to the monkey bars, determined to make it across to the end.

Unlike a lot of the other girls my age, I didn't play with dolls, I wasn't into the colour pink and was certainly not into dresses or girly pursuits like letting Mum do my hair, which was disappointing to her given she had her own hairdressing business. She'd let me tug on hers instead, firmly knotting it up in a hairbrush as she sat on the sofa in the room we called the yellow room, with its golden sunny-colour carpet that they'd inherited from the previous owners and a TV that Mum and Dad would sit and watch in the evening.

Ours was a lovely detached house on a quiet street with a garden big enough for goalposts and a trampoline. I do not remember wanting for things, and I understood young, through the principles my parents instilled in us and the people that I met, how fortunate we were and how rare that was in the world.

Dad had a high-up director-level job in a big corporate dairy business, running five different sites, when they'd bought the house, and they'd invested well in doing so but we weren't flush: we had smart-price cereal for breakfast and Mum would pay with coupons and buy-one-get-one-free vouchers when we went out for family dinners, much to Dad's mortification.

His job meant he'd be up and out early and back late, sometimes travelling for a couple of nights at a time, leaving Mum to manage us and her part-time mobile hairdressing.

On work days, she would often get us up and drive us over to Grandma's (my mum's mum, who lived half an hour away) still in our onesies or pyjamas in order to miss the traffic. We'd all have breakfast together and Mum would set off to start her appointments so she could finish in time to pick us up at the end of the day. Grandma would get us dressed and drop us at nursery or, later on, school.

Once Annabelle was born, Grandma would sometimes come and stay over at ours the night before to do the morning run from there, then look after Annabelle at home. And at weekends or in the school holidays I loved going over to hers for a sleepover. She'd make me a mini Sunday dinner, even when it wasn't a Sunday, and let me eat it in front of the TV (eating in front of the TV wasn't allowed at home) and watch my favourite cartoon, *Arthur*, about a bespectacled aardvark who wasn't afraid of a challenge.

I felt my childhood was idyllic, a safe household where Mum and Dad would find a way to do and fund whatever we wanted to do, getting us wherever we needed to be, so long as they could see we were gaining happiness; or better still, learning from it too.

But it was a strict household where rules were in plentiful supply. Shoes came off inside; there was no playing in our socks outside; and Sunday dinner was eaten as a family every week at 4pm. There were rules about how to conduct ourselves and rules about how to treat others; everything was values-led, designed to make us into good, principled people.

Only since I've grown up have I come to think that there were maybe too many rules, tiny measures that meant that although home was a happy and secure place to play and thrive as a child it was probably run a little bit by fear. While Mum was the gentler parent – even though having to endlessly wash our socks from playing outside in them drove her understandably mad – Dad was more harsh with his words.

I sought his approval all the time, through my good behaviour and, once I started my many sports and hobbies, my will to improve and achieve. As the eldest of the three kids, both my parents expected me to set an example; my behaviour needed to be impeccable because, if I slipped, the others would copy me. Dad said I was to take it as a compliment that they demanded higher standards from me because it meant I was capable of meeting them. It frustrated me enormously, but that's just how it was and I toed the line. Disrespecting authority was absolutely not tolerated in our household and they didn't want to see me do it outside either, so it simply wasn't in my consciousness to do so.

Nor was dishonesty. After family, honesty mattered above all else, in whatever form it came. Even ugly truths, which it seemed to me that Dad would readily dish out, were not something to be feared but something to use and learn from in order to be better.

We were a close-knit family unit – just us and Grandma, and Dad's mum, my nanna, until she passed away when I was eight.

We had fun together and I was taught, by example, that blood was thicker than water. I saw that whatever happened or was said in the house stayed in the house, that it was our business alone and not the concern of anyone outside. Emotions were something else to be kept under wraps too.

That worked fine for me while I was that little: I enjoyed all that I did at primary school, and my teachers liked me. They'd say that I talked too much but my end-of-year reports always commented on how easy I was to teach. I was popular with the other kids and their parents would hand me back after a play date or when I'd been invited over for tea saying how much fun we'd had. Why wouldn't we? I didn't have anything to complain about, other than that singular tearful moment in the cardboard chimney at nursery.

In fact, it wasn't long after that festive upset, while we were staying with Grandma for a few months as some building work was being done on our house, that I was in a show with the local dance class I'd been going to near her home. We'd learned a *Flintstones* routine and were all dressed in furry caveman outfits to match. At the end of the recital, as all the little kids lined up to take a bow in front of our parents, Mum remembers seeing me peer out, slightly obscured by two other girls, then pushing them out of the way to make an appearance and wave at my family.

The stage didn't faze me – and competing for my place on it was something I relished.

My competitive streak showed itself early on. At sports day I'd bomb it along in the sack race and drag my three-legged partner to the finish line, not fussed that we were completely out of step with each other, I just needed to cross that line first. And there was not a chance I was going to drop the egg in the egg-and-spoon race. If I didn't have a chance of winning, I'd laugh and let myself enjoy the experience – but if there was a shot at first place, well, that was even more enjoyable. As young as five or six I'd enter 'the zone' where my eyes would fix on the end goal and I couldn't see or hear anything else that was going on around me.

At one sports day in primary school, there was a ball-throwing contest. I was the strongest girl at sports in the year and found myself up against the strongest boy. I'd had my throw with this soft cricket ball and got a decent distance, but now he had to take his turn. As he launched it, I could tell it was about to go further than mine. I wanted the win so badly, though; so I caught it, knocking five metres off his score and derailing his chance of winning, taking the victory for myself instead.

His mum, who clearly had a competitive streak too, was fuming: 'That could have broken a record,' she shouted as I beamed with my first-place sticker, but I felt the tug of ugly truth inside me that this was not the fair or right way to win. That didn't feel good.

What I realised about myself early on was that, as extraordinarily competitive as I was, even when I wasn't the best at something and there wasn't a winner's medal waiting for me, there was never a question that I wanted to take everything to completion.

I was like a sponge, whatever I turned up to I soaked up something from it. Even if I didn't love it. Dancing, for example, definitely wasn't for me. I tried it all and moaned about it all: ballet, tap, modern. I'd go outside and practise in the garden with my tape recorder or loosen my tap shoes with a two-pence piece to make them louder and hammer away at the kitchen tiles, all in the hope of getting better, but none of it stopped Miss Susan, the dance teacher, reporting back to Mum and Dad: 'Mary's a clumsy dancer.' Where other girls gracefully pointed their feet in her class, she'd watch on, vexed, as I just planted mine down: one, two. Or she'd ask us to hold on to the barre to see how heavy our grips were and mine was so robust she couldn't prize my hand off.

But I saw and understood that if I wanted to be good, or better, at something I had to practice; not just in class, I had to work hard in my own time. And I wanted to. Besides, if you can sing and dance a 'Pop Goes the Weasel' solo at the Nottingham city music festival, as I did, if nothing else you owe it to yourself to put in the work and then to take away some character-building lesson about competing in a discipline you're not particularly good at.

Even seeing the teacher's commitment when I was a less-competent student than she'd have liked stuck with me as a valuable lesson about resilience.

The funny thing about ballet was that, when I eventually left, aged 11 or 12, Miss Susan's parting words were: 'You always lose the good ones, the ones you don't want to lose.'

As my parents continued their throw-mud-and-see-what-sticks approach to my childhood hobbies, they introduced me to swimming, clarinet, piano, badminton, judo, and – yes, soon – football. I continued learning what commitment looked like, never afraid to try any of it – and never afraid to return to the stuff I was weak at. Weak or strong, I walked away with the hunger to do better regardless.

For example, I was under no illusion that I was also a dreadful swimmer. There were a few kids in the neighbour-hood who'd go at 6am every morning before school to practise at the local pool, whereas my first swim meet – at a massive Olympic-sized thing at the university, which was very much not the local leisure centre that I was used to having lessons in – ended with me being slow-clapped out of the water by the crowd as I finished my butterfly stroke, a full length behind the other kids. It was only a two-length race – and the hardest stroke, to be fair – but with a place on the podium out of sight early doors, I nearly drowned from laughing.

I knew, as I swam on, that I could have quietly got out of the pool and saved myself the reception that was waiting for me but that wasn't me – I wanted to see it to completion.

I tried badminton, played the clarinet to Grade 4, and carried on with piano to Grade 6. I'd have a bash on the drums in the school music room, and I especially enjoyed judo, which made me feel strong and capable and it's where I showed real promise. If this roster of activities sounds like a lot, it didn't feel it back then. Between Joel and I, there was somewhere to be every night after school and I'd have done more if I could.

When we got friendly with a family whose three kids played tennis, I wanted a piece of that too. I remained extremely irritated that I never got off the waiting list for gymnastics, and one of my big superficial childhood disappointments, other than the tennis, was getting an acoustic guitar one Christmas instead of what I really wanted: an ear-splitting electric one.

But everything I did or did not take part in came with a life lesson. Whatever I wanted to try, my parents found a way and I understood the value attached to that. If it didn't fit into the rhythm of our household, like the electric guitar or a drum kit, they'd come up with something else.

Sport, music, whatever it was, when the Earps family were committed, we knew we had to be all in. If there was a kids' party at the same time as a competition or class, Mum and Dad would do their very best to get us to all of it, but if they couldn't, those weekly commitments took priority. Along with family and honesty, commitment was one of our most important family values. If I complained, they told me I could quit if I wanted to but I shouldn't expect to change my mind and go back the following week.

From all these pursuits, there was always something relevant to learn; and when it wasn't pertinent to me or my progress, only then could it be left behind.

I continued with this whole range of activities well into my teenage years until I had to make a choice, because I'd discovered a sport that I wanted to practise all the time – the one that I never wanted to give up.

TWO

RELY ON REPETITION

There were two patches of grass in our garden, separated by a narrow stone path.

I often stood in the conservatory, watching out of the window as my brother kicked a football about with my dad, usually after tea or when they'd arrived home from his training sessions with the local grassroots team, and Mum and I were back from dance or one of the many other pursuits I was now well immersed in as a child.

It was a cloudy weeknight when I was eight, almost nine, that I decided I wanted to have a go, so I put on my shoes, went outside, took a shot with the ball and joined them. From that moment on, I can't remember not wanting to play.

Now he had me to kick a football with, Dad wasn't necessary anymore and the garden became mine and Joel's domain. We always played on the right-hand patch of grass, putting down our jumpers or using sticks as goalposts and playing one-on-one until there was no daylight left.

When it was dark we'd move on to the road, where we'd play kerb-y instead, each bouncing the ball off the edge of the pavement and back into our own half of the street under the beam of a lamp post. I was so competitive that it would usually end with me finding a way to win, like insisting he'd broken a rule that we'd never agreed on in the first place. Nothing could stop me having a ball at my feet, working out how to manipulate it, improving on what I'd been able to do with it the day before.

Maybe it's because I'd already tried so many different sports and disciplines, failing and succeeding in various measure from such a young age, that I had the early instinct that football and me made sense.

The more I played, the more I wanted to play and, as I did, Dad saw how excited it made me. He started taking me down to Joel's matches with West Bridgford Colts on a Saturday morning where I'd dribble around on the sidelines a bit, more interested in what I could figure out next than what was happening in the boys' game.

By the time I was ten, I was itching to get involved in a competitive match. Dad asked the coach what he thought about me joining in, but because I was older, the league's insurance wouldn't allow me to play down an age group and, besides, he told us, girls and boys couldn't mix.

It boiled down to *Mary can't play.*

Instead, he pointed us in the direction of one of the dads, Mike, who also had a daughter my age who liked to play and had recently set up and was trying to build the Colts' first girls' team to accommodate it.

Training took place on the local pitches and I turned up on

ALL IN

a Tuesday night for my first session to find quite a few girls already down there. Mike was taking the subs and would manage on match days, and a couple of other dads were helping out with coaching. None of the girls had a position yet and we spent a fair amount of time running around like headless chickens, but I wasn't fussed – I had a football team and I was delighted about it.

We had our first fixture coming up, against Hucknall Town who played 12 miles away, and the dads agreed that everyone would do a stint, either a match or half a match each, in the only position that no one wanted: goal. I was picked to go first.

I pulled on the goalkeeper's shirt, the same kit as the boys – a golden long-sleeved top with a round black collar and the Colts' crest in white.

I took my place in net, none the wiser as to what I was meant to do in there beyond stopping any attempts to score a goal, my dad hovering behind, delivering instructions from the other side of the goal line. The ball was up the other end of the pitch for almost the entirety of the half, and without much idea about the game, I passed my time cartwheeling about between the posts, bored, while Dad hissed at me to pay attention.

'It's going to come to you any time,' he warned, as I spun upside down and round and around, enjoying my own world.

'I don't want to do this,' I whinged, peering up the pitch, wondering when I'd get a go where the action was.

'It's your turn,' he reminded me more sternly. Commitment.

The action headed my way with a fumble and suddenly a scuffle over a handball a few yards in front of me. The shriek of the referee's whistle grabbed my attention as he directed her and the ball towards the white spot marked out on the grass in front of me. The other players were gathering round now and the parents seemed excited, their attention fixed on the same place.

A penalty.

I'd never faced one, obviously, or even seen one in real life before. I readied myself, my hands out wide to feel big, and waited for the whistle to go again. I did what felt obvious, and watched as her foot made contact with the ball. As it flew low through the air I dived through the mud in the same direction. I grabbed it between my hands and held tight.

A save.

I'd saved it.

I was ecstatic. And the buzz of holding on to the ball felt great.

'See,' said Dad, proud as punch. 'Someone else wouldn't have saved that.'

This position is important, I thought. And I didn't want to leave it. I would make it mine.

So I went about it the only way I knew how: I practised relentlessly.

The once, or sometimes twice, a week training sessions weren't enough for me; I wanted to improve every day. Then I wanted to improve on yesterday.

Dad would plant the seed: 'If you can do a hundred kick-ups, you can do a thousand. If you can do a thousand, you can do them all.'

Then I'd nurture its shoots, setting myself a daily target and not going inside until I'd hit it. Kick-ups or wall-catches, bouncing the ball off the bricks and saving it in my hands; ten of them, then 20, then 50, alternating my feet or getting an unbroken catching streak until I'd seen each task through to completion.

I didn't do it for recognition because that wasn't on offer. Pushing through those standards was simply what was expected of me and what I expected of myself, so doing it and succeeding again and again made me happy. I knew that Dad saw me as able to achieve more than the others and football was another place he could push me harder because of it. The only recognition I got from that came from within myself and the idea that I had to be two, three, four, five times as good to get any sort of credit or recognition, to get the pat on the back that others more readily received, and that would follow me for the rest of my life.

As all children do, I embodied what I was led to believe about myself, and before long it was me dragging Dad and Joel out at any opportunity.

I didn't want to miss a day because missing a day meant I'd missed the opportunity to be better, so the three of us would take a ball down to the park round the corner on Alfred Street and do drills together, on the grass, most days.

'Joel, you're a midfielder–striker; Mary, you're a keeper. You two are a match made in heaven,' Dad used to say, seeing the opportunity for Joel to lob balls at me so we could both improve against each other.

Even on Christmas Day, while Mum was cooking the dinner, I'd pull them away from the TV for a kick-about. Practice was continuous, so improvement would be too. I realise now that I was training myself to be consistent.

To rely on repetition. It felt like that could earn me something. Opportunity, maybe? Or freedom?

I was different to the other kids I played with in that I wasn't afraid of doing what was needed from a goalkeeper, so while girls my age were scared to shout at their friends, I was unselfconscious about marshalling a backline and telling teammates where they needed to go. If I could stand alone on a stage doing a dance, I could tell people to move left or right in a game of football.

Standing out like that, literally being marked out in a box, isolating myself, didn't concern me at all because I wasn't remotely preoccupied by thoughts of how other kids might react to me if they thought I was too loud or too much or too different. I had my brother and sister at home, so I didn't fear or feel the threat of loneliness, and using my voice was what my teammates needed of me on the pitch, so why wouldn't I use it? I was there to get a job done, a job that my big, unafraid personality suited, and sometimes I was so eager to do it that I would wish time away, tempering even the things that I enjoyed by impatiently wanting to complete what I was there to do and do it well so I could move on to the next thing, the bigger task of getting even better at it. I saw everything as temporary.

Even at school, I'd think only of what was in front and ahead of me, being unbothered by the distractions of who was friends with who, whether someone was including me or what was going down in the playground; unless it was a game of football,

Mum and Dad had moved Joel and I from the local primary that had a little farm where you could take the chicks home for

Easter, to Grosvenor, a prep school where everyone else had a lot more money than us.

It was one of those strange features my middle-class upbringing that there was enough money to send two of us there for a couple of years (the well had run dry by the time it was Annabelle's turn) but we still ate the value Coco Pops and got our uniform from the second-hand sale.

I loved the new school yet I stood out there as well. It was an obnoxious, unfamiliar environment made up of families whose lives didn't look like mine, on top of which I was the only girl in my year who liked football, playing with the boys during break times instead of whatever the girls were up to.

It didn't feel like real life there, it was sheltered – we wore berets in winter and straw boaters in summer – and I could feel the change, but it was ultimately a happy place without much in the way of behavioural issues and it taught me a huge amount about hard work, discipline and respect.

We'd get a ridiculous amount of homework for pupils so young, and the kids across the road would often come knocking for Joel and I to go out and play but we'd be sat at the table at home with our exercise books or on our way out to another activity.

In winter, the girls would be split off for sewing lessons while the boys went outside to play football and rugby on the field. Like the times I'd stared out of the conservatory at home, I used to sit there, at the classroom window, attempting to cross-stitch and hating it, distracted by the fun the boys were having in the mud outside and thinking it was unfair that I couldn't join in. I'd end the lesson having done no work and taking the rest of my stitching home to Grandma, who'd once worked in a clothing factory and was a dab hand, asking her to finish it off for me to take in the following week.

I was so incensed by it that I even set out the injustice of it in a piece of homework entitled *Should girls be allowed to choose between the boys' and the girls' 'games' activities?*

Between that and my longing stares through the glass, the teachers must have seen how much I resented that needle and thread and, more importantly, spotted the disappointed undercurrent that my early encounter with misogyny had stirred, so they put me out of my misery and sent me outside to join in. I became the first girl there who'd ever played on the school's boys-only team. I remember a girl in the year below being allowed to join in soon after; I was too young to notice that I'd blazed a little trail for her behind me.

While parents occasionally questioned the choice, asking Mum and Dad why exactly they let me play, or why I wanted to, I never cared, and the boys never resisted – they needed me, and being the only girl on the pitch at school games was fine by me. Goalkeeping was the most fun thing I knew, as fun as scoring goals; I just needed to play.

As I moved my way up to the next age group with Colts, the games grew more competitive and the pitches and goals grew too until I felt absolutely tiny between those bigger eleven-a-side posts. But I delighted in diving, stretching and challenging myself with each new chance to play.

Change was coming thick and fast. After one school move, at 11 years old it was now time for another: high school. Mum and Dad must have had it in mind to stretch the family finances further because I sat entrance exams to Loughborough, Nottingham Girls' and Trent College, where you had to get up for the bus at 6am and go to school on Saturday. The only one I got into was Nottingham Girls'; I made the waiting list for Loughborough and had no intention of going to Trent because I'd have had to give up football on Saturdays. Mum eventually decided on Emmanuel, the new Church of England school near home, hoping they'd be stricter and have more structure than the other local secondary where she'd seen the girls walking past in rolled-over miniskirts and low-cut tops, which isn't what she wanted for her daughter.

I wasn't especially academic but I was studious enough to do my homework and answer when the teacher asked a question. I knew, from home, not to step out to authority and my conscientious-compared-to-others attitude instantly earned the attention of school bullies.

Maybe I was an easy target – I was often alone there, on the periphery of friendship groups, especially having come from a different primary school, and then cemented myself as the girl who played football, and I quickly assumed that people just didn't like me. I realise now that believing I had to be on my own felt quite normal to me back then – that's just how it was. But it was only temporary, I'd remind myself; I'd turn up, get my school days done then I got to go home and do what I enjoyed.

The problem was I was in a particularly bad year, and the mocking and taunting very quickly became daily, relentless and isolating.

The girls in my year would push and shove me in the dinner queue or tell me to 'shut the fuck up' for singing to myself, which I did gleefully and unselfconsciously. They'd punch my chair on the bus home and trip me up in the aisle as I searched for a seat.

Even my teammates on the school's mixed-age-group girls' football team couldn't extend their camaraderie to me and would dish out cruelty. On one occasion, when I was made captain of our five-a-side team, I asked all the girls what they preferred:

'Do you want to play equal time or play to win?' I offered.

They voted for the second, so one of them got 30 seconds and, when the final whistle blew, she was furious.

'Go on,' said another who was two years above me, seeing how angry she was. 'Slap her.'

And she did. I hit her back, standing up for myself, and they chased me round the school till I found sanctuary in the PE department office. It was horrifying, but I kept it to myself and got my head back down.

In lessons, I wasn't doing anything extraordinary, either good or bad, to stand out, but because I got the work done, other kids would ask to copy my homework. It became a bit of a thing, and when I eventually said 'no' it would invite more problems, more ribbing or rumours or laughs at my expense.

The teachers' interactions with me only made the situation worse.

'If the school was made up of Mary Earps it would be a wonderful place,' Mrs North, the religious studies teacher once told the class, making me want to reach out and pull her words from the air, knowing this would invite a field day for the bullies. I didn't want to be their friends, I just wanted to be left alone and survive the day. If it wasn't bad enough, it escalated during second year when they continued to chase me down the corridors, and one girl went a step further, pressing a wad of Blu Tack into my hair while the rest watched on and laughed. Mum had to cut it out, along with a clump of my hair, at home. Still, I tried to hide the extent of what was happening from her but it was clear that something was wrong. I was becoming withdrawn at home, arriving back from school without my usual smile on my face and going straight upstairs to hide away in my room.

'Is everything alright?' Mum would ask, but I wouldn't say a word. She had been bullied as a girl, too, and more than anything didn't want the same for me. I applied what I'd learned at home (what happens in the house stays there) to school life and had no idea how to be vulnerable and share how awful I felt. It was only much later that I would learn to articulate when people or situations were causing me harm and learn to draw a line that led it to stop.

'Mary's not the same,' a family friend even remarked to Mum when we spent the day together. I continued to shut it all away, occasionally trying my luck at pulling a sickie to give myself some respite but otherwise allowing myself to stay miserable on a day-to-day basis, so miserable that I don't particularly remember my life in football at that time, only what I was enduring in class.

My strong, bubbly personality had dulled. I was 12 years old and being beaten down, and I couldn't understand why so many other people would want to act that way.

It had to come to a head, and it did, when a boy launched himself across the desk in science to try and punch me after asking me a question about the difference between genes and germs. I'd answered, to placate him: 'Genes are something everyone has; germs are everywhere, everything has them.'

'Are you saying my parents have germs?' he prodded.

'Yeah, everybody does,' I said, focused on facts. He jumped over the table and swung for me as I held him at arm's length until a teacher could drag him away, kicking and screaming. My parents were called in. I was so afraid they'd be angry that I'd got into a fight when, in reality, it served a purpose and brought the bullying out into the open. Mum was clear: I was moving schools.

They put my name down for a space at the Becket Catholic school on the other side of the river where Joel had recently started, but I needed convincing. I feared it would be more of the same or even worse until, in my final weeks at Emmanuel, one girl was so horrible to me that I texted Mum telling her: 'I want to go.'

When a space became available for me a few weeks later, I transferred. It was an early experience of knowing that moving is possible, that you can leave a bad situation and take a chance on a better one, which this would rapidly become.

I could have stayed where I was and let being bullied change my zest for life, but I didn't sit in it for long enough to let it alter who I inherently was, although the experience did shape who I'd become and how I would respond when others treated me badly.

I often heard adults, then and later on, attempt to explain away bullying or experiences where I felt unliked with words that were intended to comfort such as 'they're just jealous', the same way little girls are sometimes told that a boy who is mean to them is doing it because 'he likes you'. That didn't make sense to me. In fact, today, I think it's bullshit. It's an unhelpful narrative that both excuses bad behaviour and ignores the fact that you don't have to be liked by everyone – it's OK if you aren't, provided they are not cruel.

For a long time the bullying hardened me to the treatment of others because I expected everyone I met, including in sport, to be mean like the kids at school. But I'd also learned that when I was unhappy, nothing else mattered or made sense, not even football, and that I didn't have to break myself into pieces to fit into a space that wasn't made for me because I could fit in at the next place instead.

THREE

COMPETE WITH YOUR YESTERDAY SELF

Football was fast becoming my first love. And if the early loves of everyone else's teenage years offer up lessons in adoration, heartbreak and rejection, I too was about to experience the first of many.

A coach who'd seen me training for Colts suggested that I go to trials taking place for Nottinghamshire school kids down on the astro at Southglade Leisure Centre, about half an hour's drive away.

I had no real clue as to why I was there, but Notts County had coaches along from their centre of excellence and they saw enough in me to ask Dad if I wanted to start training with other girls my age on a Monday night and play matches on a Saturday. It worked well around Colts' Tuesday night sessions and Sunday games, and all I saw was that I'd just doubled my footballing time.

I was a Liverpool fan, like Dad, so I didn't support a

local team, but I knew that Notts Forest and Notts County competed for football allegiances – where we lived, you couldn't miss that, and Dad had taken us to watch Forest a handful of times on the 'kids for a quid' match-day tickets. I wasn't so interested in the club or the brand, I just saw the chance to play in a more elite set-up as great for improving my game.

Women's football was almost invisible, other than the FA Cup Final which Dad, Joel and I watched on TV each year, and County's junior set-up was clearly not flush, for girls or boys, but the sessions were a big step up from Colts where goalie training had been Mike, the manager, grabbing a few minutes to show me some handling now and again while the rest practised their drills.

We trained on Lady Bay cricket ground, next to Forest's first-team facilities, and I soaked up the exposure to more structured programmes and the challenge of better teams and players. There was a designated goalkeeping coach, too, who worked with me and other girls in age groups either side and suggested that I get some proper, professional keeper gloves instead of the generic kids' pair I'd been playing in, which felt serious.

Being there felt like an achievement, not my future.

The future was a much shorter-term prospect at that age. Glimpses of something bigger, more structured and competitive with a higher standard in football came instead via the frequent trials, like the ones that had taken me to County, that punctuated my progress. These seasonal showcases became a familiar feature of my teen years and would determine where I'd play next, as clubs rotated their rosters of young players year after year, moving them in and out and up the ranks of training centres.

Each time kids would come into trial where I played or I'd go out to try elsewhere, I'd see a new group who were better than the last and realise how hard I wanted to work to get to the next level.

I'd often bump into the same talented kids on the circuit, like a girl called Katie, who put on these endless displays of kick-ups, juggling and manipulating the ball at just 11 years old. I recognised that you couldn't compare the two of us – I was in goal and she was outfield, so if you're judging a fish by its ability to climb a tree it will always be rubbish, but it was the talent not the position that I noticed. I wanted to meet these kids at their level and then surpass them, I wanted to be a big fish in a big pond, and I wasn't sure there was much point in anything else, so I was learning, in earnest, the dedication, hard work and life balance that was needed from me and also my parents to support that kind of ambition. Katie was the best I'd seen and we played together for a time. When she dropped out of the system a few years later it was a lesson for me in the role of circumstance and privilege in keeping opportunities alive. You can be a great player but society is not set up for everyone to win.

To keep my own progress alive, one of the big things I had to do was start understanding how to manage my time. County had fixtures all over the country and away trips could regularly be a two- or three-hour bus ride from home, so I had to figure out a way to make time for schoolwork and football practice, because I wasn't interested in letting my standards slip in either.

At my old high school I'd been put in a gifted-and-talented class for Spanish, going to Saturday-morning lessons on the university campus with some of the other kids, preparing me to take the GCSE two years early in Year 9. The Becket School didn't do Spanish but I wanted to see it through, so I continued anyway, weighing up each week how important the next lesson was to passing my exam versus how important the game was to our season and choosing which to attend.

I was still going to judo, the activity that came second, although not a close second, to football, and I was getting really good at it, attending a family-run club inside a community centre ten minutes from us every Wednesday night. Everyone there was a grafter and it was teaching me so much about what strength looked like, how to use it, and how not to underestimate it in others. There was one kid, Ryan, who was scrawny, half my height and build, but who beat me every single time from the day I started. When I fought someone with a disability, believing I should go easy on her because we weren't a fair match, she threw me to the floor and proved I didn't get to judge. I wasn't new to disability – one of Joel's friends had Down's syndrome and I already saw people's differences as a super strength that made the world a more interesting and more beautiful place. Judo reinforced this: you respected your opponent and everyone was there on equal merit. It was sport but it was also a real education, a discipline.

On top of the football and judo, dance was gone now but I was still swimming, playing badminton, keeping up with my music lessons and taking Dad down to the field to set out the cones so I could practise and then practise again whatever County had told me to.

ALL IN

I was determined to eke out everything my body and mind could do. I remember catching snippets of survival documentaries when I flicked through TV channels at night or hearing a story do the rounds at school of a mother who held back a car to save her baby. Whether it was news or a fable, I had no idea, but I was in awe of the singular strength of human beings and what they could do with it. I wondered if I'd be able to do those things if my life depended on it?

Pushing myself through sport felt like a good place to start.

The weeks were only getting busier and the kind of commitment I expected of myself required careful planning, which I could see my parents intricately executing, including balancing the financials of keeping us involved in so much. I always had a consciousness and appreciation for the effort that they went to but they were so private about money, and proud, that they preferred that us kids didn't know whether what they were forking out was a strain or not – that wasn't to be talked about.

On match days I'd meet the other girls at our home pitch or at the County ground to get on the bus for an away game, which often meant setting a 6am alarm to start the weekend, which I diligently did.

There was only ever one exception, when Dad came barging into my room one Saturday morning at 7:30am, bellowing: 'You've overslept. The bus has gone.' I'd hit the alarm and fallen back asleep, so I raced to pull on my kit through epic tears, horrified at the thought of letting my team down, threw the rest of my stuff in the bronze Mercedes C-Class Kompressor that his company paid for – I knew that much – and bombed it down the A46, Dad shouting to me to 'look out for a bus,' as I stemmed the tears, imagining the girls without a keeper. When the bus came into view ahead, Dad frantically flashed his lights, signalling for it to pull into a lay-by so I could jump on board. From then on, to this day, I set two or even three alarms, unable to fall asleep without offsetting the fear of it happening again.

I spent a lot of time with Dad, travelling to training or coming home from matches, and we talked about football all of the time. I was watching more of the professional games with him and when we could, we'd catch Liverpool on the TV, often going down to the local pub, the Willow Tree, as a family to watch on Sky. But it was my progress we spoke about more than theirs. I didn't realise it then but our whole relationship came to be built on me and football, what I'd just done or I was going to do next.

I was becoming known as the footballing kid at school, too; the sporty girl who arrived early to play heads and volleys with the boys before lessons started for the day. It was rare for a girl to be seen as good at sport there, but there was no consequence, no singling out, no cruel repercussions like the bullies at Emmanuel: the boys liked me because I played well, and one called Lewis, who was quick and a great little player, fast became my best friend. And the girls liked me because we got on – I was my smiling, full-of-fun self again. I still talked too much but I found friends everywhere. School was a lot easier for me because of it.

The hardening I'd experienced at my previous school gave me the impetus to make myself a bit more rebellious here, a protection against ever getting picked on again for being studious, which meant advocating for myself more than before, even with the adults.

ALL IN

I'd tried it out, only once, back at Emmanuel with one of my favourite teachers. I liked her so much that I'd taken it upon myself to make her a chart that would help her quit smoking not long before she told me off for talking to a boy named Joshua Dixon who was always sat next to me in class, given that D came before E for Earps in the register.

'You're not saying that to Josh,' I snapped back when she called me out. I had never challenged authority before and I wasn't sure it suited me, but the chorus of 'ooohs' that came from my classmates was probably the first time I'd experienced peer approval. I knew stepping out to a grown-up was wrong, but as a teenager it felt good to try out, even if I couldn't quite get comfortable with it.

I took it too far at a football camp with Nottingham Forest Ladies, a junior division unaffiliated to the club who I'd now graduated into after three seasons with Colts and was playing for alongside County. The word of the summer was 'wanker' and I didn't even know what it meant when I gave it a try, calling one of the girls on the team one. She was a nice kid and rightly complained to the coach that I wasn't being nice. I'd tested the boundaries, but betraying my values felt ugly. I didn't like trying to be someone I wasn't so that was the end of that; I wished I'd never tried on the new demeanour in the first place.

I learned to stick to what I knew, being my authentic self, working hard, intensely focused in sport, an unapologetic goofball among friends and still fiercely competitive on the pitch and off.

I began to realise that it wasn't other people I wanted approval from nor was it them that I was competing with;

I was competing with the yesterday version of myself. I did it constantly and in any capacity I could. Walking home from school, I'd set myself a challenge not to step on any pavement cracks, but it wasn't 'try it for five paving stones', it was 'I bet you can't do that the whole way home' when I only had myself to bet against. If there was a car about to head down the road behind me, I'd tell myself, 'I bet you can't make it to the next lamp post before that car,' and pick up my step to get there, or if I was restless at home or school, I'd wager, 'bet you can't count to a thousand without losing concentration.' I didn't need anybody else to win or lose against because, forever more, my biggest competitor was going to be me.

When Joel had a 12th birthday party at the local water-sports centre, his mates all went out on the practice lake to learn how to waterski in November. It was freezing and I watched each of them getting chucked off at the first corner then asking to get out. Not me. I pulled on a wetsuit and tried it out. I quickly realised there were no skis small enough for my feet to stay in the bindings so I'd have to use the board and stay on my knees if I was going to succeed. I took the first corner and completed a lap, then I was meant to go in for someone else to have a go, but I'd mastered it now and I had to prove to myself I could make it round again. So, round and round I went while the boys shivered on the side and the instructor's voice disappeared behind me shouting, 'Mary, time's up. You need to get off now.'

Competition was baked into me and it came from a place of wanting to max out on every ounce of my own potential. I competed with any obstacle that could stand in the way of that, including obstacles that arose from within. I was realising that one of the things I feared the most was complacency. (Well, complacency and airplanes! Our family holidays were usually driving ones to Devon or Cornwall, though, so I didn't have to contend with air travel as often as the daily fear of self-satisfaction.) Giving way to complacency felt like a certain barrier to potential – the same moment that I would stop improving – so every day I was driven by the hunger to perform to the best of my ability so that I could then raise my own bar all over again.

I had the opportunity to do just that – to raise my bar again – at my next set of trials.

County's centre of excellence had disbanded after money got so tight that we were required to pay for our own kit and so, in search of game time, I went on trial at the two centres of excellence nearest to us: Derby County, which was about 40 minutes from home, and Leicester City, over an hour away in the other direction.

Derby's trial day came first, a warm day at the end of a hot summer that had left the pitch pretty hard.

There were loads of different pitches and kids trialling, being moved up and down games according to their standard. You learned to get a feel from the calibre of those playing around you of whether you were still in with a chance or on the pitch of people about to be shown the door. I remember looking around and thinking there were plenty of decent players there, including another goalkeeper who was taller than me but technically wasn't playing better in the games.

At the end of the day, we were split into two groups, on either side of the pitch. One was in and one was out. I was struggling to get a gauge on whether I was among the better half or not; all I wanted was the news of my dreams, like a movie. Or *The X Factor*.

The coach turned to face my group.

'Sorry, you've not made the cut,' he said.

My first heartbreak. And my first brutal rejection from football. I had no idea how many more were to come and how much more they could hurt. I was young, and this felt sad enough for now.

'They only took her 'cause she's taller and she'll take up the whole goal,' Dad said to me as we drove away. Objectively, he was right. I had been the better goalkeeper, I'd saved balls where she hadn't, but this girl was more developed than me and they wanted someone who could take up space over my talent. That felt spectacularly unjust, and confused and disappointed me as a result. I understood that if you put in hard work and performed to the highest standard you earned the rewards, but I was naive and in love with a game that did not always work to those rules.

I felt deflated but I hung off every word Dad said, so when he told me, 'Don't worry, you can't always expect wonders,' and spun what had happened into a positive about what I could learn from being there, that's what I took from it.

I'd taken a step at trying something bigger and better and it hadn't gone my way. I had to accept it, respect it, dust myself down and try again, working no less hard.

A few weeks later I went on the two-day trial at Leicester, where the facilities were the most impressive I'd seen. It instantly fuelled my hunger for what that environment could do for my game.

ALL IN

I was wearing the purple Liverpool goalkeeper kit that Mum and Dad got me for Christmas the year before, a replica of Jerzy Dudek's the night he made his iconic double save and Liverpool won the Champions League in Istanbul. It had MARY 1 on the back and was the first replica goalkeeper shirt I owned. I felt confident in that shirt and I had a great first day. I went home feeling really good about my chances and sure I'd be able to get in, but the next day was a completely different story.

I had a total nightmare, and if I didn't already know it, I was moved down a pitch. Hard as I tried to play through the frustration I was feeling with myself, I was struggling to keep my emotions in check. What I really wanted to do was walk off the pitch and have a cry, and I was fighting the urge. I'd given such a good account of myself the day before but I hadn't been able to improve on it; I couldn't bear to have let myself down and be rejected again because of it.

When a woman with a short blonde ponytail, who appeared to be in charge, walked over to the pitch I was playing on and stopped the game, I didn't know yet that she was the only person I needed to impress: Rehanne Skinner, the director of the girls' pathway who had established and also managed the women's first team too. Rehanne pointed over and moved me back up to the top pitch. I instantly and intuitively responded to her confidence boost by playing better.

I was 13. I'd earned my place at a bigger club and it was the start of a beautiful development period that would set me up to seize bigger things.

FOUR

TAKE WHAT YOU NEED – LEAVE THE REST

At Leicester, Rehanne kept pushing me. She was a brilliant manager with a vested interest in her players and she saw and cared deeply about my commitment to the game. Dad seemed to get on with her, too, and he was hard to impress. I'd noticed that other adults found him direct but she didn't appear to be phased by him. She had a way of managing and appeasing him when he had questions about my progress and he had really lovely things to say about her, so when I saw them talking and having a laugh together I trusted his judgement implicitly and she earned my respect too.

Training was held every Tuesday and Thursday night, for two hours, with matches on a Saturday morning, so on weeknights I'd get home from school, have a quick tea, change into my kit and then take my homework to do on the car journey from Nottingham to Leicester.

Dad would usually take me, and on match days the two

of us would stop at McDonald's for a Sweet Chilli Chicken 'Wrap of the Day' and a Smarties McFlurry after the game for a treat.

On Thursday nights, Mum did the drive, leaving Dad to play his weekly five-a-side game near home. She'd heroically bring along Annabelle, read books to her, plough through any marking she had for the deaf school she was now working at, go for a walk round the nearby late-night Marks & Spencer, and change Annabelle into pyjamas and settle her to sleep in the car while the two of them waited to pick me up when training ended at 9:45pm.

If the long drives and the sacrifices were a step up for my parents, they saw it all as worth it because everything about the training was a step up, too, and I enjoyed all that was on offer to me. The quality of the players, facilities and coaching standards, including once-a-week goalkeeper coaching, drove me to take my development and commitment to the game to the next level, which was all that I wanted from the move.

I was among a talented group of girls, and Rehanne saw me as one of the more talented in my age group.

A lot of the girls who played there were also on the England pathway that developed players through the national youth levels, eventually selecting the best for the senior squad, the England team.

I had no awareness that such a thing even existed when I'd joined, so when Rehanne put me forward for a couple of regional and then national trials that winter, again, I had no clue where it was heading, only that it was another chance to open up more opportunities to play. Dad, on the other hand, knew exactly what was at stake and what this could be the start of but he didn't let on, keen to keep the pressure off. It's not like I didn't give 200 per cent anyway.

He and I had been on a shopping trip to JJB Sports, not long before, looking at football boots for Christmas. There was a great pair that I loved but they were expensive.

'Why don't you wait and see how you get on?' Dad said, thinking of the upcoming trials as we shopped around.

'And if you get in, how about I get you these ones instead?' He was picking up the red boots that Steven Gerrard wore; £130 and, at the time, made of kangaroo leather, so special that they came with their own little tub of wax to care for them.

I was made up, but he was more excited by where I'd get the chance to wear them. The trials went well, well enough that in February those boots and I arrived for an England training camp at Lilleshall, which had famously (but not to me) housed the Football Association's centre of excellence and was used for national age-group coaching.

Thrilled to be involved with anything run by England but none the wiser that I was taking the first step on a journey that had the potential to carry me through to the biggest stage of all, I turned up and did what I always did – made the most of every minute and played better than I had the day before. There were other girls there who I knew from Leicester: Kirsty Linnett, Rachel Williams, Remi Allen, playing in their own age groups, and I rated them highly. I wanted to mix at their level.

I remember the senior-team goalkeeping coach coming down to watch us and feeling like I wanted to impress him, which I must have done because a couple of months later I was invited to their next under-15s camp at Bisham Abbey, the national home for elite sports pitches where the men's team – Gerrard, Michael Owen, David Beckham and all the rest of my schoolmates' heroes – trained and played. This was pretty special and I wasn't just there to train.

This time, there were two matches to play against Germany. Another goalkeeper would play the first and they wanted me to play the second. I'd just turned 14 and I was about to pull on an England shirt for the first time. Now, the significance was beginning to bed in.

As they handed us the boys'-issue kit to wear, I felt a flash of pride in myself and was filled with excitement that I was there and joining an elite group of people who had represented their country even at this earliest level. I could feel the heft of this huge honour and I was happy that my hard work, my constant practise, the repetition and consistency, the work to keep complacency out, had earned me an opportunity, a spot among the best of my peers from across my country.

We lost the first game where I was on the bench 4–1, and Hope Powell, the 72-time capped former England player and now manager of the senior women's squad, walked into the dressing room to talk to us.

I knew who she was and I respected her, so I wanted to concentrate on whatever she had to say; I couldn't believe she was talking to us at all. Whatever she thought I needed to do is what would help me get me to the top, to reach my potential.

'How do you think you did?' she asked the team.

I was new on the block and not confident enough to give my opinion.

'I think we did alright,' the team captain offered.

'Define alright,' said Hope.

'We did some good things,' the captain replied, offering up a couple of examples from the game.

'You weren't good enough,' Hope answered. 'You don't get beat by Germany.'

I played the second game and we drew 1–1, and Hope came back to talk to us again.

'How do you think you did this time?' she challenged.

'Great,' everyone responded.

'I think you did alright.' Hope humbled us.

From then on, twice a year, that's how I spent my school holidays – training and playing with England during their summer phase at the end of July and the autumn one during October. If something came up in term time, the teachers were happy to grant me time off.

This was the dream. I'd seen where I could go now and I wanted nothing less than to be the greatest. I wanted to be the world's best goalkeeper, playing the greatest game on the biggest stages available to me.

It was thrilling and rewarding but we all knew that it was a dream with limitations. There was no fully professional women's national league and the game was still barely visible beyond those of us who played in it.

I'd been to see the men play at Anfield with Dad a couple of times and I loved watching football at that speed and pace, with the huge crowd and the match-day banter. Dad would alternate taking me and Joel on the odd occasion he got a ticket and we'd joke about watching out for the dog muck on the way to Everton's Goodison Park down the road. After a game, we'd stop at Anfield crematorium and sit with a bacon barm while we visited my nanna's plaque, paid our respects and debriefed on the match before heading home. It all made me feel very Scouse, a sense of belonging, of home and heritage and family that I loved.

But I'd only ever had one opportunity to watch the women play in real life, when the FA Cup Final was held at Forest's City Ground. Some of the schoolgirls from my Forest team were asked to be ball girls, so I went down in my kit and my Sondico headband and did my job, watching players like Karen Carney and Rachel Yankey from the sidelines as Arsenal beat Leeds 4–1 in front of 24,500 people. I noticed the personality of Arsenal's keeper, Emma Byrne – I wanted to play with presence and personality like that too. It was a brilliant day out, seeing women doing something that I loved and aspired to do, too, but it didn't run deeper than that because society and the sport still didn't give it the space to. The women's game had still been banned in England only 30 years earlier and I could love it with all my heart and want to make saves better than any keeper had before, but it could never provide me with a future or earn me enough money to live on or buy a house. It was a dream to enjoy and I'd have to study hard and get into university for that, to make sure I had something else in my kitbag for the real world.

A few months before my 16th birthday, Rehanne started training me with Leicester's senior team. I'd been pretty late to football – there were girls who had been in the centres of excellence and on the national pathway since they were at primary school, and because the pool of girls was so much smaller than the boys it was common to play with kids a year or two above or below you through those childhood and teenage years. Being invited to train with the grown-ups now, the semi-pros, would push my development on again and it got me extra training sessions each week too – more of those car journeys down the A453 for Mum and Dad.

Unbelievably, I was still going with all those other activities I'd been thrown into as a child and it was only around now, with England camps and senior sessions filling up my nights, weekends and time off school, that I recognised it was time to make a choice: I had to take what I needed to further my football and leave the rest.

Swimming at that average standard had served me well. In fact, a few years earlier the swimming club Christmas do had come up trumps with a competition prize on offer, to pick any Manchester United game at Old Trafford of your choice. I'd made it through the night's heats to an incredibly basic play-off game of heads or tails in which you had to put your hands on your head or your arse to win. I actually cheated and chose United versus Liverpool, which I now know was incredibly audacious, given I was unthinkingly robbing one of the biggest games of the season from someone's season ticket, but I pulled it off and went to my first Liverpool match with Dad to see us lose to a Rio Ferdinand last-minute header. I carried on swimming recreationally, as it was great practise for distributing my body weight and strength in goal and keeping up my fitness times, and I carried on getting in badminton games when I could, which was great for cardio and coordination. The one thing I was gutted to give up altogether was judo. I'd got my junior black belt – and I'd beaten Ryan, finding a method to pin him on his back that may or may not have been abiding entirely by the sport's official rules, whispering 'I got you' in his ear when my victory finally arrived. I was even told that I had a good chance of representing England and working towards the Olympics, but I was pragmatic, not sad, about walking away. You could only put in the work needed to be the best in one discipline and if it was that or football, judo didn't come close.

My confidence and the belief I held in myself as a talented young keeper only grew from being allowed to mix it with the seniors at Leicester.

Leanne Hall, the ex-England goalkeeper, was their first-team goalie and keepers' coach. Leanne was sponsored and gave me her old gloves to wear, and she became the closest thing I had to a mentor in the game and in goal-keeping – a woman who had succeeded on a path I was taking steps on, and she was prepared and able to share what she knew to help me take my next. I admired how she made me, a younger goalkeeper, feel.

She opened my eyes to a completely different mentality in training, and she could see how I beat myself up if I got things wrong and would impart her wisdom on me where I needed it. She could see where I excelled, too; the trademarks that were becoming my identity as a young goalkeeper.

My handling was best in class: I loved the feeling of catching a football so I did it at every opportunity. Repetition, consistency, over and over. Consistency of character and consistency of performance, that was the minimum I demanded of myself in my pursuit of excellence, of one day becoming number one. In training, in matches and still against a wall at home, increasing those numbers, catching till I hit my target. I didn't see many people who could catch the ball the way I could.

They'd two-touch it to the floor but I wanted it to stick. That was the feeling I loved most.

I'd been experimenting with how I played, conscious of getting too high or too low, and I was developing a presence on the pitch, too, something they call 'aura' today – leadership, fearlessness, undaunted by communicating and getting people into position, just as I had been when I used my big voice as a little girl with Colts and in the primary school playground.

My distribution was good and I was growing more and more competent on the ball too. To improve my touches, I'd joined my dad's weekly five-a-side games, with a few local ex-pros who lived in the area and went to the same pub as us. Each week, I'd play outfield, the only girl among ten grown men and Joel, using it solely as a playground to improve my movement on the ball.

When they'd bring their sons down to make up numbers, the boys would show off, trying kicks and flicks and stepovers, but Dad would remind me, before games: 'You don't need to gain anyone's affection, just do the simple thing.'

He was right. I was there to run, pass, keep the ball and keep my fitness up. No one cared what they did, whether their attempts at flare went right or wrong, or even cost them a game, but, as the only girl, if I'd gone down and wasn't any good, everyone would have noticed.

I played in those matches for years, and being around them taught me how to talk and interact with adults a bit more, on the pitch and off. We'd go to the pub afterwards and I'd order a Coke Zero and a chip butty, and allow the lads' banter to wash over me. In fact, I didn't mind it at all.

Growing up as a girl playing football in the noughties had

plenty of ways for the game to take its emotional toll. I remember one game, a man twice my age tried to block the ball and touched my boob as he did for what felt like a moment too long. I never knew if it was deliberate or not, but the memory stayed with me. My instinct told me it was probably on purpose.

When I was with the heads-and-volleys boys at school I was seen as one of them, which included being exposed to all their lads' chat about who they fancied, hearing how they viewed the bodies of other girls that we were at school with. Then when I was with the girls I was one of them, too, exploring my feminine side, chatting and listening to which of the boys they wanted to sleep with.

It wasn't me splitting my personality or moulding to fit in, I was just me being my authentic, happy-go-lucky self. Outside football, when I had time with friends, I just wanted to have a laugh and I'd chat to anyone, so I hung out with both groups. I wasn't one of the popular girls but I had boyfriends and I was the girl people liked being around. In many ways, having football and the boys meant that I fitted in with even more people than others did during high school.

But football also meant that I didn't conform with any of them. My sports clothes didn't fit in the same way that the boys' kit did when we played, and I started noticing that I didn't look like the girls either. They wore heavy make-up whereas I didn't wear a scrap. I wasn't fussed about clothes because I was always in football kit and I still didn't bother about my hair, shoving it up in a functional ponytail or bun. I didn't feel particularly pretty but then I didn't really put in the effort to be pretty.

The influence of your peers, the challenges to self-confidence, the pressure and desire to fit in is why so many girls still drop out of sport in their teenage years. That never occurred to me as an option and I was less bothered about being desirable at school than I was about being desirable in football. I still had that strong inner belief that everything was temporary; I had plenty of friends and as long as I was happy that day I couldn't see a reason not to just continue being uniquely me. But it did make me look at myself in ways I hadn't before.

In football, I saw other women's bodies more and I started to compare myself. I could see I carried more jelly than some of the girls I played with and coaches were not shy in asking me to drop a couple of kilos. 'You're moving slowly', 'You're not fit enough' or 'You're not fast enough,' they'd say, which was all code for 'lose some weight'.

On camps, coaches could see what we were eating and I was conscious of their eyes on me when I ate.

It made me feel shit about myself, like I wasn't good enough or thin enough. For years afterwards I'd try various stupid things to try and drop weight, like only having Go Ahead yoghurt bars and a bottle of Coke for lunch, thinking they were low in calories when they were clearly flooding me with sugar and providing absolutely no fuel to play on. The way football made me look at myself next to my friends and teammates in those teenage years was the start of me not liking my body, ever.

Socially, I'm not sure how much my school friends noticed the level I was playing football at after lessons; it was much more a talking point if a boy was competing, like Lewis who was good enough at football to earn a stint at Notts County and would later go on to play professionally in Sweden. There was a promise of something bigger, something to be emulated for the boys, but those options didn't exist for girls, and so it didn't bring excitement to a bunch of teenage school kids.

I didn't need that from them, though. When I was with them I loved the laughs we had and I was happy being the funniest person in the room with people who embraced the big side of my personality. When you've gone from being bullied to then having a solid group of friends, you think about how to sustain and enjoy them because you know how nasty other people can be.

Socially, I was so focused on the game that I wasn't doing what my mates were because the schedule simply didn't make time, but I remember rolling about in hysterics over games of truth or dare at each other's houses and racing round the top of the Eiffel Tower on a school trip, taking pictures of ourselves at our imaginary finish line, being way too loud and finding ourselves far too funny.

Sometimes if I had a Saturday afternoon off, I'd go into town and walk round the shops with my friends or go bowling or to the cinema – Mum and I loved doing that together, too, watching anything at all for the experience of sitting down to a movie, often by virtue of one of her vouchers. But when it came to nights out and house parties, there were hardly any for me. I was strong-minded enough to say no to drinking when everyone else was getting trashed because I had it in my head that it would decrease my reaction times at training or in a match, and I wouldn't do anything to jeopardise my football or the next day's performance. So, I felt like I ended up looking after them all night as they smoked cigs and fell down the stairs, and each time I was relieved when Mum or Dad came to pick me up at the end of a night. Whether I made those choices solely because I was an athlete, I'll never know, because that's the only version of being a teenager that I had, but I knew that it wasn't my scene.

I'm sure it reached a point where some people thought there was no point asking me to things anymore because I'd inevitably be going to bed before a match or be at training instead, but if they were talking about some night out I'd missed out on at school the next day I just joined a new conversation, unbothered. It never felt like missing out to me – I didn't pine for things or experiences outside football in that way. That can only have been aided by the fact that I had so much going on to fulfil and propel me forwards during those shaping growth years.

Within a year of going to England camps, I'd been moved into the under-17s, now known as the Young Lionesses. It was my next achievement and it made everything all the more serious again because we had championships to qualify for and take part in, so there was something more on the line. Squads were quite small, with two goalkeepers, and one clearly behind the other, which meant limited opportunities to play until you were handed enough experience to climb up to number one.

My cohort included Jordan Nobbs and Alex Greenwood, who I'd later play with in the Lionesses. Camps were longer now, usually ten days, and you were given kit – still the men's – to train in. You also got a Lucozade bottle and a few sachets of the stuff to take home, which I used for training and my games at Leicester.

Every time I pulled on my England gear I felt untouchable. I'd look around at the pitches I was training on and just feel it, being part of England, every time. It fed the hunger. Now I was in the age groups, my ambitions instinctively pushed higher – I just wanted the senior team.

After one of my early games, Hope paid us another visit.

'How many of you want to play in the seniors?' she quizzed in her typical authoritarian tone, scanning the room.

Everyone raised their hands. I looked around. This was a roomful of great players.

'How many of you are going to do the work to get there, when you're tired, when it's raining?' she asked next.

I was baffled. How was that even a question? Why *wouldn't* anyone do that? It was all that I did.

The hands all went up again.

'Yeah, right,' she said. 'You'll be lucky if one of you in this room makes it.'

FIVE

BE RELENTLESS

I always wanted to be the first, be the youngest to do something, and be the best at whatever I was going to become.

My competitive nature, independent spirit and sense of somehow being different stood me in good stead as a goalkeeper. It also meant that achieving things that other people hadn't felt natural and exhilarating, and going about achieving them in a unique way suited me. It would become a motivator and state of mind throughout my career, and I was audacious about it from the start. I didn't hide my ambition or self-belief – all I needed from an adult or coach was for them to point me in the right direction and I'd graft and grind and figure out the rest.

The difficulty with being so self-assured in my football potential is that coaches didn't always know what to do with it. My will to work hard and dig deep with a maturity that surpassed my years or the level I was playing at was often misconstrued as an arrogance or suggestion that I already considered myself the best. In fact, I was just working with confidence to get there.

Rehanne was brilliant at harbouring it but, as my footballing world opened up, I could see that it was unnerving to others who expected a teenage girl, and later a woman, to be outwardly fragile, to stay in a box.

I never wanted to be pushed into a box. I wanted to be free, and I didn't know any other way to be than to bring the whole of myself to every game and meeting in my relentless pursuit of my dream. All of myself, that is, except for my emotions, which I'd learned to keep hidden.

'Don't let them see they've got to you,' Dad would advise when talking to me on how to conduct myself with coaches.

It wasn't always easy, and England youth camps were an insight into the harsher side of football.

At the end of each camp there would be a one-to-one with coaches and, for a time, I felt like the sole ambition was to make me cry. I spoke to some of the other girls when we got older and I now know I wasn't the only one, but back then my experience felt isolating.

I always dealt with meetings by listening, respecting and critically assessing what I was being told, and putting into practice what was required of me. I saw this display of professionalism as what I needed to do to progress and get better. And I knew not to disrespect authority.

One of the coaches would tell me I was laughing too loud, so I'd dial it down because that was clearly what she believed the team needed, then she'd tell me I was sulking. When she told me I wasn't fit or fast or strong enough (code for lose weight), I'd take it and deal with the upset at home.

ALL IN

In one European camp, I'd been named number-one keeper. Camps always took the same format – for the first three games, the number one would play the two stronger matches – but this time, the coach wanted the number two to play them. I would never have raised that I thought it seemed unfair but she must have read my reaction on my face, so in our next one-to-one she asked:

'Why do you feel entitled to play two games?'

'No, it's not that,' I replied. 'It's just the usual way that it is.' I never needed emotional comforting from people, but I sought out logic and reason to explain their decisions, otherwise the actions didn't match their words. I was confused again.

'Just because you're wearing the number-one shirt doesn't mean you play two games,' I was told, putting me back into the box.

This was the other difficult thing about being a self-assured young athlete who was also an impressionable teenager. I was committed and I didn't misbehave or make a fuss, even though I saw plenty of other people misbehave and get away with murder, and I was coming to learn that when you show confidence in one aspect of your life, when you consistently demonstrate ruthlessness and relentlessness in pursuit of a goal (traits that I grew to realise people more typically associate with and accept in men), they assume that it runs throughout the whole of your life. I never projected my emotions onto others, but of course I had feelings, and insecurities too.

When coaches, both then and later in my career, took my assuredness as a cue to push me further, or even to put me down because they thought I could take it or maybe that I needed it, it had the opposite effect on me. I felt they'd taken the vulnerability I'd showed them by being so completely, wholeheartedly dedicated to football and used it to hurt instead of uplift me. They were in a position of power so I had to take it. That's how football went – they said 'jump' and my job was to say 'how high?' But it made me feel worthless.

When I was the only one of my friends at England to be pulled back into a lower age group for a camp I felt humiliated by it, even though it turned out to be a one-off.

Every camp I had been excited to pack my digital camera and bring it along, but this time I didn't bother. I felt I'd been sent backwards and I didn't want a record of it. I'd played well in our last game against France and didn't understand what I was now being punished for. I felt singled out and it reignited that feeling from school: I was doing exactly what was asked of me, but still I wasn't liked. In the seclusion of my bedroom back home, without any reason to make sense of it and without coaches or my parents watching me, I'd beat myself up over it.

Panic attacks would descend and before I knew it, I'd wound myself into oblivion, thinking over every conversation and move I'd made. I'd sob my heart out on my bedroom floor while no one else could see or hear me. The sadness of loving the game so much, wanting so deeply to be great and it not working out, and of no one seeing the potential in me as much as I saw it in myself, felt like more than I could stand.

Football bothered me like nothing else in life did. I was obsessed; unhealthily in love with playing. If I performed badly, it ate me alive for days and I'd be chomping at the bit for the next game or to get back into training and show myself I could get it right. Where I once wrote stories, I now dreamed at night about playing on a big stage or even winning a cup. I daydreamed, too, challenging myself to work out what would give me the edge. When it was my birthday, I made the same wish over my candles every year: to be the best.

Crying over the heartaches football threw me, in my room, I'd think *I have to make football work because I work so hard at it*. I'd feel this potential inside that was ready to be harnessed in the right hands and I wanted to be given every opportunity for that to happen. If opportunities were given to me, then they were mine to screw up, I acknowledged to myself, but to be deprived of them at all was a harsher, bigger pill that I couldn't yet swallow, and one I would never get used to.

Downstairs, at the dinner table, after I'd wiped away my tears, and also on the days when it was going well, my football dominated every mealtime. Mum and Dad wanted me to relay everything that went on to them and I followed their advice closely, in fact I hung off it, so, even if I wasn't the one to bring it up, there was endless talk about how I was doing, celebrating successes, dissecting what coaches had told me and lamenting when I was treated poorly. I put enough pressure on myself so it's not that it added to it, but in adulthood I've come to realise that I carried the emotion of how they felt about my football on top of my own. I'm sure it made my brother and sister feel that what they were doing was less important, too, and, while none of us let it impact our closeness, I didn't want that for them. Still, it had become near enough the only topic of conversation at home, given our whole household was now geared around the demanding schedule and all that came with it.

The focus on my football continued even when guests were over, and I remember a friend of my parents standing in our garden one weekend afternoon, telling Dad: 'She's never gonna make it. People from houses and streets like this don't make it. Why are you carrying on?'

It was true, we didn't know anyone who'd made it. Who did? But Mum and Dad, on the other hand, believed in the same thing I did, that I'd get myself to wherever I wanted to be, no matter how high. Years later my dad told me he'd been into a bookies around that time and asked to place a bet on Mary Earps playing for England seniors, just for fun, only to be told, unsurprisingly, that the odds didn't exist for a local sixth former they'd never heard of.

I was contending with my A levels now, and football competed with my study time, so I had to learn how to hack exams to maximise what I had. For English GCSE the set text was Harper Lee's *To Kill a Mockingbird*, which I can't say whether I enjoyed or not because I never read it. I just worked out that I needed to study its themes to answer the question, and I did pretty well. I decided to take that approach with me into sixth form, where I chose French, English literature, biology and chemistry at A level. They were ridiculous choices based on what I thought I liked, but subjects that did not fit at all well around sport. I dropped French after a year because the teacher didn't accommodate my football and predicted me an E, then I failed the year entirely with two Ds and an E because the school required at least Cs to progress to the second year.

I needed to see things to completion, though, even if it meant taking the scenic route to the finish line, so we convinced the school to let me redo the year and I stayed back, sharing Becket's sixth form with my brother and his friends, and trying again with English language, sociology and biology for the next two years and chemistry for one.

At weekends, I got myself a job at Inspirations, a kids' toy and stationery shop in town, working shifts around my games. I'd get £40 for a day's work and give it straight to a biology tutor to help me with my schoolwork.

I put any spare time to good use in the gym, using a cheap off-peak membership at the leisure centre to try and improve my fitness, especially running, which I wasn't particularly good at and, as a keeper, relied on less in training and games.

I had a sheet of exercises for aerobic development from the FA that I'd take along with me: four minutes on the treadmill, four minutes off, to do four times over, or speed endurance of 30 seconds on, 30 seconds off, on repeat.

I'd be breathing heavily after ten seconds on the machine, but I figured out that I could use my mentality to push myself. I could bet on myself, train myself so whenever my body thought it was done, I'd tell myself I could do four more, getting the extra reps out of myself and incrementally increasing what I was capable of.

I'd pound the rotating belt thinking *I can't fucking do this anymore*, then visualise myself on the pitch for England in the under-17 or under-19 Euros. *What if it's the 80th minute and you've got to make a save? Are you going to say you can't do it then?* I'd challenge myself.

At Leicester, Rehanne had moved me into the reserves and I'd even got a few minutes in a friendly for the first team, but she then took a job at Arsenal. I was 17 now and I knew that

I had to progress to first-team football to keep complacency at bay. Getting playing minutes was my only driving force, and that remained the case in every move, bar one, that I made in football. I only ever wanted to maximise my game time.

Forest had come in and asked me to trial for the next summer season. They were a centre of excellence now, playing in a division above Leicester and closer to home.

The move made sense so I took it, but I arrived to a disorganised set-up.

Everyone would give each other lifts to games, which was usual in the women's game as clubs didn't have enough cash for executive team travel, and I was in the back of a car on the way to Leeds with another player about my age and the co-manager, who was driving. She looked at me through the rear-view mirror.

'Mary, you know you're playing today?' she said.

That would be my first senior game.

'No,' I replied.

'Has no one told you?' she asked, eyes back on the road now.

I was grateful and extremely excited, but what kind of preparation was that from a club? I was used to Rehanne's communication and naively thought it would continue. At least I'd done what I could and had my entirely over-prepared kitbag in her boot – always the butt of jokes for being huge and stuffed with two pairs of boots, two pairs of gloves and spare shin pads for every outing.

I played a few league games and the manager, Danny Johnson, put me in for all of our cup fixtures that season.

When we made it to the final of the league cup against Barnet and arrived at Adams Park to find our names and numbers on the backs of our shirts in the dressing room, we were all touched. We'd only ever played in numbers before, and holding EARPS 21 on the green jersey was the first time I'd seen my name on a shirt other than the replicas that Mum and Dad got me for Christmas. It was as close as I'd got to professional.

I pulled it on and walked out with the team. The only problem for me was that I didn't get to play.

I'd sensed something was off earlier in the week when Danny couldn't tell us whether me or the other keeper, Claire Wallhead, would be starting. I'd asked him a couple of times after training but he was awkward. 'I haven't made my mind up,' he said, reassuring me that 'you're playing really well.'

Next thing, he turned up at my sixth form, which would never be allowed today, announcing himself with a text message: 'I'm outside.' I made an excuse to leave my lesson and headed out to find him stood, waiting, in the car park.

'You're not going to play,' he told me frankly.

'Why?' I asked

'Claire's dog's just died. She needs to be around her friends.'

Sorry as I was for Claire's dog, this felt like an absurd motivator for a football decision.

If you want to play her because she's better than me, that's fine, I thought, but I couldn't get my head around this. Someone else who'd rooted for me enough to play me in every other cup game then made a decision that undermined those results. Another person I was asked to respect but whose actions and words, felt to me, like they didn't stack up. They lost the match and it consumed me unhealthily.

The older and more resilient I got as a player, the more familiar a feature this was becoming in football, but it never got easier or felt fair reward for consistency.

I would have to wait another year for Mo Marley, the England under-19s coach and 41-capped former player, to provide the antidote that gave me reason to believe that hard work would pay off.

We were playing Serbia, Spain and Sweden in Turkey, where it was sweltering hot. I was so badly bitten by bugs that I had a huge bite under my eye that part-blocked my vision, when Mo called me in for a chat.

Alex Greenwood, Nikita Parris and Danielle Carter, who'd also go on to make the seniors, were in the team and we should have done really well but we hadn't delivered. I'd had a good tournament, though.

'I'm really impressed with you,' Mo said. 'You've shown up in big moments. You've tried to lead, I'm going to play you in the next game.'

It felt great. Then in the next meeting she told me: 'I want to make you the captain but I want to know it won't change you, it won't distract you from your job?' I said it was an honour, but my priority was to perform and the armband wouldn't change my approach to the game. Getting to walk out and play for my country at any level was an incredibly proud moment, but this was something more, beyond what I'd imagined.

She saw what I was doing, my relentless pursuit of excellence, and wanted it to work in my favour. To be endorsed, harnessed and uplifted felt wonderful. I was so proud I could have burst at the seams.

She asked me not to tell anyone, including the existing captain who was also my roommate, which felt horribly uncomfortable to me, but I gave her my word and didn't say anything, not even to my parents, who then watched in the stands, surprised and delighted as I walked out in the armband and did my job, the same way as always.

It was my proudest moment in football up to that point. I made a series of great saves that game, good enough for the Serbian players to comment on them when we walked back in.

'You're a great captain,' Nikita kindly told me after the game.

By then, still in the throes of A levels and with that England captaincy around the corner, I had left Forest for semi-professional Doncaster Rovers Belles, where I'd get £25 a game – £12.50 if I was on the bench – and, at 17, become the youngest keeper in the new Women's Super League. A first.

SIX

SACRIFICE FOR RESULTS

That summer I had taken on six jobs to pay my way. I didn't want to take a penny off my parents and wanted to carry the cost of playing myself, so I added shifts at the local Showcase cinema along with telesales calls, holiday camps for Notts County Football in the Community and hours for a private coaching company on top of my weekends at Inspirations and then Doncaster Belles.

I enjoyed working and the independence that it gave me, and those jobs taught me much more than having money in my bank account. They showed me how much I wanted a life of freedom one day and the self-discipline and care that was required to reach it.

At the toy shop, I saw how each interaction and transaction kept this small business going. Paul, the owner, paid me 50p more than the minimum wage and I carried on my shifts there for years. It may have been a small-town business but it started an education in business forecasts and trends which fascinated me. The shop would be dead throughout the year, then Christmas would be rammed; every transaction had to be tapped into the old-fashioned till and if two of us were serving at the same time one was on a calculator and we were both keeping an eye on the door for shoplifters. Staying afloat depended on that Christmas period and every item in and out helped forecast Paul's next 12 months. I cared deeply about getting it right for him.

Plenty of Saturdays I'd clock off at 5pm and go down to the Willow Tree to meet Mum, Dad, Joel and Annabelle for tea, where we'd order a sharing platter of some kind with nachos and chicken wings and a pint of Coke Zero, no ice – not exactly elite-athlete nutrition but I didn't have a good nutritional education at all. Mum would be hoping for some family time, something becoming more seldom as we got older, while I went along desperately hoping to watch the football being shown on TV.

The Notts County community coaching job was glorified school-holiday babysitting in that it required no real football or technical skill, like I imagined when I took it on, but was more about interacting with and entertaining the kids. I enjoyed what that entailed, which was the opportunity to bond with young people clearly looking for an outlet via sport and a new appreciation for the diversity that existed on my own doorstep.

It was attached to a government scheme where kids could go for 50p a day, and there were children whose behaviour or the way they turned up showed how much they and their families needed the structure and support. It was the opposite of the privileged environment I'd grown up in and I could see there were kids who just wanted a bit of time and attention from the coaches they were spending the days with. One of the older boys, who wasn't that much younger than me, was getting super-frustrated playing with primary school kids who weren't as good as him. He got so angry that he stormed off the pitch almost in tears so I went over and sat down beside him.

'Do you like coming here?' I asked

'Yeah, I don't have to be at home while Mum's working,' he said.

'You have to control your reactions, then,' I told him. 'It's like playing with your brother or sister. They're not going to be as good but you have to set an example or you'll be kicked off the scheme.'

He went back softer, and as the afternoon went on even joked and joined in with the younger kids, clearly enjoying himself. I found it rewarding to watch him learn something from one conversation that might help him communicate and perform better in his future, and I learned the power of speaking to and seeing the person in front of you, whatever side of the conversation you were on, player or coach.

I had to talk to parents and my employers, too, which only added to the unofficial education I was receiving in the world of work.

I'd arrive each day just before 9am for my seven-hour shift. One morning, someone more senior I didn't particularly know stopped me.

'You should have been here from 8:30,' he said.

'I don't get paid from 8:30,' I told him.

'But you have to be here,' he insisted.

'That's not my hours,' I momentarily pushed back before accepting: 'OK, cool, thanks for letting me know.' I thought about it later that day and decided I could respect authority but didn't have to turn up for a minimum-wage job during hours I wasn't being paid. I just wish I could have articulated it in the moment – I would in future.

Those jobs helped me to save up £800 for a car, an old red Renault Clio. I'd passed my driving test and used it for the 90-minute journeys I made over to Doncaster two or three times a week, where the club paid me 40p mileage at the end of every month.

I was glad of the income and independence because the financial fragility of women's football was evident. As my first Christmas with Doncaster approached, the club had failed to pay any of us for almost three months, blaming an admin error. I was a school kid who could ask my dad to spot me to buy presents that year – and I did, the only time I borrowed and immediately paid back money from him once I'd started earning. But there were women with mortgages and kids. It was an early insight into a footballing truth that even when the budgets and game grew, the women's team were among the first casualties of financial difficulties for clubs.

I'd started at Doncaster as number two and trained hard – which was the only way I knew how – to fight for a starting spot.

They were one of the eight founding teams in the new top tier of women's football but they weren't the strongest and women were travelling from all over, sharing lifts from Southampton and Sunderland to play. There were some more professional trimmings, though: we played inside the

Keepmoat Stadium, like the men, with a crowd of a few hundred in the stands to watch us each time, and had access to a physio if we were injured, although not enough for maintenance. And so I'd work extra on my own strength and fitness, signing up for classes and hitting the spin bikes at the Virgin Active gym I'd joined on a £33 student membership, back in Nottingham.

I was in the middle of a close shift at the cinema one weekend when I got a call from Doncaster's manager, John Buckley, late in the evening.

'What are you doing?' he said.

'I'm at the cinema, working.'

'You better go home, you've got a game tomorrow, against Birmingham.'

I managed to get myself off shift a couple of hours early at 10pm, went home for a few hours' sleep and drove over to start the game – the youngest keeper in the league and that first football 'first'. It was a great feeling, one I hadn't paid too much attention to until a few months after the event when another keeper joined the league and commented in an interview on how cool it was.

I was pursuing my passion. We were fighting relegation and lost most weeks but I was playing and we were digging deep as a team week in, week out, and playing against England internationals from the likes of Arsenal and Chelsea. I enjoyed the camaraderie and it boosted my confidence and the self-discipline I needed to pull all-nighters or wake up early and complete my studies, a year behind my friends, so I could train and play and get to university.

I had set my sights – somewhat obsessively, as was my

tendency – on studying international business at Lough-borough, a top sporting university with a great business school. Ever since I'd had a training game there with England's under-17s I'd thought its sports facilities were so impressive and the pitch so immaculate I could have eaten my dinner off it.

Everything I did had to lead to something more, and studying business was how I planned to one day buy myself financial freedom. My Doncaster wages weren't going to do that so this would be a jump back into the real world whenever I was ready to use it. Being at university also gave me the opportunity to behave like a full-time footballer in an artificial environment where I lived away from home. The bills were paid by my massive student loan and I could concentrate on training and games alongside the small matter of studying full-time for the next four years.

The course required AAB grades but I'd dropped one, and I was only two marks off the A in biology, so I put myself through clearing. I could have done the same course at another university but I was so hell-bent on Loughborough that I wouldn't settle for less than going with the gut feeling that I needed to be there, so I found a place on their information studies and business management course instead.

I settled myself into flat 3C in Butler Court, a sporty 1960s block near the gym, where I shared a top-floor flat with a cricketer and a rower.

I barely even attempted a social life. I think I went out a total of four times during my entire time at university, one of which was a foam party I had to be talked into, because once my season started, the scheduling I required of myself was off the charts. It made those school days with all the extra activities and the help of my parents look easy. Again, I had to work out what I was prepared to sacrifice, where, when and how much, in order to do the only two things that I was there to do well and to completion: get a degree and play football.

I remember doing my first group project and figuring out what working like that involved, with people I didn't know on a subject I was still wrapping my head around. I contributed what I could, but training meant that I couldn't be present for all the meetings, so one of my course-mates got a first and I was marked down for putting less time in.

Whereas my school accommodated and was excited by my football, university was less coddling. When I had an England camp the same week an assignment was due and asked a lecturer for an extension, it wasn't granted. I rushed the work out early and got 50-something instead. In my first year, where the marks didn't count towards my final degree, I had to accept that respectably passing was sufficient to get me to the next phase and that balancing my time well, by making sacrifices in the right places and only where necessary, would require constant fine-tuning and re-prioritising in response to the changing demands around me.

I made the most of Loughborough's sports facilities and, through England, had access to the English Institute of Sport high-performance centre, which was based there. I used all the resources I had access to, not wasting a second of the day. I'd get up and head over there when it opened at the crack of dawn, doing extra physio and gym work, creating my own strength and conditioning sessions and making use of ice baths to recover. It was a whole new world of elite facilities. Top athletes trained there and I loved being in the vicinity of winners, fascinated by high performance. Outside my studies, I read up on stories of marines and athletes or sports coaches who pushed themselves and their teams to the limit and to the top, fascinated by the mindsets of 'mentality monsters', inspiring and informing myself to drive what I felt inside me even further, the way that they did.

The Loughborough girls' football team wanted me to sign up to train there but the hours didn't work and my contract with Doncaster didn't allow it, so I trained with the boys' seconds, who were out at 6am instead. When I moved into a houseshare off campus in second year, I'd cycle there in the rain and snow. Anything to turn up to tomorrow 1 per cent better than yesterday; that was never up for debate.

My second year at university coincided with moves in football too. An opportunity had come up halfway through my first year to play at Birmingham City for a few thousand pounds a year and half the distance that Doncaster was to Loughborough. I'd loved Doncaster but during my second season with them they were struggling to get a regular goal-keeping coach in, even once a week, so I was turning up unable to train properly, relying only on playing and the work I was doing independently to improve my game, with no coaching to help me address technical issues. That would never get me to the next level. When Doncaster wanted to renew my contract, I negotiated a move to Birmingham instead, where the team had qualified for the Champions League and I'd go on to get my debut in the competition, playing the first two rounds.

During that season at Birmingham I received my first call-up from the England under-23s into the senior squad as a fourth keeper, with one of the regular keepers out injured. I'd played consistently in the 23s, which had been a tough age group to get into, given there were four years of players and only a couple of dozen spots, so the gap from the 19s was big. There was little in the way of competition other than a friendlies tournament each March and training camps that took place at home or abroad, usually in La Manga, a golfing resort in Spain. It was the final step before seniors, a place where you turn up, earn your trade and keep your place, desperately hoping each time that you'll be asked back to do the same again.

So, I was ecstatic when I was at home for the night in Nottingham and looked at my phone to see a voicemail from the team admin saying Brent Hills, who was serving as caretaker manager following Hope Powell's departure, wanted to speak to me.

I ran into the other room to tell my parents. 'Brent Hills wants to speak to me!' I yelled.

'Why?' Dad asked.

'I don't know, I haven't rung him back,' and I did so immediately, from the conservatory window where I'd once watched Dad and Joel play.

'I would love you to come in,' Brent said. 'I'd love to give you your first call-up.'

Birmingham's manager Marcus Bignot had been told too, which was protocol so that managers could release their players, and he called to congratulate me. The email from England confirming squad selection followed. And it said I was being picked up in a car rather than having to make my own way there, which was more standard. This really was next level.

I was fourth keeper, which means you're not going to get game time, so you're basically there to assist with drills, and I eagerly wanted to get on with anything they'd let me be involved with. I was now training alongside women I'd seen in the FA Cup Final when I was a teenage ball girl, all the while managing a nervy pressure circulating in my own head to give a good account of myself and make sure that the more experienced players never had reason to think I was lowering the standard of their work.

Just do not fucking get involved in anything but the football, I said to myself. *It's a senior environment. Speak when spoken to; do the drills.*

When I got back to Birmingham, my confidence was sky-high because of it and I was even more excited to train than usual, which was a pretty high benchmark to begin with.

I trained with the other keeper, Rebecca Spencer, and the goalkeeping coach.

'No!' he shouted as I sprinted off, jumping a hurdle a moment too early. 'I haven't said start yet.'

I went back, then I did something he didn't like again. He went off at me once more.

'It's not about you, you selfish little prick,' he barked.

'Why are you speaking to me like that?' I shouted back. Now, this was a whole other kind of first.

But he kept repeating himself: 'Who do you think you are?' he demanded.

I stood up for myself. 'I don't know why the fuck you're speaking to me like that.'

As I walked off the pitch I couldn't stop myself from crying. Kirsty Linnett, who I'd played with at Leicester and England

and was a friend at Birmingham now, too, headed over to try and calm me down.

When the coach came over to me some time later, at the suggestion of the manager, and told me 'I didn't mean that,' it turned out he was annoyed I hadn't called him to tell him about my England call-up. He felt unappreciated, while I thought, after Marcus's call, that I was meant to wait to hear from him. It taught me something about everyone's need for recognition, for a pat on the back. We moved on, and I don't know about him but I didn't hold a grudge. I never held a grudge when there was a job still to do.

It's one of the many ways I was realising that my brain leaned into its more masculine domain, something that had longed marked me out as different to other girls I knew and was now showing itself in a professional environment too.

That same season, Marcus told me during the course of a meeting: 'I know you're gonna make it 'cause, don't take this the wrong way, but you're kinda like a bloke.'

He wasn't saying I looked like a bloke or was physically like one, which I would have been insulted by. He was saying that the way I approached the game was more akin to how a man would and, while I wasn't at all impressed by the idea someone with a 'more female' mentality couldn't make it, I know exactly what he meant about me. I came in, did my work and progressed. I was matter-of-fact, logical and pragmatic, and I was unapologetic about my mindset and approach.

I was concerned with doing my own job and less so with what other people's responsibilities were – that was for them to contend with. This extended to making friends in football.

I wasn't too bothered because I didn't need the comfort of that to do what was required of me.

I could see that people found that unusual. Women so often feel they have to change themselves to fit into a certain environment. I saw lots of players my age growing pally with one another and with coaches, either because it came naturally to them or in the hope that it would help them to stay in that world. While still semi-professional, there was plenty of space for that kind of influence. That wasn't my style, though. I didn't know how to try to be something different just to impress another person. I think that was so foreign in the way a young woman presented herself that it confused or alienated people or made them think I was aloof or didn't care enough to put in the effort to be liked – that was never my intention. I felt it when people viewed me differently, but I was more concerned with being respected than liked. I enjoyed other people's company and if I made a friend, I was happy and grateful to have them. I hoped I was a good teammate regardless, and I was learning how to be.

I remember one game when the captain, who was having a hard time with the manager, had refused to take a penalty in order to stand up for herself. They'd had an argument in the middle of a game and she had been annoyed afterwards when no one in the team checked in on her. I thought that her seniority meant she wouldn't need to hear from me, but telling us that she felt upset by it taught me to always send a message and check in – better to have done that and be rejected because it wasn't needed than leave a teammate to think that no one cared. It was a small but memorable and important lesson in treating her how I wanted to be treated by people at work and by the women I played alongside. But I knew the difference between being a good workmate and establishing a friend for life, which was never what being in the game was about.

This was business, and my only focus and the only thing required of me was to turn up and to play.

In a man's world, that leads to results. When you're a woman who behaves like you're in a man's world, that gets results too, but it also brings discomfort.

SEVEN

DISCIPLINE IS THE HIGHEST FORM OF SELF-LOVE

After a single season, aged 21 and coming to the end of my second year at university, Birmingham made way for Bristol, a higher salary but – still four figures – and more travelling back and forth again in search of minutes with the first team.

The women's seasons were still played during spring and summer, and one of our early games was against Oxford United in the Continental Cup on a Friday night in early May. It was exam time at university, and my grades now counted towards my final degree.

It was unusual for the first-choice keeper to play in the cup, and I told the manager the week before the game: 'I have a really important exam the day of the game.'

'Do you really need to go to it?' he asked. This is why I didn't know any other women playing in goal in the WSL each week and studying full-time for a business degree: the two did not mix and I found a lack of understanding and appreciation in both directions. Lecturers didn't typically care for sport, and coaches didn't particularly care for academics. It wasn't easy.

I explained that I'd obviously love to be playing but the game was three hours' travel each way, plus prep, eating in the car, navigating traffic, none of which was easy or conducive to a good performance.

He thought for a moment then decided: 'No. I'd like you to play.' He gave me the Thursday off training and the next day I went from my exam straight to kick-off for our 9–1 win.

The juggle was hard, but it proved to me that a belief I had unknowingly carried over from childhood had now crystallised into something to which I held steadfast: discipline is the highest form of self-love.

I exercised this principle over and over again, and committing to it was all about strategy. I couldn't allow myself to get into a pattern of missing lectures or an exam because I'd be letting myself and my future down.

If there were 18 hours of lectures a week, the least I could do was attend because there was still the possibility that football would one day disappear and the material inside those textbooks and exam papers would be my lifeline.

Those experiences at university were my version of the women around me who paid to play, working jobs so they could sustain their semi-professional football careers just as I was working towards my future when I couldn't see an option of living it solely on a football pitch.

Even today, as the women's game grows exponentially, it is still not in a place where most of its players can rely on earning their futures from it. I see an opportunity to do things differently, differently from how we see it play out in the men's game, where academy kids come through and have to end their education by 16, swapping it for huge pay cheques, big nights out and fancy cars while they're still young and impressionable and unprepared for a quick influx of cash that can suddenly vanish. I think that girls who come through the system can pursue the dream of playing wholeheartedly at the top but there is a chance, still, to shape a system that is set up to give them space to continue their studies, even if that's online and at a far slower pace than their peers, taking care of their after-career as they take their first steps into the professional game.

I didn't have that option, which is why I had to fill my kitbag for life myself, but now, women's football is at a crossroads where it can choose to grow in a more sustainable, responsible way, allowing its players to make decisions differently, so they can give everything to the game without their lives depending on it.

For me, creating that future for myself meant some isolation: the other girls would train together every day, whereas I needed to come in and out based around my studies. I fine-tuned the balance again.

I'm sure it held me back from more opportunities to connect in meaningful ways with teammates and course-mates in either place but those were the sacrifices I had to make and, like everything, they were temporary.

My third year brought about respite from some of the intensity with a year in industry, which I spent interning at a sports marketing firm in Bristol, where accommodation and bills were paid for by the club and work and training were a much easier and more local fit.

When I'd joined the season before, Bristol had finished second and qualified for the Champions League, where we'd had a good campaign with a respectfully average team. The game was becoming a little more professional and you could feel it around you, especially there. Bristol was a great city, and a whale of a time in the sun, and the club had a particularly special connection with its fans, which was bigger than I'd seen before in the women's game. There was a loyal family vibe in the stands, where they'd sing the same songs, and it carried into the streets too. It was the first time that I'd played in a place where people would occasionally come up to me because they'd been to watch the games. There was one time, on the train to London, when the ticket inspector offered me an upgrade because he was a fan.

The goalkeeping coach there, John Granville, really believed in me. We both believed there were no excuses for anything but hard work and we worked relentlessly, doing extra training and repetitions together. I really appreciated the time and care he put into my development.

I joined a local gym and I'd go to spin classes or stay late, doing 45 minutes on the cross trainer before it closed, eagerly trying to stay fit and still desperately wanting to lose weight. I'd exercise at 9pm at night but not eat anything before or after, imposing a 7pm cut-off for food, even if I'd just played a game. The insecurities about my body that I'd developed as a teenager had never gone away, and the more women I was around in football, the more coaches I'd hear use that coded language, telling me in meetings that I wasn't fast enough when my times on the pitch were just fine, and I'd scrutinise myself because of it. I worried that the way they saw me physically reflected what they thought of me, and being in changing rooms full of women I noticed how they clocked one another's bodies or spoke about their own. Glances or whispers if someone was carrying more or not enough weight, or conversations around managing it, would continue among players at all levels I played in.

Away from home and living in a houseshare with my Bristol teammates, I was eager to do anything to keep another 0.1 kilograms off, all still with a total lack of understanding about food, weight, hydration, fuel and healthy cyclical fluctuations in women. I tried fad diet after fad diet, taking fat-burning pills from the pharmacy or health-food store, training on digestive biscuits or counting out seven Minstrels from the packet to give me an energy boost, with no nutritional meal to back it up. It was stupid. I did it in spurts for as many days or weeks as I could sustain it, losing a few kilos then putting them straight back on once I inevitably started and needed to eat normally again. I appreciated the concern and care of one of my housemates, a Spanish girl from the team, who noticed what I was doing at night and explained to me how vital it was that I fuelled before and after a game, even if it was just an omelette.

It amounted to an odd, lonely and not especially healthy situation where I'd work from home designing match-day programmes and other stuff for clients while still in my pyjamas, probably feeling a bit depressed, then turn up at the club and switch it on professionally, giving a hundred per cent to my football.

My mood wasn't helped by the fact that into my second

season with Bristol, players didn't seem to be treated kindly and I definitely wasn't among the manager's favourites.

I felt that he put me down on a day-to-day basis, so I started to ask him outright: 'Do you have a problem with me?' I was now able to articulate my concerns pragmatically enough to search for what I hoped was a reason so I could go away and address it in my game.

'No, why?' he'd answer.

'The way you speak to me gives me that impression,' I'd offer honestly, but the put-downs would keep coming, so my motivation had to come from within.

At the end of the season, fighting relegation to the recently created WSL2, the Women's Super League second tier, we played Liverpool at Widnes. They were looking to win the league that day on goal difference and we were drawing 0–0 at half-time, which was a great result for us.

When I walked into the dressing room he was already handing out tellings-off to a few people, so when he said: 'And you, why are you diving everywhere?' I looked up, thinking he was talking to one of the strikers.

But the girls were already looking at me, and then, I noticed, so was he.

'Why are you diving every time a shot goes wide?' he asked again.

He wasn't looking for an answer but in my head it was logical: Fara Williams, Liverpool and England's star midfielder, was good at shooting from distance, so I wanted to cover the goal. He'd already dismissed me and half the rest of the team. We went out and lost 3–0. At full-time, I went up to my mum in the stands and cried into her shoulder.

ALL IN

My experience has been that try as you might to hold it in and hold your nerve, as businesslike as I was, those moments of heartache and emotion come regardless in sport. It's the inevitable flip side to the elation. While I still knew not to project it onto others in football, I also knew I couldn't hold it in entirely any more.

Some of those heartaches were big, some were small, like that one against Liverpool, but repetition gave these moments the capacity to build up.

When I was put on standby for the 2015 World Cup squad that season, it felt like a miracle to be named at all. Everyone knew you weren't going to get off standby but I was ambitious enough to harbour a little bit of hope, just a tiny flicker left over from that year's birthday-cake wish that some unbelievable lucky break would arrive and I'd be needed at the last minute to fly out to Canada with the team. I know that was emotionally immature but I couldn't help the pang of disappointment when it didn't come. Watching the team get third place, I told myself to enjoy being one step closer to my wish, my dream of playing there too.

I continued in my disciplined league performances and soaked up the progress I was making in goal at Bristol too. With a new interim manager in charge, I walked away from the 2015 season with Players' Player, Supporters' Player and Manager's Player: my first cluster of individual awards and in a season in which we'd just been relegated. The team always supersedes the individual but awards made space for that kind of recognition and being acknowledged by my peers and by the fans for my impact on the team; especially as a goalkeeper, the position people paid less attention to when it came to celebration or glory. It was also a first lesson that while awards feel wonderful for a minute, it is the sense of walking away with the appreciation, the value you take from knowing that your art matters, that lasts longer than the excitement of holding a statuette or a trophy in your hand.

The mood of recognition was extending far beyond personal accolades and certainly beyond Bristol. With the WSL now well-established, there was the loudest talk yet of more money coming into the women's game, and with it a sense of standards and opportunities slowly moving forwards to reflect and respond to that.

I'd played for Bristol week in, week out, but they were one of the clubs who didn't show any sign that they were looking to invest in the same way. Either they didn't yet have the capacity or the finances or they chose not to, but the dial was moving forwards and I wanted to as well, so in February, 2016, I signed for Reading, who had just won promotion into WSL1, the Women's Super League top tier.

I was in my fourth and final year of university, still balancing two punishing schedules in a final push of self-discipline that I hoped would reward me one day soon, and living at Mum and Dad's back in Nottingham for the year. To minimise the effect of travel on my legs, body and mind, each week I'd do my Tuesday lectures in Loughborough, drive over to train in Reading that night, and stay over in the spare box room of a club houseshare (where five players were sharing a bathroom). I had Wednesdays off university, so I'd drive back at 5am every Thursday to be back on campus in time for my morning lecture.

Leaving Bristol felt hard. I had a strong sense of connection to the city where the fans and community had been such a big part of playing, but signing for a new club was always great – it always felt like the future and that motivated me to keep working as hard as I did, to be better, to be the greatest, to keep aiming for number one.

I arrived to find my own peg with my name and number – 19 – at the training ground, which delighted me, but I still had to earn my stripes. I was, unsurprisingly, a very serious trainer, not allowing anything that appeared like distraction, even a smile, to cross my face. That's what my dad had taught me, that professionalism looked serious, so I'd be doing drills with this intense, unmovable facial expression that backed up my bona fide 'I'm here for business' mentality.

Keeping footballs out of the net was, of course, my job but I was obsessed with it to the point that when we'd start a drill or reset before the next, and a coach would tell us to put all the balls in the back of the net in preparation, I simply didn't want to see them there. So, instead, I'd spend an extra 30 seconds or a minute, sorting them to the left or the right of the goalposts. *Why am I gonna start with the ball in the back of the net when my entire job is to keep it out?* I'd think to myself.

Every day I wanted to do more to further my quest for greatness. I wanted to put in half an hour extra in the gym or one hundred more repetitions than everyone else, so I was one hundred repetitions better. Repetition, consistency, competing with my yesterday self; that was my formula and it worked for me. It fulfilled me, pursuing my ambition, even in isolation. There were times when it also seemed lonely but I was content doing 'me'. I was used to not fitting in and already hardened to people not liking me and, both defensively and because I didn't want to lose a second of time I could be improving, it made me make even less effort than I already was to join in socially. There seemed little point.

Within a couple of months I was given an FA Cup game to start, against Sunderland, swapping into the number-one shirt and taking over from long-term keeper Grace Moloney, who was understandably not happy about the change. If being a keeper marked you out as different, goalkeeper groups could create places of belonging and great support but they also had the potential to be complicated environments: the same three or four personalities, keepers and a coach, working in close proximity every day with only one, the number one, who could play the games.

It was clear that there was a festering tension between us, in fact I wasn't sure by now if the fabled goalkeepers' union, the alliance and shared understanding that is said to exist between keepers, was a myth altogether or just a unicorn, rarely harnessed or even found. I had already established in my mind that a group where everyone at a club who played or trained in the position could be themselves and drive their standards together was something I aspired to be part of, whenever I earned the right and seniority to set the tone: somewhere welcoming, where competitiveness and difference were harnessed and accepted so everyone could thrive, whatever their experience and role.

Picking up on the strain, the goalkeeping coach had stopped both of us in training one day and commented on it: 'It doesn't bother me whether you and Grace talk or not,' he concluded, caring only what we did on the pitch.

'Me either,' I replied, abruptly. 'I'm just here to do my job.'

ALL IN

Having come up through the academy and helped them earn promotion, Grace sat on the bench while I inherited her spot and I understood how difficult that must have been.

A little while later she asked if the two of us could talk and told me: 'I didn't react well when you came in.' I thought that was so gracious, as nothing about that experience could have been easy for her. There was no grudge to hold and we became closer after that; when I made Professional Footballers' Association Team of the Year at the end of the season, Grace was whistling and cheering in support.

My biggest achievement that summer, though, wasn't in football – it was graduating university. Because Joel and I had ended sixth form only a year apart, and I did a longer, four-year degree, we wound up graduating on the same day in August, 2016, so Mum and Dad reached the only fair agreement that they could and decided that the family would split itself in half: Grandma and Dad would come to my ceremony in Loughborough and Mum and Annabelle would go to his in Kent. Mine was at 10:30am and Joel's was at 2pm, so I arranged with Dad to get my gown on, walk on stage, pick up my scroll, then walk straight out of the fire exit of Loughborough's huge sports hall, put Grandma in a taxi and jump in the car with Dad in a bid to make it down and catch Joel's, a three-hour drive away. We arrived two graduates after he'd been up on stage but we got to share a family meal afterwards to celebrate as a five anyway. Graduating my degree with a 2:1, with all the graft and grit and juggling it had taken, might have been the proudest I'd ever felt about myself.

I'd seen it through. I'd sat out all the uncomfortableness of the travel, the changes, the debt, the early mornings and the late nights, the not having a social life, all for the sake of a bigger goal of continuing with my football dream and getting a degree – a backup plan for when goalkeeping and I had reached our ultimate destiny.

It wasn't the quality of the education that I left with that would serve me best from then on, it was the ability to think critically and to be resourceful – things I want for all young girls growing up and coming of age in football's modern, exploding ecosystem. It was the chance to work at what I wasn't good at, like the accounting modules that jumbled my brain, and excel at the ones I was. It was that future freedom that I'd earned for myself to jump into a version of life that a future self would one day thank me for.

It had been so tempting to quit at times, to fast-forward to the dream of training every day, but I had forced myself to stay focused on my dual ambition.

A few months before I graduated, part way through my final year, I'd taken a call from Chelsea that exemplified the kind of self-discipline I'd required of myself.

'Emma Hayes wants you to join,' the coach had said of the team's manager. I'd been instantly thrilled and excited. Chelsea were forward-thinkers in their vision and investment in the women's team. But they trained full-time, the voice told me next.

'Do you realise I'm still at university?' I asked them.

'No,' came the reply, and when I asked next if there was a way I could join without giving up my final year of study, it didn't seem there was a way.

It could have looked like insanity to turn down that club and that manager but I believed in my ability to achieve what

I'd set out to do so. I had made countless hard decisions like that and proved to myself that I had the capacity to do so, to decipher when and how I could push through and how far. Sometimes that meant making sacrifices in my studies, sometimes it was in football. Neither was ready to accommodate the other yet, so I'd had to carve my own path through, twice. I wasn't the finished product but I knew that I would outwork anyone to give myself the greatest chance of getting there.

EIGHT

MOTIVATE FROM WITHIN TO MOVE FORWARDS

I must have taken something from my studies into life almost instantaneously, because I was already putting a little of what I'd learned about business into practice.

I'd brought an idea with me to Reading that I started up towards the end of my time at Bristol, a kids' coaching business called NextLevel Goalkeeping. Our visibility as players was increasing incrementally and fans would come to games with their sons and daughters and tell me afterwards or comment online (albeit in far fewer numbers than now) that their kid was a goalkeeper or that they watched me play and wanted to give it a go. I thought that was wonderful, but nothing existed for them to hone those skills so I wanted to create a place where they could learn and experience the importance of goalkeeping like I had when I was ten. If I coached them, they were already ten steps ahead of where I had been at their age, learning from a player with real-life and real-time experience in the game.

For the little girls especially, that kind of representation wasn't easy to come by and I saw a gap in the market where I could contribute value and make space for them. It wasn't about changing the world because it was only me, but I thought maybe it could change somebody's world: giving one young person hope, an outlet and some guidance was something that took away obstacles.

I trialled it with one-off sessions that people could give as Christmas presents, then established it as a regular offer, setting up my own website, business cards, leaflets and coaching tops once I arrived at Reading.

The women played way out of town there at Adams Park, which belonged to a local men's team and wasn't even in the Reading postcode, so we were fairly unknown. My priority was to contribute towards changing that by establishing a girls-only goalkeeping clinic using the club's more central training centre, known as the RTC.

So, when I renegotiated my contract for a second season I told the club: 'I'd love a little corner of a training pitch that I could use, for free, to coach goalkeeping.'

Unbelievably they said yes and gave me part of an astroturf pitch, off to the side of the main coaching area at their RTC sessions, to use for an hour every Thursday night, where I could train up to ten kids, charging £10 per child. They helped me to advertise it, too, using my graphics in match-day programmes or in their mail-outs.

It became a safe space for those girls and I felt a real connection to them. One of them had just lost her dad and I could see how she needed the escape that weekly goalkeeping practice offered her. I took my responsibility as a role model seriously and I realised that it was an honour to have anyone look up to you.

Among the girls was Robyn, who was ten and playing for Reading's under-11s. Her dad, Steve, had been a goal-keeper for Brighton Hove Albion and he and his wife Christina bought her two sessions plus a pair of gloves as a Christmas present.

Steve and I clearly had common ground and he took me into his own goalkeepers' union. Despite there being 20 years between us, Christina and I got on straight away, too; she was grateful that Robyn had someone to look up to in football and I was glad of something that felt like family in my new home town. I wasn't looking for it, but I found friendship, in fact a best friend in Christina; for years after I'd moved on from Reading, I looked forward to visits and dinners at their home, turning down their invitations until I'd finished playing there for fear it would appear unprofessional of me to mix work and pleasure. That's how intense my mentality was towards the game!

Over the years, time with their family would become highlights of life outside work. Their profoundly deaf eldest daughter Georgia and I would sing Cher songs together that I'd learned from Mum's time teaching at the deaf school, and both girls grew to call me 'big sis'. With Christina, they would follow me around the world for all that was to come in my career later on, joining the close ranks of my nearest and dearest.

As part of the contract renegotiation that had won me the pitch space for my goalkeepers' clinic, Reading had also offered me the vice-captaincy, which was, of course, very tempting but I had turned it down off the bat.

'You can't commit to that in writing, you have to do that according to the squad,' I said. 'You can take it out. I'll do my job anyway,' I promised them.

What I did accept was the reasonable (for where the game was at) five-figure salary that I was now being paid and, after years of working hard, being diligent, having no social life and squirrelling away whatever earnings I could from my toy shop and coaching jobs back home and from football, I saw the opportunity to buy my first house.

I knew that it didn't make business sense to rent and I didn't want to be in a houseshare anymore. If everything I did had a performance motivation, I was clear that being on an inflexible cleaning rota and sharing a bathroom were not helping me to become a top athlete. Through every imaginable workaround and a whole load of determination I managed to defy the mortgage advisor who'd told me I needed to double my deposit and moved heaven and earth to get enough together for a one-up, one-down in Earley, an enormous estate a couple of miles outside central Reading. Getting a mortgage as a low-earning footballer was hard, given you're expected to retire by 30, but I knew from my degree that I wasn't going to make money from leaving it in the bank, I needed to invest and property was a smart choice. I was 24 and being a homeowner along with being a graduate became another extremely proud moment in my young life. I felt that my hard work, planning and consistency were allowing me to create freedoms.

I didn't have a single penny left so there was no furniture, no sofa and no Wi-Fi. That first night after picking up my keys I walked to the local Asda for some chicken and a packet of 19p chips, reduced in the hot deli section, took them back to my house and sat down, the carpet as my chair and the cardboard box that contained a microwave Mum had bought as a moving-in gift as my table for dinner. It was perfect, and the year still had more in store for me.

During the past 12 months, I'd been getting called up more regularly to England as the senior squad's fourth and then third keeper.

I'd trained and played with them at incredible places, which provided more pinch-me moments, including Real Madrid's complex, and been called up for fixtures against France, Spain and the Netherlands, wearing 13 and 21 or whatever squad number was free for me, training alongside the biggest names in the game, women like Alex Scott, Jill Scott, Karen Carney, Fara Williams and Karen Bardsley in goal.

I wanted desperately to be a regular fixture in the first team, and knuckling down whenever I was brought into their orbit was helping to turn that into a tangible reality. By the time the 2017 Euros came around in the Netherlands that July, the manager, Mark Sampson, called me up as the 24th player, an extra, fourth keeper in a core squad of 23. In fact, I'd had the call to say my house offer was accepted the day I first met up with the Euros squad at Wembley.

I wasn't even a registered squad member, I was travelling as a training player, but being there felt amazing. I trained my heart out, happy and overwhelmed just to be a part of it.

I soaked up everything about being at a tournament, on the pitch and off: each drill, every workout in the gym at the hotel in Utrecht overlooking the canal, walks through Amsterdam with the girls, including Millie Bright and Lucy Bronze, and being moved and inspired by our visit to the Anne Frank House. I even remember my first frozen yoghurt, but mostly I remember every moment of sitting in the stands watching us reach the knockout stages then the semi-finals, so eager to learn, improve and play a bigger part and so thrilled with the one I had for now.

When we reached the semi-finals, I was so excited that we'd beaten France that I ran onto the pitch to celebrate with the girls in a pile-on.

Then when we were knocked out by the hosts in a 3–0 defeat, which saw a header from Vivianne Miedema, a chip from Daniëlle van de Donk and an unfortunate own goal seal the Netherlands' place in the final, I felt all the deflation and sadness of leaving the first major tournament I'd been taken to and, in equal measures, the pride and motivation of having now represented my country there.

When I was with England, the exhilaration of being part of it, the pinch-me of training with the national senior squad, often created a smokescreen through which it became easy to ignore how younger players could feel mistreated. There was a clear hierarchy and people in place who were happy to take the opportunity to pull rank with a young keeper whose job was basically to pick up the balls.

I kept my head down, grateful to do any of it, but after one blow-out session during the tournament, Lee, the coach, had us running up and down, up and down. Then, as I was panting for breath at the end, ordered me: 'Mary, go get me a drink.' That didn't feel like it was my job. I kicked a bottle that was lying on the floor as I walked off the pitch to fetch it.

'What's wrong?' he said, when I returned with his cup.

'Nothing,' I said, dishonestly.

'Go on, tell me. You've got something to say,' he pressed.

'You told me to get you a drink,' I confessed.

'Good,' he said, 'good,' happy to see me speak up.

Maybe he'd been testing how far my eagerness to stay there would push me; he knew I'd feel ridiculed in that moment, and that I was too green to say anything, especially carrying the scars of weeks away from home, training at my best every day, happy to be there and fearful of doing or saying anything that squandered it.

The team psychologist came over to check on me after that, a rarity outside playing members of the squad; the acknowledgement gave me the confidence to know that this behaviour was neither normal nor necessary.

In another session, he'd set us up with a handling drill. Lee had come from the men's game, which I loved, because they kicked the ball a bit harder at us and had massive game experience that challenged me more.

But when the other keepers would drop the balls, he'd tell them: 'That's my bad serve.'

If I dived the right way, I got: 'That didn't count.'

Singled out; different again.

Carly Telford, a more experienced keeper, would tell me to leave it, and I did, ploughing all my energy into my work.

But it didn't relent.

'Do you say anything other than "yeah"?' he asked me during one of our development meetings between matches.

I didn't know how to respond.

'You're too enthusiastic, you want it too much,' he gave back, leaving me feeling belittled.

If a coach had something technical to say about my crossing or my jumping I could take that, as I wanted to learn and grow. But if caring as much as I did was the worst thing he had to say about me in a development meeting and if that meant he didn't like me, then no problem, I would motivate from within to move forwards. That desire, the extra reps, the hunger that he used to beat me with is what would one day make me successful.

In other workplaces these are moments where human resources might step in, but that didn't exist in football. Everyone wanted to be in the squad, so you took those personal blows, ones which had nothing to do with your performance, because speaking up or criticising the powers-that-be brought the real risk that you were out. I didn't agree with it, but I knew that to be the case. So, I performed in spite of those people.

When Mark was sacked only a few weeks later, for inappropriate and unacceptable behaviour towards another player, and Lee resigned, Mo Marley was brought in.

'I don't know why you're number four,' she told me at her first camp. My motivation was still something to be harnessed in her eyes; my hard work to be matched by recognition.

At Reading, things weren't plain sailing either. There was a new goalkeeping coach and my intuition was that I was falling out of favour.

'You don't do anything socially with your team, you need to be liked by them,' he'd told me. It was true that I still had my guard up and wasn't sociable but I also wasn't invited when others in the group would get together and go out for food. And *why* did I have to be liked when I was there to work?

Being excluded hurt, but whether I socialised or not wasn't affecting my game. Once again the criticisms being levelled at me weren't about football and that always felt hard and personal, especially after those interactions with England.

I asked Phil, the assistant coach, if that's what the girls were saying.

'No,' he assured me. 'I'd have said if it was.'

Phil was engaged to the manager, Kelly Chambers, and she and I had a conversation around Christmas where I told her: 'Something feels off.'

'Everything's good,' she replied. But I wasn't sure that was true. Picking up on energy, misalignments, off the pitch was as important to surviving and thriving in football as understanding the energy on the pitch. It felt like something she said to placate me and close down the conversation in order to keep a lid on things. I could sense that they were ready to move in a different direction to me, and if I wanted to compete with my yesterday self that meant that I should be too.

So when German side VfL Wolfsburg came in for me with the offer of a 12-month contract, I wondered if it was the universe sending me a message, giving me a nudge to make a big move.

Reading had finished fourth in the table, my highest finish yet, but I'd been playing in the WSL for eight seasons now and they hadn't put anything on the table or had a conversation with me about extending my career there. Wolfsburg, meanwhile, was one of the best teams in the world, definitely in Europe. They'd just finished the 2017–18 season as Germany's back-to-back Frauen-Bundesliga champions and had already competed in four Champions League finals and won two.

I was 25, and making a move that would allow me to play

and train alongside women who had achieved all that was a compelling prospect.

Was it time for change?

At the end-of-season presentation, days before my contract was due to end, Kelly came over and sat down next to me.

'We want to extend your contract,' she said. 'Let's sit down on Tuesday.' I was surprised.

Tuesday passed, then on Wednesday, she pulled me after training.

'We love you, you're our number-one goalkeeper. We want you to stay,' she pledged.

'I've not felt like that,' I told her, frankly, reminding her of our conversation at Christmas and explaining how it felt like nothing had changed. I was sad about it; I liked the club a lot and I'd put down roots there but our relationship felt like it had deteriorated.

'As we're having an honest conversation, I'd like to be honest with you about something. I've had interest from other teams and there's one I'm seriously considering.'

I told her I wasn't expecting a contract offer from Reading so late in the day and was under the impression that they were happy for me to move.

'Who?' Kelly asked.

'Wolfsburg.'

'That's amazing to have an offer from such an amazing team.' She was genuinely happy for me.

Reading did come back with a counter-offer: a little more than they were already paying me, which I agreed to consider. We had one league game left to end the season against Birmingham City, away.

ALL IN

Before the match Kelly texted me: 'Can we speak before the team meeting?' and of course I agreed.

'How are you?' she asked as we grabbed a seat in the canteen.

'I was fine before I got the text,' I said. 'So come on, tell me you're not playing me.'

'We're going to play Grace,' she confirmed.

'But we were just speaking about my contract a few days ago,' I replied.

'I hope you can separate those two conversations,' Kelly said.

'But they're not separate,' I responded.

Was this because I'd told her about the offer from Wolfsburg?

I wondered if I'd been too honest; authenticity and open-ness could be such a double-edged sword. I felt frustrated with the situation. I should have kept my mouth shut.
I asked if I could be excused from the team meeting to gather my thoughts. I made two calls – first, to Dad, still the first port of call for anything related to football and business, then to my newly appointed agent. 'They're not playing me,' I told him. 'I don't think they want me here and I can't sign a contract. Push the conversation forwards with Wolfsburg.'

Until then, I'd waited out of respect for Reading. Kelly had said that she'd call in a couple of weeks to give me space for my decision but she never did. My season was over now and the universe was showing me where to go next.

There was no bad blood with Reading, but knowing when an environment is no longer serving you or bringing the best out of you has become a valuable lesson.

I remember meeting up with a teammate not long after who had recognised, too, that my time at Reading was up that day;

I found that reassuring and still do when it can feel easy to be desensitised to the way football works or second-guess your own instincts on decisions that are being made, or pushed, around and about you.

Knowing how long to stay in a situation and when to leave is hard to judge from the inside. Sometimes you might stay too long or leave too early, but only I could choose. And my instincts were proving a trusted guide.

My teenage love affair with football had now taken me into the middle of my 20s. The ups and downs had prepared and hardened me, motivated and shaped me. I'd grown from a girl whose difference marked her out into the kind of woman, footballer and goalkeeper that people didn't expect to exist in these spaces. I'd seen so many girls drop out along the way because the circumstances and conditions could not sustain them any longer, but none of it forced me back. These experiences only made me hungrier to move forwards.

I wanted to be the best in the world. So I had to get out in the world to play my way there.

PART TWO

INTUITION

NINE

UNIQUENESS IS TO BE CELEBRATED

Wolfsburg felt, intrinsically, like the right place for me to be when I moved there in summer, 2018.

I'd been there with my agent to scope out a super-small part of town: you could walk the entire route down to the stadium where we would be playing games. When I returned to begin pre-season training it was my first time living abroad and I didn't speak or understand a word of German, but everything about it spoke to me in words that said something good is going to happen for you here.

They'd brought me in as second keeper and I was to spend the season sitting behind Almuth Schult, one of the most accomplished goalkeepers in the game. Almuth had helped Germany to win gold at the Rio Olympics in 2016 and I considered her not only to be accomplished but to be the best in the world. Because she rightfully had Wolfsburg's number-one shirt, I'd take number 27.

The move meant I'd be playing far less regularly than I had in the WSL and it was the first, and only, time in my career that I chose the opportunity to learn over the opportunity to play. I was especially conscious of what that might mean for my place in the England squad, given it was a World Cup that promised the chance for me to join the team when they headed out to the biggest stage of them all at the end of the season. I knew that if England could see me playing, it would help my chances of being picked, but I also knew that I could develop my game to such a degree at Wolfsburg that it would serve my chances of representing and progressing with England better too. Learning now, in the obsessive, all-in way that was my habit, would buy me playing time in the future.

I'd been mesmerised by German goalkeeping for years. I used to watch their training sessions on YouTube and I loved the explosive, athletic training style that was very different to traditional goalkeeper training. I felt there were things in my game that I didn't do well, one-on-ones, diving explosively into corners, and learning the German way would help me to improve on that.

I was a small player in a team full of stars, a club of international names who were regulars in the German and other national sides. A group of us including Denmark's Pernille Harder, Caroline Graham Hansen from Norway, Iceland's Sara Björk Gunnarsdóttir, Germany's Babett Peter and American Ella Masar instantly became friends and we earned ourselves the nickname 'the fab six'. It still pops up now and again online and in tags on TikTok videos, and we're all still in touch – Ella and Babett's two sons, in Chicago, are my adored godsons and the girls continue to be sources of wisdom and support to me.

Babs asked me early on to be her roommate for away trips that season and, despite training together every day, sometimes twice, we'd all still end up hanging out at one another's flats in the evenings. Through both their friendship and our camaraderie as a team, this group of high-performing women taught me a life lesson that profoundly shaped who I would become: they showed me that everybody does things differently and that uniqueness is to be celebrated, professionally and personally.

My dad had instilled it into me that goalkeeping is all about concentration and I had followed the mantra diligently all these years, believing my professionalism looked like behaving a certain way: I'd never touch alcohol because that felt undisciplined and I worried it would reduce my reaction time on the pitch; I wouldn't smile on game day or answer messages because that might be an indicator that I wasn't focused, and I still turned up to all my training sessions with that same immovable expression. I felt I was cheating the process if I broke these self-imposed rules, so I never did.

But here was a group of women at the top of their game who would joke together at work, have a glass of wine with dinner, laugh and cry together. It was easy friendship and I don't think I'd experienced that in a group before. I didn't have to pretend to be anyone with them – we were all accepted. It was the first time I'd felt that, socially, within a team, a stark contrast to the places I'd played previously where I was afraid to show my whole personality, assuming everyone disliked me off the bat.

I felt extremely happy with the Wolfsburg girls and I was growing as a person and a footballer with them.

I got access to a gym that was next to the stadium and used it regularly, still in the habit of going late at night to be 30 minutes better off, or in better shape, than my yesterday self.

On the pitch, I learned a completely different training style, a new physicality that up until then had captivated me only through a screen. Almuth was incredibly generous in teaching me: she knew she was the best and she was happy to impart her experience. This was very unusual and very not English. She was so outwardly self-assured a lot of people would have struggled to work with her but I thoroughly enjoy that kind of confidence or even arrogance in a player who delivers. I wanted to know how she did these great things, and she was open to share. I considered myself lucky to learn from her.

Among other facets of goalkeeping, my time at Wolfsburg completely changed my diving style. The World Cup Final save that would one day be replayed on millions of screens? That was the school of Wolfsburg. Being there taught me how to communicate and adapt but, as is so often the case, the steepest learning curve came from my failures that season. I remember in one of the first shooting sessions getting nowhere near the balls and feeling mortified that I'd put in such a bad performance, certain I couldn't put myself through a repeat of the humiliation.

Most memorably, though – and it still stays with me today – in the February, Almuth was out injured, meaning it was my turn to start against Bayern Munich. We were battling with them for top of the table and it was a huge game. And one of my worst ever. We played terribly; my performance in particular. Worse still, the England goalkeeping coach was in the stands watching me as World Cup selection edged closer. We lost 4–2 and I walked off feeling like I'd let a lot of people down.

The obvious and incredibly exposing thing about goalkeeping is that your mistakes, conceding goals, are plain to see and impossible to ignore in public so it always feels shameful, embarrassing, and you feel responsible. 'I lost so badly,' I told Sara after the game, still standing on the pitch. 'Mary,' she said, 'we all played badly.' She was handing me another lesson: that this loss was everyone's responsibility, not just mine. It was one of only four chances I had to come off the bench and start that season but, at every turn, being there was opening my eyes to what it was to be part of an elite team and to who I wanted to be as a person and a player.

Failing in that game allowed me to succeed in future ones; that season and those moments shifted my ability to deal with pressure, too, and it's what fans and commentators saw in my performances at the Euros and the World Cup a few years later. Pressure wasn't something to fear, it was something I could harness, something to be used in the pursuit of success.

My season at Wolfsburg closed, having taught me how to be a real adult, and made way for summer and the 2019 World Cup in France. Phil Neville was the manager now, and he had played me in a couple of friendlies and started me in a Euros qualifier against Kazakhstan at their Central Stadium in Pavlodar, where we won 6–0 without the kind of defensive pressure that required much from me. I'd been thrilled to get the senior caps and the start, and pleased that he saw something of what I knew was inside me.

He called me up as third-choice keeper for the World Cup, part of his core 23-woman squad. When you're the last of three keepers, you don't go with any expectation of getting game time, you're there as a workhorse, but that was fine by me and I dutifully carried the balls in training, did every shooting drill and every penalty shoot-out practice. Going from fourth to third was another small step in the direction of meeting my potential, of getting closer to the day I could show I could be England's number one on a stage like this, and I was as grateful as ever about seeing my name in the squad and being given the opportunity to travel to another major tournament with England. It was part of the dream, but the reality check of those Euros training sessions a couple of years earlier alongside the benefit of a bit more professionalism and a different club environment under my belt meant that while I still trained my heart out, I felt a bit more disconnected, or maybe frustrated, this time, as I didn't have anywhere much to direct my efforts to help the team. I suppose I knew I could do more, it just wasn't my time yet.

My passion remained but maybe a bit of my naivety had faded as I'd matured as a person and player during my year with Wolfsburg.

I also had my dreadful fear of flying, and spent a chunk of the tournament completely traumatised by a journey we'd made between bases, part way through, when our plane nearly dropped out of the sky. Honestly, I thought we were going to die as the plane plummeted somewhere over France. I don't know how the pilot pulled us back up but I barely spoke for three days after that ordeal.

*

It must have been half-time in one of the matches when Phil told the girls: 'Let's get some goals and then I can bring Mary on.' I liked Phil and I was overwhelmingly thrilled that he wanted to get me involved, which in hindsight is pretty telling about how accepting I was of how I was spoken about. Clearly I needed to work on my self-worth because that night my roommate, Toni Duggan, asked me how I felt about what he'd said. Toni was my closest friend in the England team: she'd been called back into camp when I was brought in for the first time, and she was one of the few faces of English women's football who was well known enough to be doing some commercial work when there was barely any of it around. She was from Liverpool, and had the sense of humour and football club to match, despite having played for Everton. She made me comfortable enough to let my guard down and show some of my personality. I could have a laugh and be a bit vulnerable with Toni.

So when I answered her question by saying it felt good to be considered by him to play, she looked back quizzically. 'I think it's pretty rude,' she suggested. I felt she was right: the manager who believed in me was only going to put me on if there was nothing riding on it and he'd said as much in front of the team. Maybe I needed to rethink how much he valued me – and how I valued myself if I was still content to lap up humiliation like that.

Probably the best thing that came out of that World Cup was that I bumped into a man called Ian Willcock, a goalkeeping coach at Manchester United, as I walked along Nice's Promenade des Anglais, the long seafront that tracks beside the turquoise Côte d'Azur sea. I was with Mum and

Dad, who were there for the tournament, and Willco had come out to scout a new keeper; more specifically, he told me later on, to drive around France for a fortnight trying to pin me down between games. He stopped and introduced himself and I was immediately struck by a warm energy and an authenticity that I hadn't much encountered from many people in football before.

Two weeks later, United came in with a late offer to start the season with them. I'd already had verbal offers and was waiting for terms from teams in Germany, Spain and England. United was only one year into their women's football journey but the manager, former Lioness Casey Stoney, was ambitious and had a vision of competing in the Champions League within three to five years, which I liked the sound of.

Willco was ambitious too, for me specifically. 'I think we can make you one of the best in the world,' he told me.

I'd had that belief alive in me for so long but he was the first person in the game to reflect it back. And he meant it. I knew I had a lot of work ahead but I'd been with the best at Wolfsburg and I'd seen that I could mix with them. He believed in me and presented a whole individual development programme for how he'd get me there, which felt new in the women's game.

I've asked Willco, since that day, what he saw in me back then and his answer has always been the same: my distribution, crosses, shot-stopping ability, but also that I had the will to win and that desire to improve each day.

He would become a trusted friend, someone in football who cared truly about the person and not just the performance and knew how the two were inseparable. There were many times to come where, even when success was heady and abundant, he'd see my head down and, instead of walking past, would stop and ask: 'What are you thinking?' Or message out of the blue with 'How are you?' because he knew I needed it.

I signed for United, at a table in the men's dining room, on a modest sum, a fraction of deals regularly signed by male players. (For context, David de Gea reportedly became the club's highest-paid player and the world's highest-paid goalkeeper on around £19.5m, with sponsorship, that same season.) I was 26 and moving to one of the biggest names in global football. All I wanted was to meet my own potential; in fact, alongside flying and complacency, not doing so had become a real fear of mine, probably the biggest of all three. Now, I thought, I was somewhere with a clear direction to help me get there. *This is amazing*, I thought. *I'm going to be here for the rest of my career.*

Like motivation, that potential dwelled within me because when it came to the conditions that now surrounded me and the other girls at United there was work to be done. There were no frills for the women's team. We played and trained at Leigh Sports Village, which was open to the public, so you'd sometimes arrive for training and have to clean the dog muck off the grass on the three pitches out back before the session could start. There was nothing stopping anyone from our competitor clubs meandering up and stopping to watch our tactical work if they fancied it.

We had access to a gym which we shared with Leigh Centurions, the local men's rugby team who had priority use, so we'd walk equipment up in the lift to the top floor of the athletics track building to get some extra strength and conditioning time in.

United's men's team, who trained over at Carrington, had a dining room with a salad bar and four or five options for every meal, as you'd expect of an elite sports outfit of their standing; our food was supplied by the sports centre – scrambled egg and cereals in the morning and a pasta dish for lunch. Not awful but, nutritionally, not there.

Before I got to Manchester, I had to find and buy myself a car and sort somewhere to stay. While I looked for something more permanent, the club suggested digs for me and another player, Wales' Hayley Ladd, for £10 a night at the home of an elderly lady in Astley, a 15-minute drive away.

In return, she gave me a bed in a tiny room with patterned wallpaper, salmon-coloured carpet and no Wi-Fi, so I was going down to the local Nando's to download something to watch most nights in an attempt to wind down.

None of it was conducive to rest and therefore performance, so I spent a total of £80 with her and went to stay with Mum and Dad for a couple of nights at a time whenever I could, driving the two hours from home to training and back, listening to Mariah Carey.

When I got my first pay cheque, Willco helped me find and move into a modern upside-down terrace where the kitchen was on the top floor and the bedroom was downstairs, which I rented in Salford for £795 a month, renting out my own house in Reading to a former teammate who'd moved in as a tenant when I left the season before for Wolfsburg.

In Manchester, the team trained most days, arriving for breakfast then a team meeting where we'd prep for the next game, do half an hour's pre-activation in the gym and a couple of hours training, mostly with the goalkeepers, then join in with the rest of the team. On two of the days there would be a gym session till three or four o'clock. I always wanted to do more and there were plenty of times when Willco would either tell me 'not today' and walk me off the grass or let me strike a deal with him for five minutes more.

On the pitch I kept my number 27 shirt from Wolfsburg and my first match of the season wearing it with the United badge was a derby against Manchester City, a 1–0 defeat at the Etihad, then against Arsenal at Leigh, where I made a double save – a cross came in to my left before I stood and blocked the second. I remember Willco's face as I looked into the crowd and shouted 'Yassss!' I'm not sure they were very used to that. 'Yes to the passion,' his face was telling me, 'but deal with the corner first.'

A couple of weeks in, on a Friday night against Liverpool, I got my first clean sheet for the club – and the team had their first WSL win, another thrill. I'd made friends among the girls enough to get along but that still wasn't a prime concern in football; I knew that women like those I'd met in Germany came around only every so often and I was here to work, to make games more than I needed to make friends. After Wolfsburg, my standards for myself and the standards I wanted to drive up in my teammates had never been higher and I know that there were times I annoyed people by telling them what I thought we needed to do, bluntly. Having honest conversations with people you're competing alongside is a skill to be honed, it requires an openness and vulnerability that didn't come easily to me, and Willco had to talk to me more than once about learning to refine the way I delivered what I wanted to say to get a valuable message across and achieve results without pissing people off by being too abrupt. It was a work in progress.

The main thing was that it was going well at United and internationally, and I was about to be given a big chance in November of that year when Phil Neville announced he would start me against Germany at Wembley. I was over the moon. This was the real deal, this was the wishes over my birthday cake candles coming true, my relentless will to improve everyday coming to fruition.

The Lionesses weren't selling out stadiums yet but this was pretty close, with a crowd of almost 78,000. Phil made the choice to put me in the number 13 shirt which, again, with hindsight, was strange and sent a tough message which took away from a big moment: my first opportunity to wear the hallowed number 1 for my country on hallowed ground. But I was genuinely delighted and grateful to him for giving me my first game against a top nation at our national stadium. I played OK, but not amazing. There were things I should have done better and the goalkeeping coach made it clear to me that he thought I was to blame for the 2–1 loss. I knew I had to carry that and it felt heavy.

In my next game for United we lost 1–0 to Chelsea but, by contrast, when Casey and Willco called me to the back of bus to talk through the game, I could feel that they did it from a place of care, about both me and the team and what we took away from it. The two of them kept me focused.

The next England camp was coming up in February at St George's Park, including the SheBelieves Cup, where we'd travel to the USA and play them, Japan and Spain.

ALL IN

A week or so beforehand I was on a night out in London with friends, watching *Magic Mike Live* of all things. We'd screamed and laughed through the show, then when we stepped outside afterwards I pulled out my phone and saw a missed call from Phil at 8:30pm. Phil never called me and I knew immediately what this meant. My heart sank into the paving stones of Leicester Square, where I stood as people poured out from the shows and bars around me. I didn't call him back.

Instead, knowing that United would have been informed about selection before the players were, I called Casey. 'He's not picking me,' I said. She confirmed my intuition.

I tossed and turned all night in the hotel room where I was staying and headed down to the street outside to call him back at 8:30am the following morning to hear it directly.

'I'm not taking you to camp,' he said.

I asked him why.

'I just think you've had a dip in your performance.'

'Can you give me reasons?' I asked. I'd literally saved a penalty in a match the weekend before – I didn't understand why he thought I'd dipped.

'It's nothing,' he said. 'Just a feeling. I don't want to take you all the way to America and not play you.' He wanted to give younger players a go, he said.

'Why do I have to be the sacrificial lamb?' I remember asking, although there was no answer forthcoming that satisfied me. I was ready to meet my potential and this was a roadblock unaccompanied by what I thought was a fair explanation.

Before we hung up, Phil made a point of reassuring me: 'But don't worry,' he said, 'it's only temporary. You'll be back in the next camp.' He told the press the same.

I held on to his promise but I was devastated. I didn't want to tell my parents and watch the disappointment stretch across their faces, and I wasn't good at taking the inevitable embarrassment when my name wasn't included in the squad announcement either.

At training the next day, Willco told me: 'We're going to work really hard, you'll be flying.'

I knew I was good enough but I was honestly beginning to wonder what the point of all this was. I'd put in so much. For so long, I'd not only worked hard, I'd done the repetitions, taken everything to completion and made it my point to work harder than anyone. Wasn't that how you reaped the rewards? How you earned the chance to take your next step and touch your life's goals? For the first time ever, I began to feel something unimaginable; I felt disillusioned with football and unsure what I was doing in life, chasing this dream that was constantly in reach but never fully within my grasp. And then, abruptly, lockdown hit. And the world changed, at either the best possible time for me – or the very worst.

TEN

WHAT'S MEANT FOR YOU WON'T MISS YOU

We were each given an allotted time to go down to the training ground and collect a bag of footballs and a bit of training gear to keep us busy at home for what we thought might be a couple of weeks, tops.

Footballs were an obvious choice for an outfield player but less use for a goalkeeper living alone with no one to hurl them. I had a bit of decking and some shrubs out back but what I needed was a wall for drills. I took the balls back home anyhow, shut the door and barely saw a soul for the next four months.

I certainly wasn't going to be able to train as a goalkeeper, which took away the thing that had consumed me every day for more than 15 years. More damaging was that, after what had happened with England, I wasn't sure I even wanted to anymore.

I didn't know what it felt like to be unmotivated before this.

I was always the person who tried too hard, who'd rather try and fail than fail to try. But now I could feel the absence of football, in just the way I was so used to feeling its presence. Football was shut down and my chance to play for my country was gone. With the world on fire, I didn't see how I would ever get it back. My mental strength was collapsing.

The world at large was a frightening and unsettling place, with death counts mounting, and I was terrified of something happening to people I loved, especially Grandma.

Mum and Dad asked me to go home but I didn't want to be with them or anyone else.

'I'll stay here in case football starts,' I told Dad, making excuses. I'd never really told him 'no' before.

My life had been built around a structure for when I trained, ate and even when I slept for as long as I could remember. It was my scaffolding. Suddenly, after rarely ever having had more than a day off at a time, I could do whatever I wanted.

I threw everything I knew out the window and did all of it, in any measure, whenever I wanted, kidding myself that this break from the grind could do me good. I stopped answering my phone, watching friends' and family's names flash across the screen then waited for the backlight to dim as I returned to whatever I was watching on TV.

I barely moved from the sofa, shovelling down biscuits instead of meals, and developed horrific sleep patterns, watching the final episode of *The Last Dance*, the documentary series about Michael Jordan's Chicago Bulls, then looking up to realise it was 5am.

I told myself that I was enjoying making decisions for myself for the first time in adulthood, choosing what I did with my time and what I didn't.

In reality, I was taking the isolation we'd been forced into and letting it do its worst and it didn't take long to realise that this whole situation was a dangerous invitation to demons.

My whole life I'd believed that vulnerability and huge floods of emotion were weakness, but now that the doors were closed I could be as vulnerable as I chose, on my own, away from everyone. It was like the times I used to cry in my bedroom over my frustration at my hunger to play.

The truth is, I was in pure survival mode but barely surviving at all.

About two months in it became clear that the league wasn't resuming. The manager set up challenges via WhatsApp which were designed to keep us connected, maybe motivate us in an un-motivating time, with points on offer for cooking nutritious meals or posting training videos. I didn't see the point in taking part. When it came to football, following things to the letter hadn't got me where I thought it would so what was I trying to prove? Extra-curricular activities were no longer part of my survival mode, so I ignored it.

To add insult to injury, I started drinking in a way I wasn't used to. I put Echo Falls Summer Berries Vodka in the freezer and poured it out with diet lemonade and strawberries suspended in ice cubes, like another indulgent treat.

When I ran out, I'd go down to the local shop and stock up again while I queued for essentials like toilet roll.

On one of the many days that melted into the next, I remember going to the Tesco superstore round the corner where the queue was out the door and you had to follow social-distancing rules, two metres between each shopper, through every aisle of the store as you gathered what you needed. I slowly snaked that entire supermarket, not picking up a thing, until I got to the drinks aisle. I wasn't drinking myself into oblivion but for someone who usually didn't touch it at all, it felt too much and completely out of hand.

I'd never drunk like that in my life, but for now it was the perfect way of numbing, of not feeling, and that, I decided, was what I needed above all else.

Meanwhile, I was piling on pounds and annihilating my fitness, and that old body-consciousness about being big and bulky was back with an angry vengeance, so I stopped eating as much. Relying on junk food wasn't making me happy anyway, so instead I underfed myself, which was just as destructive. I told myself I was experimenting with fuel, working out what my body needed, but that was nonsense. Not eating was also getting me drunk and therefore numbing my feelings quicker. For two weeks straight I ate nothing but soup, drank Echo Falls at night, and continued trashing my body and my self-confidence.

I had withdrawn into a shadow of myself – and then become someone I didn't recognise at all.

The only person I'd check in on occasionally was Grandma because I was so paranoid that she'd get Covid and I wouldn't get to see her again, but I hid the depth of the darkness that I was allowing myself to sit within. And no one else who loved me knew the extent of it either, because I wasn't speaking to any of them. I just didn't have the capacity to talk or reach out. I went into my shell.

None of my behaviour was conscious. If it had been,

I'd have been horrified by what I was doing to myself. And what I was doing to my friends and family, who must have been worried.

With hindsight, I don't judge myself at all for trying to get through in the way that I did, I was just putting one foot in front of the other so I didn't give up and give in entirely. What I can see now is that I was probably struggling with depression or anxiety, maybe both. In the midst of those things it becomes hard to contextualise things, as much as you try. I understood the gravity of what was happening in the world around me but I couldn't ignore what I was feeling. I simply didn't have enough clarity to see all of it.

Football had always given me a purpose. It was the reason I'd been put on this planet. My whole identity was as an athlete and my only aim had been to be the best goalkeeper in the world. Now I wasn't sure if I had anything left to work towards and weeks of solitude had given me all the space I needed, or dreaded, to question what it was that I'd committed my life to: this pursuit, this game, a career that didn't seem able to give me anything back anymore.

Without football, I realised I didn't fear anything any longer. Nothing. Not even death. It sounds strange to say that now, especially when death was such a real threat then for so many people fighting for their lives. But to me at the time I felt if I wasn't going to achieve what I was meant to accomplish then what was there left to be afraid of? I lost the will to fight and, in some of those moments, I lost the will and the desire to live. For the first time in my life, I wondered if there was any point in me being here any longer. I don't believe I was ever going to end it all but I thought, too many times, about how I could.

My demons had stepped in and replaced my passion, so by the time we were allowed to meet people outside I hadn't touched a football in weeks. The FA had sent out exercise bikes to players with central contracts and somehow I was still entitled to one, so I'd jumped on that a few times. I was ten kilograms lighter from the awful eating habits I'd developed, which is a pretty dramatic loss, and clearly I wasn't healthier nor did I have much ambition to be. So when Willco turned up in his purple Nissan Qashqai and presented a ball launcher on my doorstep I wasn't especially enthusiastic about giving it a try.

He'd asked the club to buy them with the hope of having goalkeepers who might be somewhere closer to match-ready whenever games resumed, so he'd put three £2,000-machines on his own credit card, forking out from his own salary until he could be reimbursed.

He set it up in the street to show me how it worked and the motor propelled a few footballs into my hands. Then he ramped it up till they were bouncing off the cars, which was a clear cue for us to stop. He sent me a plan to build my reactions back up: I'd drive it down to the nearest field and do 400 catches one week, 500 the next, then 600. Joel came to stay with me for a couple of weeks once that was allowed so I got him to feed the machine while I put myself in the firing line, remembering how it felt to put my gloves on and to catch a football in my hands: comfortable, familiar, and the best feeling I knew, but still, I thought, pretty pointless. If England didn't want me to do that for them, then my dream had come to a grinding halt regardless.

When we got the call to say the season would start up again

in September, I was still less than enthusiastic. I wasn't drinking like I had, but still not eating particularly well and decided my best option was just to focus on going into training and getting paid so I could get back home again at the end of the day. If the ambition I'd had each day of my football career to improve was still there, it was resting dormant somewhere deep down where I couldn't reach it.

I did OK back in training, although I couldn't muster the energy to care in the way I always had. But being back was forcing me into the swing of things and I remember, during those sessions, in the fortnight before our first match, sensing the potential for me to be replaced and wanting, innately, to rally against it and to remain number one. Whatever embers were left flashing inside were buried deep yet they'd begun burning a little brighter.

There was an England camp in the middle of September. A couple of weeks before, at the start of the month, the FA had invited me to take part in a YouTube series called *Pass the Gloves On*, asking keepers to track the journey of their England careers. I was surprised to be asked and took it as a good sign. It was a Monday night and I was logging on to a video call to record it with Mark Mason, the goalkeeping coach. Phil was announcing his squad the next day, the one he'd promised I'd return to, but I'd lost all sight of that possibility during lockdown. I took this as a clear indication that he was going to stick to his word. I began to feel hopeful about getting an email in my inbox, bringing me back into the squad. That would be enough to reestablish that my dream was worth living. What's meant for you, won't miss you, I told myself, remembering the old proverb.

I was in my kitchen late the next morning, scrolling Instagram as I plated up the eggs and avocado I'd made myself before my afternoon training session with United, when a post from Phil appeared on my feed. It was the squad announcement and I wasn't in it. I read, then re-read the words on the image: three goalkeepers' names but not mine.

That tiny, bright spark that had been holding me up was extinguished in that second. I'd made it through months alone with my demons, through the accumulation of disappointments. I'd climbed out of the hole that had made me question what the point of anything was anymore and I was trying to get back up again. To be smacked in the face with this news was too much. It sent me back. My already crumbling world broke apart entirely. And so did I. Whatever small part of myself had continued in the belief that I'd still make it was now, finally, in ruins.

I let my grip on my plate loosen. I put it down on the counter then felt my back slide down the kitchen cupboards until my body touched the floor. I sobbed, deep guttural sobs.

I'd spent months living in the darkness that came with relinquishing my dream only to find the dream was still alive and it was still in someone else's power to take it away from me.

I felt he'd made me a promise, and this felt like a betrayal, not only of that, but of the journey I'd let myself go on in football, of all the work and all the effort that I expected to be rewarded for, of the belief or the occasions people had told me that my time would come. I didn't have the stamina to withstand the disappointment of reaching the end but never my potential. It's a feeling that others in sport must experience when their journeys come to an end but their ambition and commitment does not.

This was my lowest moment.

I was due at the training ground but I couldn't keep the pain in, I couldn't hide my vulnerability anymore. I left the food I'd made, drove to work, through tears, and saw Willco in the corridor. He'd had the news, too, and took me into the staff room, where I broke down again.

He called Mark Mason, angry on my behalf for having had the opportunity to look after me and tell me the night before to prepare me for the shock.

'She needs to speak to Phil,' Mark said.

That September camp came and went without me, then another in October before I had a message from the manager.

'Do you want to talk, then?' Phil wrote. To me that read as 'Do we have to?'

We spoke on the phone and he explained I wasn't in his plans anymore, including for the Tokyo Olympics, which had been postponed until the following summer. 'How do I get in those plans?' I asked, my voice shaking. I tried to advocate for myself but didn't feel able or confident enough. 'What can I work on?' I queried, but I was given no clear areas to address. The conversation wasn't heading anywhere and I felt defeated. 'I don't know why I'm playing this game anymore,' I remember confessing to him.

'No, you can't give up,' Phil responded, earnestly. 'You're such a good kid and I wish you all the best. This isn't personal. You're too good to give up. I'll be so mad if you stop playing, you're better than that.'

He wasn't horrible, I just don't think we were compatible.

'I don't hate you,' I told him, acknowledging that. 'I'll always appreciate the chance you gave me at Wembley.'

The England dream was dead. I tried to make peace with the fact I'd never play for them again, that I would never achieve what I knew for certain I was capable of. I had been so open about my dreams that it was OK to strive for them and to say so out loud. I wanted to raise the bar, but I'd fallen short.

For the next few months, I couldn't look at England anymore. And for a game that I loved, that just felt extraordinarily sad. I couldn't see the badge or watch the games. I muted people and removed accounts from my social media – not out of spite, it was that the pain was too much. I didn't feel bitter, I just felt a sense of sadness and injustice.

I'd bump into England players in league matches and struggle to speak to them. I remember seeing Steph Houghton, the Manchester City player and England captain, at the derby match that season. It was a Continental Cup game so we were both on the bench and she said a few kind words to me, but I just felt hurt.

I began to question who, around me, I could trust. I felt Phil had gone back on his word, so anyone could. Maybe he'd never rated or liked me in the first place? Maybe no one ever did or ever would. Maybe they all thought I was delusional that I could make it to the top.

I wish that back then I had been able to better articulate how upsetting it all was, to have said, after the first time he dropped me, this is difficult to deal with and I'm not ashamed that I feel hurt. To say, 'I think how you've treated me is terrible.'

But in football, as in other workplaces, how often do you feel afraid? Especially when you're young, or, as I was, only just making ends meet despite the globally recognised organisations I was working for. You're afraid that if you speak out you'll be replaced. It's hard to have open conversations when someone else is in control, and that's how it is in sport: other people's decisions and opinions will shape your whole career. Someone has to give you the opportunity, then they have to give it to you again. Sometimes those opportunities never come, sometimes you don't deserve them, but I knew, based on the work I put in every day and the sacrifices I was still willing to make over and over, that I did. That's why it hurt as much as it did.

In those months, for the best part of that year, no one knew how to pick me up, not least me; but what I couldn't see then is that I was unlearning patterns of the past and learning lessons for the future.

That period taught me that you can't choose the cards you are dealt but you can say 'This is how I want to play my hand'; you can control what you do with other people's opinions and where you let them take you as a person.

I discovered that while I would never wish anyone to be plunged into darkness the way I had been, and so many others are each day, allowing myself to sit in it and stay there was the only way I could reach the clarity I would eventually use to pull myself out. I discovered that you don't always have to be noble when people are behaving badly towards you. Instead I allowed myself to do what I needed, which was to feel.

I was learning that an athlete was not all that I was and that to move forwards, I had to separate my identity as a person from who I was in football in order for both to thrive; if I didn't, one – the latter – would swallow the other whole.

I was finding out how to draw boundaries that I wouldn't let others cross, and how to communicate what those lines were. I was learning to be unafraid to start over and that hard work does pay off, just not always in the ways you expect. And when, in a couple of years, I would re-emerge on the other side and achieve a level of success that I convinced myself I'd never get to feel, I would do so with the unwavering belief – or maybe, delusion – that whatever was thrown at me, I could make a triumph of it.

First, though, I had to get there. I had to learn to reframe my reality.

My goal had changed. It was no longer to play for England but to prolong my football career. I couldn't change what happened but I could let the hunger back in, I could do the work I'd always done and believe in moments of success again: clean sheets, shot-stopping, distribution.

'Work hard in silence and let success make the noise,' Willco taught me. It became powerful.

We set to work on marginal gains, all the 1 per cents we could introduce to make a difference to my game. In goalkeeping, there are so many ways you can do things and do them well. We looked at where I placed my foot when I landed and where I needed it to be in order to recruit more inches to get to the top corner, for example. We noticed that when I dived to the left, I was using my right hand to make the save, which was inefficient, so we focused on my left shoulder. I'd warm up on the pitch with a glute band round my ankles to keep them narrow and we examined where I wasn't making saves that were within my range, changing up the exercises we did in pre-activation to feed those gains: that ball launcher came into its own.

'We know you should have been in that squad,' Willco would tell me. 'Somewhere along the line, someone will see what you're doing. It could be two months, six, 12, but people are going to talk about how you're playing.'

There were weeks where my confidence would dip and frustration would take over. Sometimes, after training, I'd just stay on the grass and offload while he listened and offered opinions. Whenever an England camp was approaching there would, inevitably, be tears: I just couldn't extinguish that little glimmer of hope that I'd see my name in there again, that certainty that I was good enough to. I did things in games that I didn't need to do as well, hoping it'd get me noticed: catching a cross I didn't need to be involved with, kicking a ball that looked a great pass when a more simple one was the option, hoping it would get me seen. But when you strive for perfection, at some point you have to realise it's a moving target. It's not always perfection, it's progress.

And in goalkeeping there is no such thing as the perfect performance. You can have a great game that's damn near it, but you'll have two or three moments where you misplace your hands, feet, body.

I had to keep doing what I knew, improving every day.

One of the dangerous things about women's football is that when your place in the game changes or you're suddenly dropped, as I had been, there isn't the same support structure in place as the men's game or even in more typical workplaces. Still today, managers are not making those choices about players with millions in the bank but women who've bet their lives on playing, so losing my England salary had left me significantly worse off on a club salary that was covering my rent and bills but very little beyond.

I was feeling the ramifications, watching the money coming in and not covering what was going out, with a maxed-out credit card stashed in the bottom drawer.

I was due to sign a new contract with United and my agent was confident it would be good. I got the paperwork two days before Christmas while I was at my parents' house in Nottingham. I don't remember exactly what their first offer was but the game could afford to pay me more now. It was disappointing. Not only was it way below where I wanted it to be, it was clear I'd struggle to live on what they were offering once I took out car payments, insurance, rent, bills. Football is a lavish lifestyle. Nowadays, some girls at the top end of the game can afford to indulge a little more than they could, nothing close to the way the men can, but they will have the odd night spending silly money on bottle service at a club after a big win; they will buy designer clothes and drive something a little closer to the cars that they saw in the car parks of men's training complexes when they started out. Don't get me wrong, I indulge occasionally, too; I enjoy elements of that lifestyle at times, and I've bought myself beautiful things from Louis Vuitton once I had the means, but I didn't back then, not even close. I am still, typically, extremely frugal with myself. Even my financial advisor has to tell me to spend money, reminding me I can enjoy my life and the fruits of my labour from time to time. So, when I went back to renegotiate, I wasn't after the good life, just a comfortable one that reflected my hard work and meant I didn't have to continue to get by on credit cards.

We pushed negotiations into the new year and United had me under pressure to sign swiftly. If not, they said, they needed another goalkeeper.

'OK, look for someone else,' I said. I think they thought it was a negotiation tactic, but remember those lessons around boundaries – I knew the difference now between losing interest and finding respect for myself and I was brave enough to assert it. I could work hard in football but go home and be Mary. I could look forward to a meal and just one glass of wine if I wanted, do my gym work but not be in PureGym all hours of the day and night. I could deliver without killing myself in the process and that included stopping to ask myself if the juice was worth the squeeze, if there was enough money in this game I could love but not blindly anymore.

I remember the manager walking past me at training, asking: 'Are you going to sign it?'

'I can't sign that,' I said.

I'd known for years that I'd pursue this crazy dream until it didn't make sense anymore. It had already threatened to consume me, so if that was now my worst-case scenario then I'd walk away and use my business degree, like my friends who had settled into corporate jobs in London, and having played for United and England would be a great conversation starter on my CV.

I'd had experiences that others would have killed for, travelled and played the game I loved. There would be no shame in having given it my best shot. I had prepared myself to be thrown into the real world even if I wasn't quite ready.

I remember discussing it with Dad over the phone, telling him that, all considered, I thought my football career was drawing to an end and it might be time to retire. I found that so difficult to say out loud to him after all the effort he and Mum had invested in me making it.

Dad understood but, like me, he was disappointed.

'Is there any way you could make it work?' he asked, as we settled on the idea that I'd be best off to carry on for just a couple more years, taking whatever was on the table and playing some more so I could set myself up for a life beyond football and build something else to walk into.

In February, United came back with a final offer. It still didn't set the world on fire but I ran the numbers and it meant I'd be able to pay my bills without constantly looking over my shoulder. They'd included more performance bonuses and, if I hit them all, I'd get a little closer, financially, to where I was when I had the England contract.

I signed a new two-year deal with the option to add on another 12 months to 2024.

For the first time, United also offered me the chance to switch from my number 27 shirt to the number 1. At the start of that season they'd given it to Emily Ramsey, who was younger than me and had come up through the academy a couple of years earlier, but she'd since left. It had disappointed me at the time not to have been offered it as the starting goalkeeper, but I'd quickly moved on and had come to really enjoy seeing fans with my number 27 on at matches.

So when they finally gave me the opportunity to swap, I asked myself whether I really wanted that famous '1' on my shirt or if I just liked the idea because it's what people expected of a goalkeeper? It didn't take me long to work out that it was the second – and that it felt completely unreasonable to buy into a big business model that hooked fans into forking out for another shirt with a new number on the back. I turned them down.

After weeks of negotiating, I think that might have been the first time that I realised, when it came to the business of football, I could do things Mary's way. I could work, once again, at being the best goalkeeper in the world, and I could wear 27.

ELEVEN

IF YOU'RE GREAT, YOU'LL GET IT; IF YOU'RE CONSISTENT, YOU'LL KEEP IT

I'd earned myself enough to make ends meet, but only just, and I was still on less than I had been when I was under contract with the FA, meaning I didn't feel any significant uplift to what I was taking home each month.

I'd looked at downgrading my car and considered selling the house in Reading, which was costing me a grand a month in mortgage payments and still being rented out to my old teammate for half that. Instead, I told her I was sorry but I had to get someone else in to make it pay. I changed my already restricted spending habits and found new ways to make some extra cash.

With the men's squad on a total player payroll apparently just shy of £200 million, I bought food from the markdown shelves in the supermarket and realised I could make a bit of money by selling off kit and boots for £50 on eBay. Entirely against the rules, I scraped off the personalisation on my boots using scissors and listed them online, packaging them up and taking them down to the post office for some buyer who had no clue they belonged to a professional player.

I employed my business head, did some research online and went out to find myself a commercial agent too. I came across Tina Taylor, who was based nearby in Manchester, after seeing a video she'd done with a client of hers, Tom Malone Jr, who was in one of my favourite TV shows, *Gogglebox*.

Tina had the ability to spot trends; she ran a community dance school alongside her business and had a strong sense of purpose and social justice, especially around girls and young women. We instantly saw that we shared that and a passion for business and I could see that she believed in me too. I told her that I needed to think about earnings outside football and prepare for my post-career because it was never going to sustain me financially. I wanted to use what I knew, which was the game, and do something, especially for young goalkeepers. I wanted to make goalkeeping cool and I wanted to leave the women's game, as a whole, in a better place.

'You need to be on TikTok,' she told me.

'I don't even know how that works,' I replied, and Tina explained how I could lean into the goofy side of my personality, let it all show there and have some fun posting videos. She told me to go away and give it a try and come back to her when I'd worked out what my lane was. If I could be my authentic self on there, do it well and build a following, there was scope for brand deals down the line.

If the price of entry is embarrassment, I decided I was willing to pay. British footballers were all over Instagram but they didn't have a presence on TikTok and I was worried that teammates, United fans or anyone else watching would think, *Why is she spending her time doing this?* But the women's game didn't afford the luxury of doing nothing and expecting a stable future, and beyond a core following, the wider world still knew so little and carried preconceptions about what we did and what our standard was. So, I used that as my jumping-off point and gave a few hundred followers a glimpse into what being a female footballer was like, posing in a dress and heels and asking them to guess what I did for a living, poking fun at the team bus breaking down or the different tax brackets in the players' car park when the men and the women pulled up, and jumping on TikTok trends that had nothing at all to do with football. It was a great way to switch off, and the more stupid and unselfconscious I was, the more unapologetically me I was and the quicker the follower count grew. I batted off the misogynistic trolls who showed up in an instant with their comments of 'Get back in the kitchen' and 'You can juggle my balls' and kept posting, watching the numbers creep into their thousands and hoping I could soon make it pay.

Meanwhile, still finding ways to stretch my monthly income and cover the household bills and feed myself, I realised that I could save even more on my weekly shop by bringing meals home from the work canteen. I'd seen a staff member taking a second lunch into a meeting one day and thought surely taking some home was no different, so I started asking for containers when lunch was done and boxing up just enough to make sure I was well fuelled at dinner.

Some of the girls noticed and started doing the same. One afternoon, we got a message in the team WhatsApp group from the club nutritionist asking us not to take food away until everyone had eaten as, that day, some of the staff hadn't got theirs before it was all gone. I felt absolutely awful and rang her almost in tears to explain and apologise profusely. I told her that, because of everything that had unfolded over the past year, I was struggling to make it all stack up financially and was trying to be smart. I was so afraid that I was about to get a proper bollocking. In fact, she took it seriously. 'It's imperative that you fuel,' she said, caring and grateful for the honesty. I mustn't have been the only girl in that kind of situation and her priority was that we were all properly fuelled. From then on, the club increased the amount of food, making sure there was enough for all players to take extra portions home.

As I opened up about my practical struggles, I talked more about how I'd been struggling over the past year mentally too. The anxiety of lockdown and my distress about England hadn't altogether disappeared and I'd suffered an episode I'd later learn was called dissociation: a complete memory gap where I'd driven Mum and Dad home from a game one night but couldn't recall any part of the drive or indeed anything from the final whistle to climbing into bed at my house.

Someone had said something in the changing room at Leigh, just before it happened, that had felt like mocking, and it sent my brain into shutdown. I walked out of there in a trance-like state, skipping my post-match recovery. I never cut corners at work but the whole episode of involuntarily emotionally checking-out was the latest symptom of the overwhelm I'd been carrying around since lockdown and that was still creeping in and blurring my days.

The club were entitled to punish me for not doing my ice bath that night and they hit me with a fine. I really didn't have space to lose the cash but they were right to hold me accountable to team values. Nonetheless, they were concerned with behaviour that was so out of character.

'You're not in a good space, this is not the Mary I know,' the manager said to me afterwards, and offered for me to begin seeing a clinical psychologist. The access to that help is one of the best things that United ever gave me and I started regular sessions that would help me embed the lessons I'd taken from the months that had just passed and learn more about myself as a person than ever before.

Being resourceful and vulnerable enough to open up and accept help had delivered change on a personal level and for my teammates. I would emerge with higher self-worth and prove to myself that I no longer needed to take the verbal or emotional punches of my past in order to continue in football.

I opened myself up emotionally in my personal life too, something I had neglected for a long time, paying all my attention, as I had, to my first and biggest love, football. I was spending more time with a friend, Kitty. She had been a physio at United but had left the year before and was living and working in Scotland. At the club, Kitty had always been supportive of all the girls when we talked to her on the physio table, listening to our problems and helping find work-arounds that would help our recovery or our minds.

We'd been out for brunch with Willco and his little girl a couple of times, but lost touch for a while, then reconnected when she came back to Manchester to visit friends. We started messaging and I found her to be fun, frank, caring and astute, noticing where I needed my confidence rebuilding and where I just needed to be Mary the person.

It was Lewis who picked up on the possibility that there was something between us before I did by the way I spoke to him about her over the phone.

'Do you *like* Kitty?' he asked, as I drove over to meet her one night.

'No, don't be ridiculous. She's just my friend,' I said.

But we were drawn to each other in a way that is hard to explain or describe and, as the spring progressed, we went on a few dates, Kitty driving down to Manchester around my training and her work schedule. Our first was at minigolf but often we'd head out to the countryside and take picnics so we could sit somewhere restful and just talk.

It was a slow build. Kitty had never been attracted to a woman before and I was hesitant to let anyone into my life. I didn't usually let people in, not in any meaningful way. I'd dated men, in fact I loved going out on dates – meeting some-one new always felt like a great way to spend an evening – but I never felt like my personality or my football was something they could handle. And when I'd dated a girl, years earlier, my parents hadn't approved. I'd remained paranoid and fearful, even now, about dating seriously again, particularly a woman.

For me, though, sexuality isn't linear: I believe you love who you love without any need to label or fall in line with other people's labels around it. Love doesn't discriminate. I was confused by what I was feeling but I couldn't ignore the instinct that Kitty was good for me. I enjoyed all the time that we spent together, and the more we did, the more I saw how she understood who I was in a way that no one else had before.

She was organically helping me to come even further out of the protective shell that I'd built around myself. The security and stability that our relationship brought was also having the unintentional positive consequence of helping me with the work to build myself back up as a person and that, in turn, was building me on the pitch too.

In fact, it was learning how to no longer to be a slave to my dream that was bringing it closer within reach than ever before.

Those experiences during lockdown, the disappointments of England and negotiating with United had made me wiser to the game, on the pitch and off. And United's other goalkeepers helped me to improve my game in sessions, and I theirs. It was the supportive goalkeepers' union at its best.

Opening up my shell was also helping me open myself up to better friendships in football among the girls I played with. Girls are led to believe that friends should come easy but when you have difficult experiences and you're guarded, as I had been in the past, that was harder. It's important for those same girls to know that if you don't find your friends now, you will find these most important relationships later, as I had done at Wolfsburg and was doing again here.

In training and games, the stats began backing up the work that I'd been putting in. My shot-stopping went through the roof, increasing from 33 saves in the season before lockdown to 53.

'If you're great, you'll get it; if you're consistent, you'll keep it,' Willco would tell me.

He nicknamed what we were doing 'Return of the Mearps', and I ended the season feeling like I was, indeed, in comeback mode.

At the end of May, I was booked in for a small procedure to clear out my right wrist at a clinic in Manchester. I'd been struggling with a chronic pain there for the best part of two years and various treatments, including injections, hadn't worked. I wasn't needed in pre-season training for six weeks so I did what was long overdue and had the procedure, which meant not catching balls for at least a couple of weeks. I went on holiday to Portugal, where I'd be able to recover while I was unable or needed to train.

Within 24 hours of landing, I had a message from Willco: 'I know I said I wouldn't bother you but please call me when you get this. It's really important.'

He'd had a call from the Team GB goalkeeping coach. Phil had left earlier in the year after a tenure the press described as 'tepid', and Hege Riise, the Norwegian coach and former player, had been installed as caretaker until the Dutch manager, Sarina Wiegman, was due to take over that September. There were two pre-Olympic camps coming up in four and ten days' time, and with one of the keepers, Ellie Roebuck, struggling with injury, they wanted to see me there.

I was stunned.

Team GB and England had a lot of the same staff. Now, after no contact with any of them for the best part of two years, just when I'd finally said 'Fuck it, I should do something for my wellbeing' and wasn't allowed to catch a ball, they were calling me in. I had to laugh at how ridiculous it was. Then I thought about Willco's prediction: my hard work was being spoken about.

I thanked them but said I was sorry, I couldn't be in and explained why. I think it was the first time I'd dictated to someone else what was best for me at work, choosing my recovery and resolution not to derail my own progress over a fleeting chance – they needed a fourth keeper to help out in camp but I wasn't about to head out to the Olympics with them.

It was met with respect. They said they understood and hoped I could make the second of the two camps, which I did. Having convinced myself that I simply wasn't good enough, I thought, *Just go, no regrets.* So when I arrived alongside the Olympians back at Loughborough University at the end of June I felt incredibly excited to be training with a national team again, but this time it was tempered with nerves that I would face their rejection once more. A lot of time had passed – what if I'd lost it? What if my standard actually just wasn't there?

I hadn't put on gloves in two weeks. I pulled on a new pair and the coach kicked the ball at me. I couldn't get a grip of it. I knew that my handling was the thing I was well known for, which is unusual in the modern game where a lot of keepers punch and parry the ball – I like to keep hold of it. *What have I signed myself up for?* I thought. *I'm going to give a terrible account here.*

I pulled myself together. Don't let complacency in. Then, I got into it. I remember having the ball at my feet, Ellen White diving in to slide tackle and me chopping the other way; I remember a nice sidewinder pass, too, and a penalty save in an inter-house game that we won. I was back in my zone, doing what I'd always done well, and it was validating. My first instincts had been right: I belonged on this team and I'd been dropped for no named reason. After two years of feeling

I was a piece of shit that didn't even deserve a phone call from the manager, I took the confidence boost.

Towards the end of those few days, the goalkeeping coach went through some analysis with me during one-to-one feedback.

He was super complimentary and, as coaches always had done, even when they were kicking me out, picked up on my professionalism and work ethic. 'I've been watching you and I don't know why you're not in the squad,' he said about my England chances. I'd spent the past ten months focused on just feeling well and future-proofing my club career, but it was nice to hear someone essentially saying 'I'm impressed' and feeling seen. Then he warned me: 'There's people at the FA who don't like you.' That cut deep but I valued and needed his honesty; we both knew that there were people watching over the team's progress at Loughborough who were just as influential in England. 'It must have felt good to stick two fingers up to them this week,' he acknowledged next. It did.

I knew I belonged there – who knew if someone else ever would again? I'd enjoyed myself. I left thinking, *It's a shame that's done*, and taking my raised confidence back with me to United. I think, somewhere, I took the hope of a fresh start back too.

TWELVE

YOU HAVEN'T COME THIS FAR ONLY TO COME THIS FAR

Sarina Wiegman took over as England manager that September and her first camp was the same month. I suppose that renewed hope was more real than I'd wanted to acknowledge because the day squad emails dropped, I thought maybe, after Loughborough, they would be paying more attention to me this time.

The day came and went and I thought, *This is fucked, I've not got it again.*

I went to pour myself a glass of red wine to take the edge off any pending disappointment, then it appeared in my inbox. Sarina was calling me back into England.

I called my parents, excited, and before I was even off the phone, Willco had messaged, excited too: 'Have you got an email?'

With Karen Bardsley and Ellie Roebuck, the number one and number two who'd both been in Tokyo, now out injured, it would be Chelsea's Carly Telford, Everton's Sandy MacIver and me. And with an entirely different line-up and a new manager it was impossible to know in what order.

I was buzzing to be included again. Last time, I'd wanted to be number one, now I just wanted to be back in among the squad. Maybe there was something more waiting for me in football after all.

What I didn't have was any England kit, so, a bit like your first day in a new job, I had no idea what to wear when I arrived at the Hilton hotel attached to Southampton's Utilita Bowl cricket ground on a misty Monday morning exactly a year after I'd found myself on the kitchen floor, pining for the very same thing.

I stood out like a sore thumb in a black hoodie and leggings, while everyone else was in England tracksuits. I'd lost weight and my hair was blonder than the last time I'd been with the squad; one staff member even did a double-take, then telling me, 'Oh, Mary, I didn't recognise you there,' as we gathered for the first day of camp.

I felt self-conscious about being back there and back with the girls. Their lives had continued and mine had stopped; I didn't know how they were going to be with me so I told myself to go in with no expectations.

I happened to walk into the building at exactly the same time as Sarina.

'Hi, how are you?' she said to me.

It was the first time we'd met or spoken and I couldn't believe she was acknowledging me. I wasn't used to that in football's power dynamic and hadn't experienced it from an England manager.

On the second day, she called the keepers in for individual

meetings, one after the next, at 15-minute intervals. This would become routine at each of Sarina's camps, a message arriving on our phones from one of the coaching staff telling us a time and leaving us to work out where we were in the running order: first, second or third. I had no concept of how she did things but this time I was called last into the space with a projector screen on one wall and seats set out in three or four rows.

'Where have you been? Why haven't you been in the squad?' she asked me. Darren Ward, the new goalkeeping coach, was sat beside her.

I told her Phil had never told me why and she appeared surprised, as though she'd presumed there had been a falling-out that made my absence make sense.

'I've been watching you for a while, I think you're a fantastic goalkeeper,' she said, and made references to certain games and saves of mine to back it up. She really had seen my hard work. I was amazed.

'I see you as my number one,' she said.

I couldn't believe it.

Before I'd left, Mum had told me I shouldn't be afraid of being emotional, that it was OK to be vulnerable after everything I'd been through, and so, I was, as I explained what a hard time I'd had and what it meant to me to hear her say that, to offer me that recognition and opportunity.

It was the most open and direct conversation I'd ever had with a manager and she'd only known me for two minutes. I was teary and her eyes welled up in empathy. It forged an instant bond between us that I would soon come to trust in and respect immensely.

'When they come back, you'll have to fight for the spot,'

she said of the two keepers who were out, acknowledging that she couldn't guarantee this was mine forever but she was handing me an opportunity and telling me 'it's yours to take.'

My first games with the England number 1 on my back would be that week's 2023 World Cup Qualifiers.

I started work with Darren, who seemed like a genuine guy, who could see what it meant to me to be able to put the work in.

It was his first job in women's football and he was softly spoken and enjoyed a laugh while challenging me at the same time. Apart from wanting a few too many repetitions out of me in our first session, which I of course didn't mind, you wouldn't have known he'd come straight from the more brutal world of the men's game.

On the Friday night, I pulled on the shirt – no mind games with a number 13 or whatever else was going spare on my back – and walked out in front of a crowd of 8,000 for the match against North Macedonia at Southampton's St Mary's Stadium. My family were there and Christina had travelled down to watch too. It felt good, and merited another pinch-me moment to be stood on the pitch singing the national anthem again. I could feel the nerves fizzing through me, though, so it was a good job I didn't have much to do for the 8–0 win, or the 10–0 we got at the Stade de Luxembourg four days later. But having arrived in camp delighted just to be making up the numbers, I was leaving with two clean sheets and the shirt. I loved it.

I could feel that this was the best place I'd ever been with England although I would never have dared take anything for granted. I, more than anyone, was under no illusion that doing the work did not guarantee my place the next time but being picked again had suddenly become a real likelihood and that was very new to me. The inspirational words 'you haven't come this far, only to come this far' came to my mind and settled there, spurring me forwards.

I started all four World Cup qualifier matches that year, with four clean sheets. After our 1–0 win against Austria, Sarina told the press: 'She can make the difference, and she did.'

Sarina believed in me and I delivered. Being in her squad was a huge confidence boost and it showed in my club performance, too, where I played all 22 games and kept ten clean sheets. All those 1 per cent increments were paying off.

I'd been to such a dark place to disentangle who I was as a person and who I was as a player, and as is so often the case in life and work, only once I'd learned how to stop conflating the two, to know myself better and control the personal pressure valve, did the rest fall into place. It was the process of becoming and the invisible law of progress: that growth, results and visible change come from the consistent, unseen efforts that happen before.

Return of the Mearps was well and truly on.

Selection for the summer's Euros, on home soil in England, was right around the corner and it was hard to believe that I now had a real chance not only of going this time, but of playing in a major tournament with England. Every time I went into one of Sarina's camps I wanted to cement myself as the number one and push my level again. She was clear and constructive with me every time, giving feedback I could take into my performances and championing my own will to get the best, and then better, out of myself, which was the kind of pragmatism and motivation I responded to well.

Sarina was bringing three other keepers into her squad: Ellie Roebuck, who came back in as number two and was an incredible and supportive teammate; Sandy MacIver, who I got on well with, and Hannah Hampton, who'd recently come through from the age groups. All brilliant goalkeepers who played the game differently. She rotated us in goal for the Arnold Clark Cup matches against Canada, Spain and Germany that February, but had played me in all our other matches since she'd taken over. I didn't care who I played against, I just lapped up every opportunity to show how hard I could work for my team.

I was intuitive now about almost everything in football, but when the day arrived for the Euros squad announcement in June, it was brand new to me to approach it from number one – I didn't know what feelings to trust or what to expect from it.

United had finished fourth in the table and I'd had a poor last game against Chelsea, which I fretted over as a bad omen for my England chances: every performance and every moment on the pitch mattered, and still does to me.

At St George's Park, Sarina calmly went about the day while we trained in the morning and worked through the agonising wait of her announcement that afternoon.

Camp had grown a bit tetchy, which was to be expected with a tournament right around the corner. It was an incredible group of hardworking girls and the Euros would be a fresh start for a lot of them; everyone was working out of their skin for their spot and nervous of getting injured at the same time. Particularly because it was being played at home there was a real consciousness that there were only two ways this would go: this selection will be great for those it is great for, and heartbreaking for those it isn't.

The day played out like an episode of *The X Factor*: each of us would be called into a meeting via a text message that told you it was your turn to see Sarina. If you were going to the Euros, you went back into camp and were given a time for the team meeting, where you'd find out who your teammates were; if you weren't, you took your bag and walked straight out of a back door. Brutal.

We knew now that Sarina had her harder conversations first, it's why she called her number one goalkeeper in last in the run of those three meetings that she held each camp, so it followed that the people who were leaving were likely to be called first.

Some of the United girls were in a WhatsApp group together, including Ella Toone, Alessia Russo and me, where we'd chat about camp logistics and we had a deal that we'd each send a short message when we were called in so the rest of us knew the meetings had begun. Most of them had been in as I lay on the bed in my room watching Netflix and trying to stop my limbs from fidgeting.

It couldn't have been more different to the selections I'd experienced before where I'd been on the brink, waiting for an email and not knowing if I was going at all; as the minutes went on, it felt more and more likely that it was great news. Now, I was waiting and hoping for Sarina's confirmation that I'd play and I was excited to know how that felt.

My phone pinged.

I headed to the Drum, the bright conference room on level two of St George's Park, where Sarina and Darren were waiting.

Sarina praised my performances and leadership, all good noises, then she told me:

'You can't be worried you're not going to go? You're going to be number one.'

In those few minutes Sarina did what she always did with me: she made me feel invincible, like I could run through brick walls.

I was chomping at the bit to start.

As I walked back through St George's Park, I was filled with so much pride and quickly called and messaged my family, overjoyed to be sharing good news with them where I'd once resigned myself to the sadness of telling them 'I've not made it.' This was a new, personal first and it was a huge one.

'Well, obviously you have!' was the general tone of their delighted replies. I just wanted to get down to business now.

In the players' meeting there was an incredible buzz, another new experience I now knew from the inside.

'I'm really excited about the squad,' Sarina told us once we'd sat down.

We felt it too. There was a sense that there was something special about this group of players who'd been brought together. There was a wealth of experience, in players like Bronzey, Jill Scott, Ellen White and Fran Kirby, mixed with people like me who had their first shot at playing and younger girls like Alessia and Tooney who were going to their first major tournament. There were players like Millie and Nikita who I'd known for years, and Leah Williamson, the team captain who I got on well with.

You couldn't always control the outcome, Sarina continued, but she was looking forward to us doing everything we could together. 'I think we can win,' she said, a motivation and a very real belief.

We watched the video that the FA were about to put live on their social channels, revealing us as England's squad – a creative and poetic account of what it was to be a little girl who dreamed football, assembling each of our names in a tournament sticker book, with cameos from greats like David Beckham, Alex Scott and Ian Wright telling the nation a story of the sisterhood, spirit, community and pride that would take us, the Lionesses, into our home Euros.

It felt amazing waiting for your name to pop up and impossible not to be emotional.

The announcement helped us to feel a buzz around what was to come as we sealed ourselves into a bubble for the next month and a half to prepare for play.

I wasn't used to seeing my name anywhere much at all. Goalkeepers were far more under the radar than other players but there was more speculation and talk on sports sites about us as a team, how we would work and how the tournament would go, than I'd seen before. Still, though, chatter about the Lionesses was largely confined to the women's football community, and beyond online fanzines and forums we were still pretty much unnoticed by the public.

We had a couple of days to go home and pack and I headed back up to Manchester, where I had moved house from Salford to a new estate a few miles south of the city. I put my stuff together, then rejoined the team at St George's Park for our pre-tournament training. Later in the tournament, after our opening match, we would move to the Lensbury, in Teddington, a grand hotel set in manicured gardens with a grid of perfect pitches by the banks of the River Thames, where we would set up our Lionesses' training base.

We didn't take it over but we had a big chunk of the hotel for exclusive use, including a play room put together by Nike with basketball arcade hoops, table tennis and a little corner where some of the girls sat and watched *Love Island* at night.

Around the training schedule I'd sit in the grounds and read my book in the sunshine or we'd go for walks into Teddington, where no one paid much attention to us, and grab a coffee. Back at the hotel, between games, there were team bonding activities: I was paired with Lotte Wubben-Moy for a challenge night, and Jill arranged a brilliantly ridiculous one where you picked names out of a hat and dressed your partner in the worst clobber imaginable for dinner. I was paired with Tooney, whose only request was that I didn't choose anything too hot, given Britain was sweltering in a particularly hot summer. So, thinking outside the box, I ordered her an inflatable lobster costume which I hoped would be both entertaining and airy but was, in fact, stifling. She sweated through the evening and caught the leopard print heels I'd put with it in the hotel decking. It all left us in fits of laughter and banking memories like that off the pitch only helped to bring us all closer as a team when we were on it.

More than anything, there was a shared ethos that permeated the camp, a philosophy that we'd all agreed to live by in the joint pursuit of success, from work ethic to trust to the way we treated one another.

Sarina took absolutely no nonsense when it came to bad behaviour and created a culture where it would be addressed head-on to the point of isolating or removing people from camp who wouldn't adhere. She created a space where roles and responsibilities were clear and respected and the result was a squad who lived, breathed, slept and dreamed by our team mentality. We hung our hats on the mutual values of Sarina's England.

THIRTEEN

EARN THE RIGHT

The opening match of the 2022 Euros was on a Wednesday night against Austria at Manchester United's Old Trafford, and we arrived at the city's Hilton hotel a couple of days before.

Opening the tournament in Manchester felt really special. We'd done our tactical session at St George's Park then travelled up for a light training session at Old Trafford on the day before kick-off.

I remember noticing big things, like the banners and billboards announcing the game, and small things, like grains of sand within the pitch and the choice to allocate us the away team's dressing room, but everything else was comfortingly familiar to me.

My biggest regret about the Euros and World Cup I'd been to years earlier, when I was on the periphery of the squad, was that I'd wished the time away in anticipation of what I could do next.

This time I wanted to remember to enjoy every minute, including the pressure of it all, because it was a privilege to carry that pressure and expectation on my shoulders. It was what I'd dreamed of – this time I was going to feel everything, smell the grass each time I stepped onto the pitch, take in the sounds of every stadium and not let a single moment pass wasted or unnoticed because no one could guarantee me the next.

Above all, I told myself the opportunity was in my hands now, just as I'd asked for; I had to make sure I could translate everything that I'd worked at for two decades of my life when it mattered most – on the biggest stage yet.

I always carried a Fire Stick with me to hotels so that I could feel the comfort of picking up whatever drama or reality TV show I was watching on Netflix and, as I lay on my hotel bed on 5th July, match day minus one, I felt the right mix of excited and nervous before I switched off the TV and turned in for the night.

We met the next morning at breakfast, where our chef had an omelette station set up, then a few of us went for a walk into the city and strolled around with a coffee, a common part of the match-day morning routine.

Then, I entered game zone – the grown-up version of that competitive focus that I'd first let in as a child on sports day.

Everyone prepares for a match, of any importance, in their own unique way, knowing innately what works for their own psyche, and I was unsurprisingly pretty intense in my pre-match rituals. While some of the other girls had a laugh and a joke at the back of the bus, harnessing the endorphins as soon as the team meeting is done before we've even sat down for the drive, I put my headphones in and stop speaking to anyone.

If any of them were looking at me on that short journey from central Manchester to Old Trafford early on in that dry and breezier-than-usual summer's evening, they probably thought that I was staring right through them.

And if you listened to the lyrics of the songs that played through my ears in those moments, and before every match of the tournament, Stormzy's 'Big Michael' ('Not top two, top one'), Kojey Radical's 'Talkin' ('They throw shade on my name') or Rita Ora and Sigma's 'Coming Home', you would hear journeys of being written off and rising up.

I carried the intense energy through the changing room, breaking for Sarina and Leah's pre-match words, then into the tunnel where the mood was matched outside.

I'd never played to a full Old Trafford, but the stadium was at capacity and it was filled with smoke and the heat of fireworks and flares that had been set off during the opening ceremony. This was how it felt to play big-occasion football. It was magic, it was the stuff that my dreams were made of.

I let the national anthem run through me as we lined up to kick off the tournament. Whatever I did first in that game, I just knew I wanted to do well and set my intention with my performance from the first whistle.

It started nervy and scrappy from both teams and there was a lot of space in the wide channels for Austria's full backs; I distributed a lot in those early minutes, left and right.

Neither side was playing their best but Fran set up Beth Mead, who chipped the ball into the net in the 16th minute, a goal that had had to be confirmed by VAR, adding to the nervy atmosphere. The England fans – and all of us on the team – breathed a collective sigh of relief as it was confirmed. Austria came in with some chances in the last 15 minutes, calling me into action more; I tipped away a shot and made another good save to keep it 1–0. We held the game. We'd got the job done, won our first game and the pressure momentarily abated.

We headed down to Teddington, where base camp had now been set up for the remaining games, and five days later we were at Brighton's Amex Stadium, preparing ourselves for an intense, defensive battle against Norway. There was a lot of talk about their forward line and I could feel the extra nervous energy circulating within myself as I planned to face their captain and striker Ada Hegerberg, who had just made her return to the national team, and my old Wolfsburg teammate and friend, Caro Graham Hansen.

As it turned out, the game came and went quickly with an 8–0 victory in which I barely touched the ball, confirming our passage to the quarter-finals with a game to spare.

We played our final group game against Northern Ireland four days later, in Southampton, without Sarina on the sidelines after she'd tested positive for Covid and following a panic over our red socks and their green tops, which were apparently a worrying combination for anyone watching with colour blindness. I was called on for a save in the opening minute followed by a few waves of attack but we walked into the next round with a 5–0 win.

Now we were into the knockout stages, it was do or die.

We were playing Spain in the quarter-finals, back at Brighton, on 20th July. They were a phenomenal team and we were proving that we were too. I knew I'd be needed from the jump, but I didn't feel any nerves this time. Through the group stages, playing to the pressure of a major tournament had done what I always thought it would: it had moved me into a space of high-octane confidence. My mentality as we went into our biggest game so far wasn't 'Can you translate where it matters most?' It was 'Try and beat me.'

I'd done the work and all those extra repetitions for as long as I'd been catching a ball, now I was ready for whatever one of the biggest teams in Europe had to throw at me.

I was needed for the entirety of the 90 minutes and the 30 of extra time that followed. For the first time in the tournament we went a goal down when Esther González put a shot low into the far corner.

I was infuriated.

We cannot go home, I thought. *We're too good, that's just not possible.* That would have felt like injustice; we had to meet our potential.

Beth equalised then, six minutes into extra time, Georgia Stanway scored a rocket to put us in the lead. Spain's Athenea del Castillo gave them one final chance with a close-range cross, which I took with one hand. I got absolutely walloped in the melee afterwards but I felt invincible. I loved the feeling of spoiling their party with a save.

I hadn't had the right before to be as obnoxious as that because I hadn't earned it yet, but I believed that I did now. This is what it looked like to earn the right, for all of us.

We won 2–1, we were into the semi-finals, one game away from the final of a home Euros, and I'd conceded only one goal in four games, a record I was proud of and an indicator of what I could do in two more.

The feeling after that match was the most excited we'd allowed ourselves to get all tournament.

ABBA was playing in the changing room, 'Mamma Mia' and 'Voulez-Vous' were becoming a bit of a soundtrack for the team, and we all sang and danced. We'd done well, defended well, we'd been resolute in our defeat of a European giant and we'd matched them like for like. It felt incredible and the energy carried us through, again, to the semi-final against Sweden at Sheffield United's Bramall Lane.

Sweden was a very different type of team, a counter-attacking side who played four-four-two. They started brighter and I had a one-on-one within 25 seconds of kick-off when Stina Blackstenius showed up with an immediate low, close shot. I instinctively stretched out my leg to block it; I knew a goal so early could threaten to change the course of the game and our chance at the final. I felt dominant, that earned-confidence and the instinct to put into practice everything I knew that I had been consistently working on all those years coursing through me. After that, it was like a game of ping-pong, as crosses and saves went back and forth.

I was focused on keeping a clean sheet, allowing the girls to go up the other end and attack. Beth had scored, putting us 1–0 up, and as half-time approached, Blackstenius was back; Sweden had won a corner and a cross came in, a messy one that bumped around in the box. Blackstenius pushed it into me with a header that powered towards the top centre of the goal. I needed to move backwards, something that's really difficult as a goalkeeper and I'd been working hard on.

I leapt back and up and got my fingertips to it, tipping it over the bar. I landed back on my feet to see Millie and Rachel

Daly celebrating; Leah came running back to tell me how big and important a save it was.

Seeing what it meant to my team was everything.

We won comfortably, 4–0, thanks to Alessia's unreal and now-legendary back-heel kick and a fourth from Fran.

Roebuck grabbed me afterwards and said: 'I've never seen a female goalkeeper take crosses like that in a game.'

Nikita, who'd been on her England journey alongside me for so long, told me: 'I'm so proud of you.'

Everything about the experience felt new. We'd just earned ourselves a place in a Euros final, but more than that you could feel the power of the fans celebrating in a way I never had before, because there were so many more people behind us now. Although we were in a bubble and didn't let social media infiltrate us or even have Sky Sports on in camp, for fear of getting too high or too low, you could sense the appreciation and fervour for what we were achieving as a team and then as individuals within it, spilling out far beyond the buzz of sold-out stadiums.

The noise was getting louder, and there were indications everywhere, even on the smallest scale back in Teddington, where people now stopped to wish us good luck or in the streets we drove through, where flags were coming out. Most meaningfully, though, was the sense that each of our moments were being noticed, en masse, for the very first time.

That extended to my own moments and my personal experience. I was used to making saves that twisted momentum in games and the unspoken response being 'Of course, that's her job'. Within this team and this tournament, I felt as appreciated and noticed as every other player who was doing exceptionally well: Meado, who would become top goalscorer, Ellen running people ragged, Hempo for her speed, Georgia's penalties and goals. You could name every starting player and every substitute for her contributions including me, as keeper, and that meant a huge amount.

I had always wanted my contribution, my goalkeeping, to matter, it's what I'd longed for when football broke my heart. Now I was beginning to know how it felt and how powerful it was when others knew what I did: that goalkeeping was important.

I had translated what I knew I was capable of. My saves had made a difference to the games and the delusion I had that I was destined for the big stage, and high-pressure situations, that gut feeling I'd carried since I was a little girl was on display – my intuition that this was where I belonged was right.

This was the job at its best, and feeling celebrated and part of something in a way I never had before made me feel I could run on water as we headed into the final. We would face Germany, at Wembley, and earn the chance to bring home England's first major trophy since 1966.

The day before the biggest game of our careers didn't look much different to any other match day minus one. Everyone was tired; we'd played five games and a lot of energy had been spent, so looking after our bodies and minds was a priority.

Our mentality was only focused on one thing but somewhere, in the back of all of our heads, was the first reassuring sense of certainty that we'd had for a long time, in knowing that whatever the outcome, we'd be going back to our families in a couple of days, going on holiday, resting our bodies. It's just that no one wanted to do it without winning a trophy first.

ALL IN

We spent the night before the game at Spurs' training ground, the Lodge, which is closed to the public and might be the nicest place I'd ever stayed. We had our own coffee barista, and everything was controlled by an iPad, from the lights to the sound system to the curtains, and all the glass-fronted bedrooms arced out in a crescent overlooking serene gardens.

I felt unusually calm, as focused as ever and still reassuringly confident about what was needed from me the next day. I really believed we could win; in fact my mindset was now, 'Fuck it, I'm going hell for leather on that pitch.'

We had our team dinner, hung out together a little then went to our rooms. Willco had sent me a video montage of some of my best moments, from the tournament and beyond, set to music that he knew I loved, with words of inspiration written over them and messages from my family. He'd done a new one for every match and it made my heart swell with determination, pride and potential before turning in for the night.

If there was ever a clearer sign that I was prepared and composed about what lay ahead it was the fact that the iPad-controlled curtains pulled themselves open at 5am, briefly waking me, and I dozed back off, unbothered; some glitch meant they'd done the same to every one of us.

I woke properly a little earlier than my alarm and soon had a knock on the door while I was doing my morning skincare at the bathroom sink. I went to answer in pyjamas that conveniently said Go FUCK YOURSELF across the top and found the team general manager stood on the other side.

'Hey, Mary, are you OK? Are you able to come for a meeting?' she asked. 'Sarina wants to speak to you with the goalkeepers. Whenever you're ready.'

She stood at the door, waiting, which meant whenever was now.

Darren was facing an emergency and had no choice but to be out of action for several hours, maybe the whole day, meaning he couldn't do the goalkeepers' warm-up. Darren had my warm-up routine, my penalty technique, he knew it all; the whole thing would have to change.

'Don't worry,' people were trying to reassure me, hurrying together contingency plans and scrambling around for other FA-eligible coaches to step in on the day of a Euros final.

It was enough to throw someone. But I was unfazed. I knew my warm-up routine and my penalty technique, I knew exactly what I needed to do and I knew that I could deliver; that was all the reassurance I needed. Roebuck stepped up to help me and, as it turned out, Darren arrived in time for the final warm-up at the stadium, but nothing could shake me now.

We got on the bus to Wembley early that afternoon. It was an hour and a half's drive away and I put my headphones in. I tuned into my music as we approached the stadium but this time I spent most of the journey inhaling mindfully and listening to the Calm meditation app.

Jess Carter was on the other side of the aisle; Jess was in a long-term relationship with Germany and Chelsea's keeper, Ann-Katrin Berger, so she understood my job and how my mind worked particularly well. 'You're on your way to a European final and you're asleep on the bus. Could you be any more relaxed?' she said. I can't remember if it was an observation or a question.

I was surprised at how relaxed I was too. For such an

intense teammate, who usually intentionally wound myself up as part of the pre-match process, I was, it had to be said, finding composure a different way at the biggest moment, but it was the product of doing something bigger that always worked for me, going with my gut, and that's what my gut told me I needed as we made our way across London to meet our potential.

FOURTEEN

BUILD CHANGE IN THE MOMENT

The tunnel at Wembley was hot and humid. If Spain were all about possession, Germany were mentality monsters; physical, tactical, they had everything.

Alex Popp, their captain and prolific striker who'd scored six goals in five matches to lead them there, had withdrawn from the team at the very last minute due to injury and I remember standing there beside Leah and Millie, thinking: *This is ours for the taking; this is our time.*

England versus Germany was *the* biggest game to watch when I was growing up, the biggest climax to a football competition, and I was impatient to take my turn to play it.

I remember nothing of the build-up and concert that took place on the pitch before we walked out. I couldn't see the people I loved dotted through the stands, only the smoke that filled the stadium and the pride that ran through my veins as the festivities cleared and we lined up to sing the national anthem.

We were under the cosh immediately, the ball pinballing between players in the box in front of me. We needed to be resolute in our defending from the off and I remember a slew of crosses, blocks and saves in quick succession.

It took until the second half for a goal and Tooney broke the deadlock in the 62nd minute with a fantastic chip over their keeper, Merle Frohms, set up by a brilliant through-ball from Keira Walsh.

We were seeing out the game but they were throwing everything at it. I denied Tabea Wassmuth a dangerous shot, then they scored a decent goal, bringing it to 1–1 and sending the game to extra time.

When Wembley's hot, it's stifling, and I was sweating through my shirt as we went into another 30 minutes.

The moment that Chloe Kelly scored her close-range finish in the 110th minute is now etched in millions of minds, but the event itself was a melee that I could barely make out from the other end of the pitch. I watched as she scored, pulled up her shirt and ran on to celebrate then paused, as though she was unsure if it had crossed the line. When she kept on running, the stadium erupted again and the girls piled on to celebrate. We were on.

While her and Bronzey worked majestically to keep the ball in the corner, I looked up at the Wembley clock to work out how long we had left. I was so worn out by then that I completely miscalculated what I thought was a couple of minutes remaining for the eight we actually had left, including stoppage time. I wasn't even sure if I could see straight for much longer: if the ball came my way, I thought I'll be seeing four of them instead of one. I forced myself through to the final whistle.

It went. And I collapsed to the ground.

Champions.

Every single thing had been worth it. Every repetition, every heartache, every comeback. Every game, every save. The tears, the self-belief, the determination, the improvements every day, the team. I felt all of it as I sat on Wembley's turf, depleted – and complete too.

I'd fulfilled my wildest dreams. We all had. We'd dominated, we'd steamrolled teams and we'd embodied and lived by our values to a T. We were in the history books. No one could ever take this away from any of us.

I sat in front of the goal and cried my eyes out as the stadium bounced with England's victory around me.

This was the bit in a movie where the music plays and everything comes together beautifully, where it all looks so easy and effortless, and in many ways it was because I was finally where I felt destined to be. Those scenes playing out around me were real now but, inside, a whole life's work came to my mind, all those moments that had prepared me and given me the strength to dig deep and form this resilient core that I'd come to think of as normal that had allowed me to overcome and perform.

Darren came over and picked me up off the grass.

'Have you stopped crying yet?' he asked. We hugged and I ran to celebrate with the girls, then into the stands with my family.

It was electric, the fairy-tale ending to all the stories I'd written as a little girl.

This was unreal.

My work, and our work, was truly seen.

We lined up to receive our medals. As I reached Prince William in the lineup, he shook my hand and congratulated me. He'd been to visit us during a training session at St George's Park a few months earlier and I remembered him telling me something about Charlotte not wanting to be a goalkeeper.

'I bet you Charlotte wants to be a goalkeeper now,' I said and we laughed.

We lifted the trophy to an ecstatic Wembley as confetti rained down on the pitch where we, the women, had brought football home to a nation. I did a knee-slide through the silver ribbons but the grass was so dry, I didn't get very far and fell in a heap instead. I didn't care. I just wanted to stay out there and feel the pitch underneath me for as long as possible, to take in every last moment.

Inside, ABBA was on in the dressing room, which was as alive as the stands, and we danced and sang at the tops of our voices. I must have popped out for a moment because as I walked back in, everyone was making their way out the door.

'Where are you all going?' I asked

'We're going to see Sarina in the press conference,' one of the girls called back.

We piled down the corridor and conga-line'd into Wembley's media room, singing 'Three Lions'. I was the last to make my way in.

I didn't even look up at whatever was happening around the room; I went straight towards Sarina, who'd broken off from speaking and was beaming at us. Something urged me to put my foot up on the table that she was sat behind and launch myself on to its unsteady top. 'What are you doing?' she asked me. I paused for a split second, wondering if she had a point and not quite sure if it would take my weight, then clambered up anyway and carried on dancing, wiggling my hips and pointing my fingers in the air.

Then I looked out.

I had only ever seen that room less than half full, with the same dedicated journalists punctuating rows of empty seats.

Now it was packed out with reporters and every camera, phone, light and flash was going off in our direction.

Fuck, I thought. *I've made a complete tit of myself now.* Then, I figured, *I'm here now, better stick with it.* Sarina found it hysterical as we crowded round her, in front of a bunch of strangers. Bronzey got up with me for a few moments more then I rapidly mumbled to Sarina, 'OK, we're done now,' as we climbed down and flocked back out of the room.

When I looked at my phone later, I had a message from Tina, who was in Los Angeles, telling me she'd been walking past a shop with TV screens in the window and the same thing was playing on every single one: me dancing on the press conference table.

I'd only ever wanted my goalkeeping to be noticed; now our success was so visible that our celebrations were playing on the other side of the Atlantic. It was a clear, early sign that everything was about to change and a whole lot already had.

The team headed back to the Lensbury for a party that went on until the early hours.

Our families were there and I FaceTimed Grandma, who told me what she always did, that she'd waved at me on the telly but I hadn't waved back. Mum and Dad sat outside for most of the evening, but the person I really wanted to celebrate with, Kitty, wasn't there. I knew then that Kitty was the person I wanted to share my life with. Her fierce loyalty and fearlessness to say what she thought were qualities I really admired. We brought out the best in each other and the conviction she gave me was a big feature of the happiness and grounding that was allowing me to thrive and implement all I knew to succeed. She had sat among the players' friends and family at the game but I didn't yet have the confidence to mix business with my personal life at the party, even if it felt obvious or came easily to others. I had never brought anyone into my football world – I'd grown up being extremely private, so I didn't know how to. And I'd only introduced her to Mum and Dad a few months before. I didn't know how to adjust or remain undistracted by the idea that my love life might be known and talked about by more people still, because I feared everyone would react badly towards it. I kept us safe in a bubble a little longer while she went back to Christina's in Reading.

The two of us had a flight booked to Greece 48 hours later, so I knew we would soon have ten days to unwind together, and I soaked up the celebrations with my teammates till I couldn't stay awake any longer. It must have been about 2am when I turned in although I could still hear a couple of the girls, steaming drunk, sat in the corridor outside my door eating McDonald's hours later.

If I'd slept soundly the night before, the adrenaline of the final and the win had a hold on me now and I woke up, restless, at 7am, each of us gradually emerging for another party, this time for the fans in Trafalgar Square later that morning.

ALL IN

Thousands of people turned out in a sea of red and white that we later learned was 7,000 deep. Among them were men, women, people in suits passing through and lots and lots of little girls wrapped in St George's flags and England T-shirts calling out our names beneath a cloudy sky with the National Portrait Gallery and Nelson's Column as our backdrop.

They were all there to celebrate our victory but, even as we danced and sang to 'Sweet Caroline', wearing the flags around our waists and sunglasses to protect most people from their hangovers as much as the sun's beams, there was a strong, immediate sense that washed over everyone that this was about something so much more than football coming home – this meant something far bigger to the people who were there and the millions more watching on news channels at home.

On the bus out of central London, Lotte came up with an idea that we all thought, instantly, was great.

'We have to do something now,' she said, eager to harness what we'd seen and heard.

There and then, she penned a letter, addressed to the two politicians vying to lead the Conservative Party and the country at the time, Liz Truss and Rishi Sunak, urging whichever of them became prime minister to ensure every girl had access to football in school PE lessons.

She asked Leah then Sue Campbell, the FA's director of women's football, if they'd be on board, then recruited each of us for our signatures, which we sent a photograph of to include alongside one another, all 23 squad members resolute in using our fresh-earned platform to achieve something far longer-lasting than the euphoria of lifting a trophy.

'Throughout the Euros, we as a team spoke about our

legacy and goal to inspire a nation. Many will think that this has already been achieved, but we see this as only the beginning. We are looking to the future,' Lotte wrote on behalf of us all.

Many of us, like her, had spent a lifetime accepting the bare minimum and being told to be grateful for the chance to play; if little girls were going to pick up a ball, inspired by our triumph, we didn't think that was good enough for them.

'We want every girl in the nation to be able to play football,' the letter went on, citing the sad fact that only 63 per cent of girls had access to the game at school, and we asked to raise that standard so that every girl has access to two hours of PE each week. 'Women's football has come a long way. But it still has a long way to go.'

Lotte had thought about what bringing joy to the nation actually looked like: the physical, societal, cultural and psychological barriers to girls playing had to come down if our win was to have any real impact and we were to achieve our ambition to leave the game in a better place for the next generation.

I thought anyone who could come up with what she did and build change right there in the moment was super-special.

We didn't delay, and sent it out on social media, writing openly to the fair-weather politicians who had turned out to Wembley and were sending out public messages of congratulations.

We didn't know then that it would become a catalyst for change for girls' and women's sport the nation over, that the win followed by an instantaneous call to action would become a new standard to inspire women playing rugby, cricket, netball in what they could achieve and further for their sports if they could win a major tournament too.

We planted a seed and left it in sunlight to grow, ensuring the best conditions we could. For now, though, we had another party to get to.

I headed over to Christina's a little over an hour away and got changed for a team night out, rapidly organised by Leah, at Pizza Pomodoro in Knightsbridge that evening.

I hadn't drunk much the night before but tonight was a different story. Alessia and I were on the tequila shots and I told anyone who'd listen that I had a flight to catch at lunchtime the next day and, no matter what, to please make sure I was put in a car at the end of the night to get me back up to Manchester by 9am.

The night moved from the restaurant to a cordoned-off area of Cirque Le Soir nightclub on Carnaby Street. Somewhere along the way, someone sneaked a sambuca shot into my hand, which was a recipe for disaster.

When I left the club at 2am to flashes from the paparazzi – which I had never seen in my life before – I could barely stay upright in my heels, and photographers were conveniently there to capture me being a mess. Their pictures, of one of the FA staff helping me into the taxi as I hung myself off his shoulders to stand up straight, appeared online in a carousel of photos from the Lionesses' boozy night out the next day, querying who Mary Earps' mystery man was, which Kitty was not at all pleased to wake up to.

He put me in the cab with a few more flashes of the camera bulbs and two sick bags, which were put to good use on the drive back up the M1.

I arrived in Crete nursing a tequila hangover and a far bigger hangover of euphoria that I didn't know what to do with.

People were coming up to me at dinner and by the pool to ask if I was Mary Earps and celebrate with me. This was brand new and I wasn't sure what to do with it. I was really touched that they wanted a photo and I liked meeting people and hearing their stories, but I was also incredibly self-conscious.

I was at an all-inclusive hotel, mostly in a bikini or doing the kind of goofy stuff I usually did on holiday, like joining in with folk dancing at the Greek restaurant, but now people were watching and filming me.

Inwardly, I was trying to prolong this mad high I was on while realising that I didn't have a clue how to either maintain or process it. I don't know what taking drugs feels like but I imagine what I was experiencing was something resembling a comedown. I was trying to hold on to the elation of the environment I'd just been in while entering a new one that felt suddenly and unexpectedly alien.

People like to say it's imposter syndrome – that's what they want us to believe as women, and as female athletes, that we don't know how to sit in the product of our own success because we don't or shouldn't believe we have a right to it.

It wasn't that. In fact, I don't buy imposter syndrome, I think it's another tool used to keep us in our box. I'd just never experienced the recognition I had over the past few days and I had to get used to it, quickly.

I stayed off my phone as much as I could, doing a handful of interviews or responding to requests coming into Tina in the mornings, then attempting to rest in the afternoon.

ALL IN

As the exhaustion abated and I came home to Manchester, I found it harder still to come back to real life.

I'd been on top of the world, in a love story with romance and fireworks going off, and now I had the laundry and the cooking waiting. We may have suddenly been getting the kind of visibility the men were used to but we weren't living in gated homes with staff to take care of us like they were. I was out of the England bubble and back in control of my own life now. I wasn't entirely sure how I was meant to get back to the mundane, and a day job at Manchester United was anything but; still, I was feeling really quite flat about it.

I have spoken to other athletes since then and it is not uncommon to find it harder to come off a successful tournament than an unsuccessful one. I think it is something that translates to high-achievers in the world of work too. When you lose there's an immediate focus on what wasn't good enough and what you have to work on. This time, I had completed the thing I'd dedicated my life to – I was England's number one and I'd won a trophy on an international stage. I was no longer chasing that huge ambition and I knew I was still only as good as my next save and my next game. But I didn't want to grow complacent. I was going to have to find the next big thing to chase.

PART THREE

GOING ALL IN

FIFTEEN

BE UNAPOLOGETICALLY YOURSELF

I'd developed a reputation as the TikTok Queen, a nickname that did the rounds and then stuck after the Euros.

My follower count had already grown well into the hundreds of thousands before the tournament, before anyone knew me as a Lioness, with most people turning up for my dance trends or pranks on teammates, enjoying the entertainment of me goofing around rather than that I was England's goalkeeper. The videos that had nothing to do with playing football, and were pure personality, were usually the most popular and racked up millions of views.

After my table-top turn at the press conference, which had shown that side of me to far more people than I intended, I had almost half a million people following me on there. This was considered a stand-out presence among English players, so brands were beginning to show up to do business with me and reach my ready-made audience, just as Tina had predicted.

Spinning business out of being just exactly who I was as a person was perfect, in part because it was attracting people who genuinely liked me, which felt refreshing but it meant even more now because even with our recent success, women's football was nowhere near ready to set any of us up for life.

The Euros bonus had been my Manchester United salary and then some, but that Manchester United salary was still the same as it had always been, and only a year earlier I was living in credit-card debt.

I still wanted to exercise my business muscle and build something that could help me live freely in the future. The powers that be at TikTok had spotted what I was doing pre-Euros and collaborated with me during the tournament. Until then, JD Sports had invited me to a screening they were hosting and paid me to post about it, for the first time, which I'd been absolutely delighted with and we'd worked really hard to pull in a few other deals. Now brands like McDonald's, Superdrug and Nocco energy drinks all wanted to work with me, paying tens of thousands of pounds for a series of posts which was adding up to become a significant income boost.

Straight out of the tournament, the girls had all seen an uptick in commercial interest: businesses hurriedly sent us 'Congratulations, Lionesses' emails, inviting us, via agents, to Disneyland and on Virgin holidays or to spa breaks and holiday parks in exchange for photos and social media posts.

Ironically, my reckoning with the end of my England career two years earlier had given me the need to start building a platform for it earlier than I otherwise would have done.

As a direct result of Tina and I working together to grow my profile, I was a step ahead of most other players in terms of how many people they could get their products in front of.

Women in sport are often made to feel ashamed for pursuing those kinds of opportunities, as though they distract from the expectation that we prove ourselves only as athletes, but there is no humiliation in being multifaceted and certainly none in carving a life and business for yourself. Those opportunities to do better, financially, are ones we had earned the right to after years of accepting so little for giving so much of ourselves. Putting in extra work off the pitch was, and still is, a welcome necessity for players who want to capitalise on a public profile during their short footballing years in order to prepare for later. It doesn't take away from wanting to be the best on the pitch, and if anything, it gave me more fuel to fight harder, work harder to be even better for everyone who was now invested and watching us play.

In fact, now that a nationwide spectacle had delivered the spotlight, women's football via TikTok and Instagram was proving to be good business. It brought new fans and added visibility to the game, which translated into greater support for players and especially, as far as I was concerned, goalkeepers. It also brought new followers to brands online, and, on TikTok, I was the most followed Lioness they had. Marrying the two was ideal and I didn't have to change my formula, which was to work at and grow my reputation as a world-class goal-keeper first and foremost, and my reputation online second.

The football season was about to kick off when the Queen died and our anticipated return to the league was delayed by a week. I felt a real affinity to the Queen, as a lot of people did, but in truth I was grateful for the extra week to get myself back into a familiar routine. I was still struggling after weeks of adrenaline coursing through me and the adjustment to post-Euros life. They say that getting 'it' is the easy part, although I definitely couldn't relate to that, and keeping it is the hard part – now that I could relate to. Now that I was known and respected for what I brought to the table, I wanted to stay that way. I wanted to learn and rise for as long as possible to make it harder again to catch me. I was conscious of carrying that pressure and privilege into matches. Like tearing off a plaster, I just needed to get started.

United were due to play Spurs in the first match of the season and we had a Lionesses camp beforehand with qualifiers for the following year's World Cup against Austria and Luxembourg.

I was out for a walk and a stretch pre-game and Sarina asked, 'How are you finding it?', alluding to the change that we'd all experienced.

'It's different now,' I said. 'I don't know how to feel.'

'I told you your life is going to change,' she said. 'It's so rare for a goalkeeper to do what you've done, to perform as you have.'

England felt like such a safe space for me.

It was usual to have a team review after a big tournament and we came together in the Club England meeting room at St George's Park.

The emotional security that I felt within England was bolstered by the culture and values that had underpinned and contributed to our success. Non-collegiate behaviour was not tolerated. We came back together to the news that Hannah had been dropped from the squad: her behaviour behind the scenes at the Euros had frequently risked derailing training sessions and team resources.

Ellie Roebuck and I had buckled down and I'd given the performances of my life, and she had blown it out the park in supporting me. We got on well but what happened around us had not been easy at all and the conversations about it, within camp, had been an endless source of distraction.

As a result, Sarina announced the September camp, without her, explaining to the press: 'She has some personal issues that she has to solve, so for her at this moment it's better for her to stay at her club.'

The following month, the press would speak to multiple people and report that behaviour and attitude at age group and senior levels and at club, where she was now sitting out games in the stands in what that manager described as 'the best interests of the team', were behind the decision and she was not expected to return to England under Sarina.

In our post-Euros review at St George's Park, we split off into groups and reported back on what had gone well – which was pretty clear, given the win – what hadn't and what we could do differently in the future. It was an eye-opener into how a group can live the same event or set of circumstances with such variety, with those of us who'd played every minute understandably having had a different experience of the victory to those who hadn't played one. Nobody was right and nobody was wrong, it was just a solid lesson in remembering and acknowledging how there were 23 different players and 23 different personal versions of the same summer, with space for it all.

The only negative that each group reported back on was that behaviour, which was overwhelmingly considered disruptive and unreliable, with a risk of being destructive, taking energy and time from coaches who needed to work with the rest of the team on set-pieces, mentality and of course goalkeeping sessions. It affected us all in a domino effect to an extent that was extremely unusual in a successful elite team environment. It also completely contradicted my professional values, which included preserving everything I had, mentally and physically, for performance and for a goalkeeper union where everyone, whatever their role, had the space and support to be great at their job.

'I accept this was negative,' Sarina acknowledged. 'This has been dealt with and it's not appropriate to speak about one individual anymore,' she said, drawing a line under it.

I had often shut down conversations in camp about it too. In the feedback session, I praised Roebuck instead: 'I really couldn't have had the tournament I did without you,' I acknowledged while we were with all the girls.

Back at United, we had our first home fixture, against Reading, in front of over 7,000 fans, which was 2,000 more than we were used to seeing at Leigh. The goalkeepers always went out early to warm up and I remember going out ahead of the midday kick-off on a Saturday and hearing all these little voices, girls and boys, chanting 'Mary' from all through the stands where once you'd hear 20 or 30 scattered among the seats.

Oh my God, I thought as I looked around and took in all the new signs bearing my name and asking for my gloves.

The support was incredible; I needed to carry on my

warm-up and prepare for the game but I wanted to stop there and then and thank every one of them. I was blown away. From then on, the club had to have an extra security person come out with the keepers to make sure all went smoothly. The change was instant.

Willco describes it as there being a different aura around me, Tooney and Alessia, with bigger and louder crowds, and a bigger energy in the changing room and in our conversations with management at the club that demanded the higher standards we brought back with us from the Euros.

When we played Arsenal in an almost packed-out Emirates stadium that November, it became one of my favourite ever games with United.

The more pressure and noise there was, the more I loved rising to the occasion. It was that state of mind that I'd taken from Wolfsburg, that pressure wasn't something to fear but something to harness, used in the pursuit of success, and the Euros had proven that. I demanded the best from myself anyway, so it suited me perfectly and the buzz from this was the closest I'd got since Wembley.

Arsenal were top of the table and we were level on points. We played out from the back beautifully, dominating and going 1–0 up before half-time. When they scored two decent goals, I pulled the girls in: 'Do you want to fucking win this game or not?' I shouted and we did, 3–2.

Horribly, Beth, playing for Arsenal, was badly injured, which would rule her out of next summer's World Cup; I was devastated for her and knew how badly she'd be missed by us all at the tournament. The adrenaline of that day's win, though, stayed with me – I can always feel the energy of games running through my body for hours afterwards. Kitty and I went out to a beautiful Italian restaurant in Shoreditch that night and I woke up, still buzzing, at 4am, resorting to some silent yoga in the hotel room to try and bring myself down from the high.

I loved playing at iconic stadiums and was excited to be back at Old Trafford to play Aston Villa just before Christmas. It was a record attendance for our home games but the ground was still less than half full, and the marketing that went into the game reflected what was going on at the club behind the scenes, where everything was a bit topsy-turvy and change was far from instant.

Meetings between players and executives had been going on for well over a year, and long before the Euros, as we constantly tried to break down barriers that seemed to stand in the way of this global giant of a club investing more in their women's team.

Casey, who'd come in as manager and started the team from scratch the year before I joined, had resigned as we fought for change from the inside, battling the club over conditions at Leigh.

It was true that the women's team brought in little financially but the promise of doing what was needed to help reverse that wasn't coming to fruition. There had been a commitment, for example, to move us to a more elite training outfit at the club's Carrington complex where the men trained, but it wasn't happening and the stagnation around what we did often left us feeling like a publicity exercise rather than benefitting from a real will to integrate us.

After Casey's departure, we lost two of our biggest players

in Christen Press and Tobin Heath, both USA World Cup winners. While playing at a juggernaut like Manchester United, I felt disappointed to be facing the kind of hurdles I had encountered in my early days at Doncaster and Birmingham, and when the will to seize the momentum of the Euros didn't appear to be rapidly improving matters I found myself among one of the more experienced players and felt I needed to use my voice.

If we, as Lionesses, had set out our legacy as leaving the game in a better place and improving conditions for young girls that didn't mean only within schools, it extended to everyday conditions and conversations in our current workplaces too.

Besides, I had maintained good relationships and still wanted to see out my career there. I was United ride or die. And I wanted it for my teammates, future players and younger goalkeepers who would follow me into the union there for years to come. I was determined that by performing on the pitch, a European champion in goal delivering clean sheets week in, week out, and applying internal pressure off it, they would – and could – come good in their vision to be something great.

Where I was once afraid of appearing to bosses to be biting the hand that fed me, I was now about to turn 30 with a record that I felt gave me the right and the responsibility to advocate for better.

I sat down with the new manager, Marc Skinner, in January, and told him players needed to see the club's ambition if they were to have a chance of keeping them, which was a huge priority.

Other players were negotiating contracts and it didn't look

as if they were being treated particularly well or there was any great urgency to get them to stay. Meanwhile, I had one year left on mine, with an option to extend for another 12 months. I wanted, above all, to stay at United so I needed clarity around whether they wanted me there, too, whether I was part of their future plans.

As a leadership figure in the squad, I knew that if I was proactive in renegotiating a better deal for myself then it would set a precedent for others, too, and could also help to attract and retain talent by setting an intent to be a club of champions.

I was pretty frank, pointing to how other contract negotiations were going and how they seemed to be left to the last minute. I wanted to know that my future there was a secure one, where I would pursue what I'd always chased, to play at a club that pushed my level. Maybe they didn't like being told what to do. Or maybe it wasn't high on their agenda, but they were slow following up and the negotiation was left on the back-burner. I just needed to look back on those conversations and be satisfied that I'd said all I needed to while I continued committing my best on the pitch.

At the end of February, I was invited to Paris for FIFA's The Best awards, which recognises the top male and female footballers in the world. I had been nominated in the Women's Goalkeeper category by fans, team captains, coaches and the media, then shortlisted in the final three with Germany's Ann-Katrin Berger and Chile's Christiane Endler. I was buzzing to be in such talented company. There wasn't a chance that I'd win but being held in that regard and going to the ceremony, alongside greats of the game including Lionel Messi, Kylian Mbappé and Karim Benzema, who were nominated in the men's categories, Spain's Alexia Putellas, who had won Best Player the previous year in the women's, and Beth who was deservedly nominated for the same award that year, was an honour in itself. I was just so happy to be a contender.

The trip was another fairy tale and a view inside life at the top of the men's world too. FIFA put me (and any guests I wanted to invite) up in a five-star hotel, with everything taken care of. Kitty, Mum, Dad, Joel, Annabelle and Lewis all joined me for the ceremony.

It was the first time I'd taken Kitty to an event with them, which meant a huge amount to me. I hoped that being there together to enjoy something special would be good for us all.

We were coming from different parts of the country, so we planned to fly out separately and meet in Paris. At Charles de Gaulle Airport, Kitty and I were greeted by a FIFA escort and taken to a waiting car that would transfer us into the city.

'Is there anything you want to see before you go to the hotel?' the gentleman asked.

It was gone 9:30pm on a bitterly cold evening but we both wanted to see the Eiffel Tower sparkle.

I'd been there once before but in the daytime, during that school trip, and now I was excited to see it twinkle on the hour. We pulled up with about 45 minutes to spare and found it already lit up beautifully in blue and yellow for Ukraine. So, we stood in the Parisian frost, freezing the tips of our noses waiting for the light show that was scheduled for 11pm, only to find as the hour came and went that there wouldn't be one that night.

Oh well, luxury awaited at the spectacularly grand Hôtel du Collectionneur – we'd have to find our sparkle there.

We arrived to macarons and champagne and autograph hunters who were waiting outside for players far better known than me, so I passed through the doors without any requests for a signature.

Hair and make-up had been scheduled for me the next day and I had a laugh in the chair at the hotel alongside Sarina, who was nominated in the Best Manager category, and Ann-Katrin. 'Who's going to win?' the girl doing our make-up asked. 'Mary,' said Sarina and Ann-Katrin, having a laugh too. *Not a chance*, I thought: you don't go from zero to that trophy in a matter of months.

I'd been for a coffee with my family earlier that afternoon and Dad had also mentioned it: 'I don't think it will happen, but have you thought about what you'd say if you did win?'

'No,' I said. 'It'll be short, I'd thank people. But I don't think it's going to happen.'

'No, me either,' he said, 'but don't be caught out.'

With my hair and make-up done, and the opulent setting and all the fancy thrills and prestige of heading out to the ceremony, I felt like a queen. I also felt sick with nerves. I was dressed up in a tighter-than-tight sparkly gold dress with chain straps and tall block heels and I'd had to spend some time in the room watching *Harry Potter and the Goblet of Fire*, my comfort film, to calm the raging anxiety inside my stomach.

I had never been anywhere like that before, dressed up in a grand room with such huge names, people I admired and respected. I was way out of my comfort zone as we pulled up at Salle Pleyel concert hall, a couple of minutes from the Arc de Triomphe, and I wriggled out of the car.

ALL IN

I got to my seat and saw Beth and Sarina, both positioned on the end of rows. They both deserved to win and I suspected that meant that they had. I walked on into the middle of the row where I'd been seated next to Jess, who was Ann-Katrin's plus-one.

Women's Goalkeeper was one of the first awards of the evening and I'd been quietly chatting to her when Canada's Olympian goalkeeper Stephanie Labbé and men's Premier League legend Didier Drogba started to introduce the category. There was barely a moment to tune in before I heard my name 'Mary Earps'.

I felt astonished and sick, immediately and at once.

Then I heard my mum let out a short, shrill scream at the back in pure shock.

Normally, I thought, you're nominated for a few years then maybe you win, but I hadn't been on the scene at all, I hadn't played in the Champions League or major tournaments until the Euros seven months ago. Now I was walking up the steps to a stage in Paris as the best women's goalkeeper in the world.

The trophy was a hell of a lot heavier than I thought and I didn't know what to do with it, so I looked around awkwardly for somewhere to place it down, found nowhere and propped it up with both hands as I began saying words I suddenly wished I had taken longer to prepare.

It forced me to speak from the heart.

'Thank you to everyone who voted for me. I feel really honoured to be holding this really heavy trophy,' I began. 'I just want to say thank you so much to my loved ones who have picked me up off the kitchen floor to be here today – not specifically tonight, but a few years ago. Thank you so much to all of my teammates, without them this wouldn't be possible. The coaching staff at Man United and England, but particularly Ian Willcock and Darren Ward, who I'm pretty sure deserve a trophy of their own for putting up with me every single day, because that isn't easy.

'Sarina, I run out of words to say thanks to you for the opportunity you have given me to chase my wildest dreams and for believing in me the way you have.

'This is for anyone who has ever been in a dark place, just know that there's light at the end of the tunnel. Keep going, you can achieve anything you set your mind to.

'Sometimes success looks like this, collecting trophies, sometimes it's just waking up and putting one step in front of the other. There's only one of you in the world, and that's more than good enough. Be unapologetically yourself.'

I returned to my seat to feel my phone already vibrating in my little handbag. Sarina won and Beth lost out to Alexia, which felt unjust to me: Alexia is a phenomenal player, but Beth had had the year and tournament of her life.

Little did I know that the words I'd just spoken on stage were already making their way around the internet, generating a reaction I couldn't have predicted any more than my win.

Messages started arriving in my inboxes, mostly from young women and girls, but dads, mums, grandparents and young men too. There were even teenagers undergoing psychiatric treatment who felt inspired to get well. They all explained how they'd been in the darkest of places and related to my version of what courage and success looked like. Whether they shared their whole stories or not, they all said 'Thank you'.

They wanted to save the words on their phone screens and

put them on T-shirts, so we made them, and with it the idea for my clothing line, built on purpose and authenticity, MAE27 – Mary Alexandra Earps and my shirt number – was born; wearable messages of positivity harnessing the words of my speech for a community that grew around the shared experience of emerging from darkness and into light. Later it would grow to provide something for inspired young goalkeepers to wear and draw a sense of shared identity from too.

I believe that those words came to me that night because I didn't want to be defined only by that most visible, shiny version of success, when a couple of years earlier success had been as hard to reach as just getting dressed after sitting in pyjamas for three days because I had no reason to leave the house. One experience made way for the other. I hadn't known back then that a new trajectory was waiting right around the corner for me and having the resilience to meet that opportunity was as big an accomplishment as the trophy that I now took home in my hands.

I had learned that that vulnerability is strength and being unapologetically who you are is your power, and I wanted others to share in that lesson too. It turned out many more people than I imagined resonated with the message. My own life had become a lot better when I had embraced my vulnerability, and when I had understood that who I was was good enough. I hoped that someone who heard those words would not be fooled by the darkness, as it had once threatened me, but instead that they would find the light.

My light had now catapulted me to my greatest performances and an accolade that confirmed it. It spelled out exactly what I'd always dreamed I could be: the world's best.

When I blew out the candles on my 30th birthday cake a couple of weeks later at dinner, with the words TikTok Queen iced on the top, celebrating among the women I loved most, my old wish was complete. So, now I wished to do it all again.

SIXTEEN

LIVE BY YOUR PRINCIPLES, DIE BY THEM TOO

The season that started in the afterglow of the Euros ended with a run of career highs.

At United I won the club's first Player of the Month award, broke the record for league clean sheets, keeping 14 in 22 games, and received the WSL Golden Glove for the season's best keeper.

I made it my mission to turn the new spotlight that was on me to goalkeeping as a whole.

With each award came the reminder that while keepers were pulled up on their mistakes, they rarely commanded attention for their positive contribution to the sport. Commercially, too, the goalkeeper had never been a poster girl or a focus for sponsors, choosing strikers who scored rather than saved goals instead, and that followed into grassroots and what little girls could see and wanted to be. I'd lost count of the number of times I'd gone somewhere and been asked if I could convince a girl to go in net. Those requests and messages had dropped off a lot since the Euros, which felt like a direct response to winning trophies and to the growing visibility of my position within the Lionesses, in the game and online. I wanted those little girls who saw heroes like Superwoman and Catwoman on their TV screens or in stories to feel like they could be superheroes, too, arms outstretched, diving across a goal.

And so it felt unjust to keep any added attention to myself. Goalkeeping was a sport within a sport and my team were keepers. I made it my mission to share the future gains with them, telling any journalist or content creator who'd listen that 'Goalkeeping is cool,' hoping the message would filter through to young players and those with the power to invest in them.

Talking about my own accomplishments was nice but it was also ephemeral. I was keener to generate long-lasting change and give them an opportunity to be seen and rise higher with me and then long after I'm gone.

As a team, United had finished second in the table, our highest ever finish, and we reached the FA Cup Final; it was all a huge improvement on paper, although behind the scenes there was a mess of loose ends in urgent need of tying up.

We'd lost two more of our best players, Ona Batlle to Barcelona and Alessia Russo on a free transfer to Arsenal, and the club wanted to pick up the conversations around my own contract extension that I'd tried to start with them six months earlier.

We still weren't in the new training building, there was real concern about player turnover. The problems felt acute but they were not unusual in women's football and teams and players variously faced struggles like these throughout the professional game and the world. I just wanted to stay at United and I wanted my future at United nailed down. I needed to know their intention was the same and I held out hope they'd come good on the ambitions they'd used to bring me to the club in the first place. 'We've got a big summer ahead. We'll have signed new players by the start of the season,' I was assured by the powers that be as we entered the summer transfer window. I was expecting that a contract would be waiting for me then too.

'OK,' I said. 'Let's continue talking after the summer.'

I had a World Cup to play.

At England, I was in a flow state. After that camp debrief and the World Cup qualifiers so soon after the Euros we'd come back together for a showpiece match against the USA at Wembley and won 2–1. I was convinced that we were unbeatable. We were a ridiculous team with an incredible amount of talent and, most importantly, a special cohesion: we felt like we could do anything together, including winning the biggest trophy of them all that summer.

In April we'd won the Finalissima, against Brazil, between the champions of Europe and South America, and we did it on my first penalty shoot-out for a trophy.

I'd been disappointed when Brazil scored in the 93rd minute of the game, then I'd been unable to save the first penalty. I thought, *This is not going to be my day*, then swiftly told myself, *Fuck that, I'm going to make it my day*. Negative talk or a bump in the road weren't going to derail my meticulous penalty preparation. I went on and saved the decisive shot, almost pulling my shoulder out of its socket with a reach so far to my left that I felt like Superwoman.

Leah asked me to lift the trophy with her.

'No, don't be daft, you're the captain,' I told her.

'Grab the handle,' she insisted and I felt honoured to raise it in the air, but more so that my teammate and captain recognised the role I'd played in us winning it.

If there was one disruption to the year with England it came as I was driving in Manchester in the spring.

Sarina called me to bounce the idea of bringing Hannah back into the squad. Sarina now routinely called me into leadership meetings and would take my opinion into consideration on team matters beyond goalkeeping. I was happy to be part of those conversations and no matter whether you were among the more experienced or junior players in her squad, feeling like you had a say was a part of our success.

'It doesn't make me feel comfortable,' I said in response to the idea of a return, not needing to remind her of the disharmony that the squad had felt before. I felt protective of the good energy we now had in goalkeeper training and the morale of the wider team.

I wished that this situation wasn't what it was but I had been asked my opinion, precisely because the decision would affect my work and performance space, too, and I was both expected and needed to be honest. The progress and development of younger players had become a huge feature of my professional value set in football. I'd experienced and assessed how I was or wasn't supported when I was coming through: it's why I set up those sessions for budding goalkeepers in Reading and committed to it in my goalkeeper unions as soon as I had some seniority to do so. Equally, to reward certain behaviour went against those same fundamental values of creating a healthy and happy space for players of all experience to work and thrive, not least in a team environment before a World Cup. I saw, too, that other hard-working keepers would miss out on that space as a result.

'I think everyone deserves a second chance,' Sarina said, and another call followed a few weeks later with a wider group, in which she reiterated the same, confirming she wanted to bring her back in.

There was a genuine concern about breaking something that wasn't broken but we respected the manager's decision and I kept my focus on retaining my standards and those within the group.

As the summer and the World Cup drew closer, my big thing on the pitch and in training was 'don't change what got you here,' but I questioned what would happen if I couldn't hit the peak performance that I had in the Euros and my mind would unwillingly challenge itself – *You've gone ten games this good, you can't keep it up* – driving its own internal competition as it did when I was a little girl.

Consistency was everything and I'd maintained it when no one was watching. Could I continue to do it with so much pressure and anticipation? People expected the extraordinary now and a certain facet of success is that the higher you go, the more expectations rise alongside.

I leaned into the belief that carrying that pressure was my privilege and that their expectation was a product of the knowledge that I could deliver.

I was on a big, pre-World Cup shoot with Adidas, who sponsored me at United and personally as an athlete, when Sarina was due to call confirming her squad for the tournament, nothing at all like the *X-Factor* build-up of the Euros.

I told Tina I'd have to be available between certain times to speak to the manager and let Adidas know that I'd need to excuse myself when the phone rang, so I kicked myself and panicked when I spotted a missed video call. I called her straight back.

'Obviously you're going' Sarina said on the other end, 'let's go win this,' giving me not only confirmation of my place but the vice-captaincy for the tournament, too, with Leah out injured, another huge loss for the team, and Millie stepping up as captain.

I had never been to Australia and didn't know what jet lag might look like until we were presented with an expert in it during preparations at St George's Park.

He handed each of us two pairs of glasses, one that let in blue light to mimic daylight and an orange pair to block it out and release melatonin that would help us sleep, alongside instructions and a protocol of when to put each on, placing us in a frankly nightmarish rhythm that involved going to bed and waking up progressively earlier each day in the run-up to our flight out there, until I was starting my mornings at 4am.

I followed it to the letter, obviously. I had no experience of that kind of travel before, and wanted to give myself the best shot of getting ahead of the jet lag, if not beating it altogether. But I felt absolutely terrible as we arrived at our first base, a hotel and training complex across the road from the beach on Queensland's blissful Sunshine Coast.

I felt like I'd left my eyes, and my ability to be a goalkeeper, back in England. For days I couldn't see a thing properly, including a ball, until it was right in front of me, and I was 'seeing' no improvement whatsoever.

I really needed my vision to do my job. 'Your body language is off,' Sarina noted after one of the training sessions, reminding me I was a big personality in the group and they needed it present.

I explained to her how on edge and frustrated I felt, being unable to pick up the flight of the ball, and she told me to give myself time and grace. 'It'll come together,' she reassured me.

We played a friendly against Canada as we acclimatised for games and I still couldn't see a damn thing clearly until two days before the tournament opened.

'I'm not going to lie,' Darren said in a warm-up ahead of our first game against Haiti, having told me he wasn't worried about my sight at all every time I'd asked during training. 'I was worried but I'm not now.'

As we prepared to begin our World Cup campaign on 22nd July in Brisbane, I had something else ruminating in my mind, and knowing whether to speak out on it had been occupying space inside my head for months.

It had unfolded around February time that England's main sponsor, Nike, had no plans to make my green goalkeeper shirt available for fans to buy during the tournament.

The issue had first fleetingly come up before the Euros when things were different and it had never even dawned on me that they might, but Nike had informed England back then that an ordering mishap meant it wouldn't be on sale alongside the rest of the Lionesses' white home shirts. Who was I to complain? Goalkeeping wasn't celebrated that way and I hadn't achieved anything to convince them that it should be. *That's a bit shit*, I thought, and I wondered if it were more likely a choice dressed up as an admin error but, they volunteered, it wouldn't happen again.

So when I began picking up in conversations that Nike were saying the replica goalkeeper shirts were now not going to be ready for the World Cup, that was a pattern, and definitely a choice, so I started asking questions.

I took it to Sarina's right-hand woman, who was a problem solver, and to the commercial team at England, who worked alongside Nike, and said surely that couldn't be the case. Participation in girls' football, including goalkeeping, had rocketed since the Euros and so had match-viewing; demand for Lionesses gear had soared alongside but keepers were clearly not part of Nike's commercial strategy.

I, on the other hand, had been talking about goalkeeping anywhere I could and I felt a responsibility to all the kids who were now being sent a clear message by this that they and their position didn't matter.

As I saw it, anyone who played keeper or had any ambition to do so was being excluded from a room: the message that Nike, and England by default, were sending with this was your friends and teammates can have Bronze 2, Mead 7 or Russo 23 on their back but you can't get into this World Cup party because you're different.

You literally cannot field a team without a goalkeeper, a specialist position required for a game to kick off and you're telling them they're not respected enough to deserve a shirt, so go and be a striker instead? I found that to be absolutely unacceptable. And unjust. I pictured all these kids giving up goalkeeping as a result of what they couldn't replicate or celebrate about themselves and their dreams.

As the months went on and the tournament drew closer, I tried to push every channel I could to get a replica in stores and online, holding meetings with Nike and England and discussing any kind of alternative they could come up with, a T-shirt celebrating goalkeeping perhaps, as time ticked away while the mismatch with my values ate away at me.

'We'll think about it, we'll see what we can do,' was always the answer.

On a smaller personal level, players were being asked how many shirts they wanted making up for their family and friends to wear to games, whether they wanted home, away, personalised, with a number or not, and mine, with nothing on offer, would be showing up with my old match shirts or none at all while everyone else queued at the customisation stations Nike set up at our hotels out in Australia to ensure they were kitted out for each fixture.

We'd been such a campaigning team, and our commitment to creating change in every area of football that it was needed in order to leave the game in a better place was as celebrated and pawed over as what we accomplished on the pitch. In fact, the press were following closely at that time as we fought the FA as a squad, demanding equity through bonuses for tournament wins; the dispute was paused and unresolved as we'd gone into the World Cup.

I felt that this approach to parity had to extend to keepers in a commercial setting and I had raised it with Leah, Lotte, Lucy and Millie to check if I was overreacting and understand if the team agreed it was an issue to continue pushing with

Nike. They were a hundred per cent behind me; Millie's niece was among the kids who'd wanted my shirt and I'd had to tell her 'You can't, it doesn't exist.'

Those private efforts continued until we left for Australia and I was beginning to hear that a few journalists had noticed the absence of green jerseys on sale and had been quietly querying if there was more to the story.

I started to think about whether I should be talking more publicly about it, whether that's what being unapologetically myself looked like.

I asked the people closest to me what they thought, and everyone said: 'Don't do it'. It was seen, unanimously, as a pointless quest. Playing in a World Cup was pressure enough, they all said, global conglomerates didn't U-turn and, besides, no one takes on the sponsor. There was a bigger risk of reputational damage to me than to them. Worse still, if I performed badly at the tournament, I'd have created a distraction onto which anyone could hang blame.

It was true that speaking up takes energy and I felt I should be using all of mine on the pitch. I was team and performance first and I didn't want to do anything that could distract from them and the team goal at a major tournament. But it was also now my waking thought every morning and had been for weeks – one day concluding that I had to speak out and the next thinking, *No, it's not worth the backlash.*

When I was called into a press conference two days before the Haiti opener, I still didn't know if I was going to bat the question away or answer it truthfully.

I let my principles dictate what came next – honesty above all else. All you have is all you are, your character.

If I didn't speak my truth I'd have to look at myself in the mirror for years to come and question why I wasn't brave enough to speak up when it mattered – that wasn't what going all in looked like. I'd have let aspiring and future goalkeepers down when I had the chance to leave the game in a better place for them.

Live by your principles, die by them too. This was too important *not* to speak out on.

As sports reporters assembled in a semi-circle on one of the hotel floors that had been taken over for our media day, and the question of how I felt about not having a replica shirt on sale left one of the mouths in the room, I paused and took a breath.

'I can't really sugar-coat this in any way, so I am not going to try. It is hugely disappointing and very hurtful,' I said.

I felt something close to tears prick in the corners of my eyes, not because of the hurt but because of the passion with which I now advocated for my sport within the sport.

I explained how I had desperately tried to find an outcome with Nike through private channels but it had become evident there would not be one despite those talks or the rise in goalkeeping participation in the year since the Euros. 'There is not going to be an acceptable solution for the young kids out there,' I said.

I didn't yet know the power that my words would carry or how far they were about to reach but I hoped they'd achieve something. And if nothing else, I could look myself in the mirror and young goalkeepers in the eyes and tell them that I used my platform when I had it and that I had tried.

With my social media heavily filtered so no one could tag

me and a sports news blackout in camp, I left it in the quiet, sombre reaction of the journalists gathered in that room as they went away and turned it into news stories.

I called Tina and let her know what I'd said, warning her that it might become a bit of a thing, but I needed to switch off and get my head down now.

I felt like a weight had been lifted. That I chose to speak out at all joined my proudest moments. My head and my conscience were clear, leaving space to kick off a World Cup.

SEVENTEEN

CHOOSE PRESENCE
OF MIND

One of the most beautiful things about playing a World Cup is that you get such varied opposition, and I enjoyed the challenge of taking on different styles of play from across the globe.

We won our first games against a counter-attacking Haiti in Brisbane, then Denmark's defensive four-four-two in Sydney, both with clean sheets, then our third, 5–1, to a technical China in Adelaide.

The stadiums were full of Australian English speakers and ex-pats, as well as travelling England fans who'd made the long journey, so they felt like a home away from home in the southern hemisphere's mild winter.

Each time we played, I loved looking down and seeing a World Cup football in my hands. The weight of it felt extra special because of what it represented.

And in between games I didn't have to look hard to see what a beautiful life it was out there. We'd been whale-watching, coming up close with humpbacks in the wild during our prep camp, which had blown me away, and the days there, for locals and for us, were fuelled by fitness, fresh food, good coffee and sunrise and sunsets on the beach.

So, when I spoke to Kitty late at night, a couple of days before our next game against Nigeria, she was dealing with a situation that threatened to burst my bubble, but I couldn't let it.

She'd left the apartment she was sharing with my family and was sat in a corner of Adelaide airport, in floods of tears, after begging a guard to allow her in hours before her flight out to Brisbane at 6am the next morning.

We always FaceTimed before bed but she hadn't been answering and when I messaged, hours away at our training base, in Terrigal, she'd tried to deflect.

It was very normal in tournaments for family to keep things from players, people being ill or difficulties playing out at home, in order not to distract us from performances, and I could tell that was what Kitty was attempting.

When she wouldn't tell me what was going on, I called her. She was as distressed as I'd ever heard her as she told me about a conversation she had overheard between my parents in the apartment that night and the hurtful things that had been said about us. She knew how much it would have upset me and had confronted Dad about it. The two of them had an almighty row.

It felt horrifying and extremely upsetting to hear what she had dealt with, but it wasn't the only problem.

A few days earlier, the FA had put a note on the friends and family group reminding everyone about words and conduct in the stands and I had to have a conversation with him about things that had been said in the heat of matches, seated among everyone else's loved ones. My dad wasn't the first person to make comments like that, and I'm sure he won't be the last, but I did need to speak with him about his part in why that warning message was needed.

Now I had my partner stranded at an airport with all her stuff after his words had hurt her and me too.

You can contain things inside a bubble for so long but when that many human beings are concerned, things will inevitably begin to spill out. No family is perfect, but the timing was awful.

When someone you love hurts, you're a person not an athlete. It threatens to affect your sleep, thinking and capacity, all of which I needed full access to so that I could play my best football. I couldn't allow this to go on.

This was almost certain to be my only World Cup – I'd be 34 when the next one came around, I couldn't jeopardise it for myself and I certainly wouldn't let personal problems derail anything for the team: to do so went against our squad morals and my own. I had to handle the personal myself and keep it out of the team so I could do the professional and deal with the consequences within my family later. I still don't fully know how I managed to perform at such a high level while carrying so much strain, but it taught me something important: even in the darkest times, we all have the ability to find light. Pressure and turmoil can feel overwhelming, yet they can also bring out strength we didn't know we had. It's a reminder that resilience isn't about avoiding hardship, but about rising through it – and that we're capable of more than we often believe.

I went into problem-solving mode, rapidly and instantly, and moved Kitty into an Airbnb near the training camp, reassured by the knowledge she was nearby and OK. I moved my parents out of the friends and family seats to minimise the impact of any of this; the first time I had laid down boundaries like that. It was important that Kitty knew she was my priority and, vitally, it was essential that I needed to be more concerned with my World Cup performance than their experience watching.

I look back and think how incredibly distressing it was to deal with this conflict in the most personal parts of my life, but I didn't take it that way at the time. I had learned from competing and fostering consistency in professional sport that when your career has its share of roadblocks, including emotional ones, finding routes around them becomes alarmingly normal. It's almost too easy to numb yourself to the drama because you know you can overcome it – and you want to, in order to focus on performance. I faced the situation with athletic pragmatism, using the tools I had at my disposal: from the inner resilience that was so familiar to the material resources I was fortunate enough to have, to the support of Kate, the team psychologist, who helped me to quickly understand what I felt and move on.

If I could safeguard my zone of mental quiet and reseal the bubble I was as capable as ever of performing at the consistently high level expected of me.

I would need calm and clarity going into our round-of-16 game against Nigeria, who were physical, capable, fast and really difficult to play against.

It wasn't really coming off for us in the game. I had a few saves to make and with the score still 0–0 edging towards fulltime, we were down to ten players when Lauren James was shown a red card.

I knew if we hung in and reached penalties we could win.

ALL IN

I'd inflicted myself on a shoot-out in the Finalissima and I was confident I could do it again as we pushed through an ugly 30 minutes of extra time without any goals.

Before the penalties I went inside to the toilet, and as I walked back out at Brisbane Stadium, in front of 50,000 supporters, I thought: *Beat me, then.*

I had researched penalties thoroughly, studiously, endlessly. I'd pushed penalty meetings and strategy at camps and even had a say in designing the notes that were taped to keepers' water bottles with prompts of which way players would go.

I dived left for the first one, forcing her off target, then knew that Alozie's second was going central as she sent it over the bar. The third and fourth went in. England were on their fourth, and when Chloe scored for the win, we celebrated together.

We won 4–2 on penalties and headed to the quarter-finals against Colombia in Sydney, where the remaining stages of the tournament would take place.

Colombia had just beaten Germany. They were a physical, technical, hard-to-play team, and added to that their fans were unreal. Their fans had already booed and trash-talked us passionately in Spanish as we walked through a park in central Sydney earlier in the day. The stadium felt like a Colombia home game, with everyone giving it a bit, which I absolutely loved about football. The atmosphere was incredible, in their favour.

I blocked a shot from Linda Caicedo, who was on fire, before Leicy Santos looped it over me as I got my footwork wrong. I was so disappointed, as I'd been working on that in training and was furious with myself that I didn't get it when it counted, making it more difficult for the team who were now chasing the game 1–0 down. Across the Euros and

World Cup I'd had a run of ten tournament games like never before, and I felt disappointed now by the mistake.

I wanted to apologise and rectify it but, in a game, the opportunity doesn't arrive instantly so the only option then is to flip what you feel on its head immediately, giving it no space to ruin the rest. *Perfection doesn't exist*, I told myself. On to the next. I made a save in the final minutes of the game which kept us 2–1 up and luckily helped make up for earlier as we went on to win the game.

ABBA was back on in the changing room, 'Mamma Mia' this time, and we had settled into a beautiful routine in Sydney, staying at the magnificent InterContinental Hotel with views out over the water and across to Sydney Harbour Bridge.

If the opener had felt like a home game, with Aussies cheering us on, we were now about to meet the host nation in the semi-final in four days' time. They were having a great tournament and everyone inside the Accor Stadium, originally built for the 2000 Olympic Games, was rooting for them.

Their star was Sam Kerr, who took an early shot that I saved, getting down low to block it, before it was ruled offside, then scored an absolute worldie in the second half. It was a tight game that required another critical save later on as well as interventions and defensive work, then goals from Tooney, Alessia and Hempo to give us a 3–1 win. That result sounds more comfortable than the battle it was, but the only thing that mattered was the outcome.

We were going to the World Cup Final and it was an unmatched feeling.

The supremely competitive side of me relished it. The little girl who stapled together storybooks in her parents' front room was finally able to play out her tale in real life. As an athlete I had reached the pinnacle of my playing career thus far and my greatest potential: I was about to play football's most prestigious game.

It would come and go in the blink of an eye. I wanted to remember every detail, storing them away in a filing cabinet in my mind for reminiscing over a lifetime to come, when I could sit back and enjoy where I had been.

I had four more days to invest all of my energy in making sure I was in the best frame of mind to play it and perform for my team, which meant sleep, hydration, nutrition, energy.

If performing at the top meant not changing what got me there, the attention to detail extended to other small things, too, so I didn't change a thing about my World Cup routine. Every match day minus one, Tooney, Alessia and I had taken the same picture with our arms around each other on the pitch inside the empty stadium we would be playing in the following night, so we did the same before the final.

Outside games, I'd worn my silver ring with the engraving 'through difficulty to the stars' on the middle finger of my left hand and the same Lionesses necklace that Alex Greenwood had given to some of us too. And each match-day morning I attentively ironed out creases in the pink Nike polo shirt we wore to travel to games, even though no one ever saw it underneath my tracksuit, to absorb a few minutes of my restless energy.

So I completed all of those rituals alongside my usual breakfast of eggs and sourdough toast and the walk and coffee with the girls, as we counted down the hours until kick-off against Spain on Sunday 20th August.

I listened to my Calm app in my hotel room as we waited

to leave, then put on my tournament playlist, full of the same hype music I'd listened to a year earlier at the Euros, with a few new ones added, and let the sounds play through my ears for as long as possible as we travelled across the city to the final.

Everything was narrowing in on what I had to do. My shirt hung on the left-hand side of the dressing room, smart and strip-lit with neon. As we got ready, Sarina spoke a little about execution and we listened. By then, what happens next is all that matters, how you feel is already irrelevant – good, bad, nervous, you simply have to do your job, translate your skills one more time because while there was some small comfort in knowing we'd leave Australia with a medal, we only wanted one colour: gold.

During our warm-up, as crowds slowly began to fill the seats, Darren, unbelievably, popped his calf and immediately began limping.

'Are you joking?' I said.

'No,' he replied, trying not to give away to anyone else that there was a problem.

'What is it with you and finals?' I asked, wryly.

Athletes are creatures of habit; anything that disturbs the fine-tuned routine forces you to adapt when you're striving for as much reliability as possible, to create conditions for calm and consistency and control while it is within your power to do so, before you enter the unpredictability of a game. I'd adapted a thousand times, and I could do it again now. I pressed on with my warm-up as though nothing had happened.

I was so focused as I walked back out again with the girls to sing the national anthem that nothing could touch me, including the sounds of the stadium or the feelings rooted deep inside me.

ALL IN

We were under the cosh immediately. Games between England and Spain were notoriously tight and neither of us had reached a World Cup Final before. When their captain, Olga Carmona, scored a low powerful shot into the far corner of the net in the 29th minute, we knew that moments of quality were needed to stay in the game.

At half-time, Sarina decided on a change in formation and we instantly got a better footing in the second half.

We created a bit, but they created a lot, and I stretched my whole body to deny Mariona Caldentey a shot from the edge of the box, which bounced awkwardly off the ground. As always, timing was everything: split-second decisions informed by thousands of repetitions.

Then, in the 68th minute, Keira's inadvertent handball. Then, the penalty.

And the save.

We had minutes to try and stay in the game and get a goal. We hadn't played our best football as a team, but even so there was such great desire and belief that we could still win. I felt so deeply that we could do it and I felt the shift, instantly, from the save.

Then the utter devastation when the final whistle blew.

Playing had been a dream but the hope of lifting the trophy was over.

I was in tears.

I crouched down.

We had played gritty, resilient, determined football and shared one another's deep sadness in an overflow of emotion and passion that we had done all we could to deliver, but our shot was now gone as Spain celebrated beside us.

We applauded the fans who had given so much to watch us because we were genuinely grateful; the moments and the memories we created were for them in equal measure to ourselves.

But the ending to my World Cup dream had been shattered instead of made and, instinctively, all I wanted to do was curl my tired body into a ball inside my bedsheets.

This was the beautiful game, though, and we had reached its pinnacle, falling narrowly short against an absolute giant of a team.

So instead, I stood, I cried a little and I clapped a lot as we were swept up into the formalities of the tournament's final presentations.

'Are we smiling or are we not?' we asked each other as we planned whether we could suppress our heartache when the time came for us to go up and collect our silver medals. I look back now and think how amazing it was that we had achieved those but none of us were ready to feel happy in that moment. We'd try to smile, we agreed.

Huddled towards the side of the pitch, the team admin pulled me aside.

'You've won the Golden Glove,' he told me.

The award for the best keeper in the World Cup.

'I'm sorry to tell you that you have to go on stage,' he said.

'Can I trade it for the gold medal?' I asked, deadpan, because I meant it. That's all I wanted to do.

'I know you don't feel like it now, but this is an incredible achievement,' he added.

He was right. It was uncommon for the keeper of the losing side in a final to win it.

I had no idea how to process it because I felt ruined but I

knew I'd look back at the pictures that were about to be taken on stage and wish I'd respected my achievement.

I took myself out of the moment and allowed perspective to find its way in. This would mean something, a great thing, one day soon, and not permitting the negative emotions that would also inevitably lift to cloud that is, to me, the definition of choosing presence of mind, of having facts and emotions and making the appropriate decision in light of the two. So that's what I chose.

I also didn't want to be stood there with a face like a smacked arse.

I'm not sure how much I achieved it on the outside but I think I went some way, and I know that I did on the inside, as I clapped towards my friends and family, where they respectively were in the stadium, grateful for all that had got me there, and raised my trophy in the air with a pride that said 'Thank you for giving me this award.'

I stood beside Spain's Aitana Bonmati, who won Player of the Tournament, as we were asked to pose for photos, then returned to my teammates and repeated the walk on stage for our silver medals, variously raising smiles.

I look at my trophy cabinet now, at the Golden Glove, at the ones that came before and, although I didn't know it then, those that would follow very soon, and I think how was I able to do that?

I'd delivered the biggest performances on the biggest stages, and delivered on my potential, and that meant more to me than any of the awards because above public and professional recognition, as beautiful and earned and meaningful and appreciated as those things are, that glove, the save, and every moment of that tournament represented strength to me: the indomitable strength of the human body and mind and the hard-to-reach place that enables you to push them beyond what you thought possible for yourself.

I had grown up with football heroes and loved to imagine achieving my own version of what other goalkeeping greats did, which this now was, but when it came to the fortitude to overcome and achieve, I still took such inspiration from those captivating accounts of people outside football too: in those marines I'd read about and survivors I'd seen on TV documentaries; the real stories of parents who'd lifted a car or held a door shut to save their child from harm; ultra-marathon runners who lived, trained and performed by the mentality that we never truly push out bodies to the limit, that no matter how many pulls-ups or press-ups you do, you will always stop before you give out. That we, as humans, are capable of such majestic things and so much more than we truly know, no matter how deep we dig, or are forced to dig to find out.

What I'd been through in the two years leading to the World Cup were of no equivalence to those who had stretched their capabilities to save a life, or others who make gruelling journeys every day to survive, but those journeys are happening everywhere, in measures big and small, in every walk of life, every arena, community and workplace, and, in football, mine had felt extreme. As we flew home from Australia, wrestling with the sense of accomplishment amalgamated with loss, I felt exhausted, as though my well of resilience had run dry. But there was further to go.

I was about to be catapulted towards the kind of success that even I could never have dared to dream of.

EIGHTEEN

SELF-WORTH DOESN'T REQUIRE OTHERS' PERMISSION

I had eight days clear before I was due back at United for pre-season, and was ready to wind down in the sun. I headed to Seville, which was expecting a heatwave, and rented a little apartment overlooking the city's historic cathedral and central square, Plaza Virgen de los Reyes.

I was being recognised far more than I was used to, but I'd gone to Spain after playing Spain, which I hadn't given any real consideration to, so when a restaurant owner, locals or holidaymakers asked for a photo I was inclined to put it down to that. Except that there was noise around me everywhere.

I'd left the World Cup bubble, had my social media back some way to full blast and I'd spoken to Tina and my football agent as soon as I'd left Australia.

There were three huge talking points from the tournament. One was the unspeakable kiss that Spain's football federation president Luis Rubiales planted on Jenni Hermoso as she collected her gold medal, which would later lead to his resignation and prosecution.

It had happened in such a way that we hadn't seen it from where we stood on the pitch, but as it played out publicly, what an injustice and what a shame it felt for those players that their incredible achievement should be overshadowed by the inappropriateness of one man, whose behaviour now dominated the headlines surrounding their win. It should have been a moment of celebration for the team. The entire game united to call out sexism against female players, aggrieved that misogyny had found another way to seep in and steal the opportunity for them to generate substantial change for women's football in their country, including their own working conditions.

The other two talking points both related to me.

The save had been viewed as heroic and, even, perfect. Even people who weren't into football were excited about the display, praising the execution, the composure and the swearing that followed, which was celebrated by women for its passion and deliverance and criticised by others who would never have picked up on, let alone noticed it, in a man celebrating the biggest save – or any other feat – of his life.

I'd been given the new nickname Mary Queen of Stops, and the way the save, or a goalkeeper for that matter, was being talked about was on a scale that was unprecedented in the women's game. I was buzzing that it had achieved that. I was also taken aback. After all, the stage on which it was seen was huge, but I'd been doing the same thing my whole career, the same repetition, same consistency, same composure, with barely anyone noticing until a year earlier.

Consolidating excitement around the save was the third big story.

The press conference where I'd called out Nike had very much not remained in the words written up and published by the journalists in Australia.

What I'd said had exploded, triggering headlines and thought pieces and interview requests from news publishers and broadcasters the world over. It had gone far beyond the loyal group of women's football reporters in the UK, and far beyond sports pages, into outlets covering news, business and women's issues.

There was even a public petition, started by a young girl called Emmy, with more than 130,000 signatures calling on Nike to do better, which was incredibly touching.

Nike issued a public response saying it was working towards solutions for future tournaments, and I replied on Instagram with the first thing I'd said about it since the tournament, asking: 'Is this your version of an apology/taking accountability/ a powerful statement of intent?'

It was picked up on by the papers all over again, another round of stories, and fans were rallying in a battle that was about goalkeeping but, at its heart, was about representation and equality, something women were fighting for in their own lives and arenas every single day. I had been unafraid and unapologetic in using my voice, and I'd backed it up with performances that demanded visibility too. It resonated.

When Nike saw how many people were listening to what I'd raised off the pitch combined with the number talking about my save on the pitch, they paid attention. A day later, and four days after the final, they did indeed U-turn, and when my shirts began to go on sale a few weeks later, they sold out with each restock.

I had taken on a global sports giant and won, entirely from a place of choosing my principles.

My TikTok following was now rocketing towards one million and Tina had the likes of the *New York Times* and *Forbes* wanting to hear more from and share a platform with the athlete who took on the sponsor and won, as well as half the magazine editors in Britain offering me their front covers. Invitations followed in tremendous volume from banks and businesses and leaders in sport and creativity to speak and offer a glimpse inside the mentality of The Mary Earps. I upped my ambitions too. With a bigger platform, I could work not only to leave women's football in a better place but women's sport as a whole: the past 20 years in goal had given me an affinity to women playing other team sports who felt underappreciated and deserved a share of the spotlight to help bring investment and recognition to their work.

In the spirit of the Lionesses, this wasn't just about change within football, it was about culture, and I was realising, helped along by those reactions and approaches from people holidaying alongside me in Seville, that this must be what it felt like to transcend your own arena, your own sport. It was an extremely odd sensation, in equal measures phenomenal, exciting and unnerving in its newness and, I discovered promptly, its scrutiny.

It was still not a week on from the World Cup Final. I barely knew what day it was, wiped out and trying to recuperate on holiday, when a whole other set of headlines about me arrived to deal with.

ALL IN

I had landed from Australia to a phone call from my football agent telling me that Arsenal had put in a bid to buy me from United and it was about to go public.

Meanwhile, I was due back with United in a matter of days and I still hadn't heard from anyone at the club since the tournament.

Chaos ensued.

When offers come in, as they do every year during the summer and winter transfer windows when players are passed between clubs, they are usually handled by agents until the point where they're serious enough for players to have a decision to make and therefore be brought into the conversation.

While in goalkeeping terms and culturally I was being hailed a hero, my social media feeds were, in tandem, now flooding with United supporters who had seen rumours that Arsenal's women's team had a put in a world-record bid for a goalkeeper. It was being reported on Sky Sports and every other football outlet, and some fans had rapidly decided I was a rat and any other name you care to think of under the sun.

Their quick conclusion was that I was trying to push a move when actually I knew very little beyond the fact that Arsenal were supposedly serious. Arsenal were a big club in the women's game and had reached the semi-finals of the Champions League the season before.

'Do you want me to find out more?' my agent asked me.

Still hoping for something new to consider from United, I answered: 'Yeah, why not?' And I sat down in a café in the middle of Seville's baroque buildings and orange trees watching it all unfold on my phone.

There is so much to say about this time but I have no desire to speak badly of a club that I poured my heart and soul into for five and a half years.

I waited for a call from United but nothing came. So I called the manager, Marc. I was disappointed I had to initiate contact as I was advised pre-tournament that things would be in place and conversations would continue. It didn't happen the way I thought it would, especially when you get an approach from the previous season's Champions League, semi-finalists, I thought that would spring United into gear. It didn't.

Conversations like this are usually left to agents. They are difficult for players, they get ugly, but I didn't mind. I understood that in business if both sides were a little unsatisfied – the seller needing to come down a bit, the buyer coming up – you'd likely hit on a fair deal and I was happy to be involved in the negotiating process. It was important to me to communicate exactly how I felt, I didn't want anything to be misconstrued.

I had always been painfully honest with him and reminded him that I hadn't wanted to run down my contract, aged 30, and render myself a free agent at this stage of my life. I wasn't a kid anymore; I had a mortgage to pay, responsibilities to take care of, I wanted my future to be secure, a request which I thought was fair and reasonable. I didn't want to go into the final year of my contract without my future locked in, I wanted to focus on my performance. It was an unsettling feeling. My priority had been to stay at United for the rest of my career and I shared some of the frustrations of those fans who didn't want to see me move clubs. I told him I wasn't getting the impression I was valued, that they didn't want me to leave but equally did they really want me to stay? My contract was due to expire and I didn't feel any sense of urgency.

ALL IN

Based on the circumstances, I didn't know what I was meant to think. 'There's no contact from the club, and a record bid from elsewhere,' I said to him. The entire situation was dizzying.

Inside a fortnight, I'd played a World Cup Final, become a penalty hero, won the Golden Glove, forced an unprecedented commercial U-turn, stood up for goalkeepers and for women, become overnight big-level famous and experienced the flip side as I was now either a pariah or an icon depending which group of United fans you talked to.

I flew back home to Manchester with a lot of extra baggage.

The reality, as a footballer, is that you are a commodity, a good to be bought or sold, and unfortunately, politics come into play when it's trading time.

Since the Euros, The Best and now the World Cup (including the Nike triumph) analysts were reporting that we had reached more people and done a better marketing job for the company than a host of basketball's biggest NBA stars. Reportedly my market value had grown five or six times.

Commercially, this kind of leap was new territory for female footballers and goalkeepers in Europe, and my business degree was working hard for me as Tina and I filtered through the stacks of offers coming in. Before the Euros, I'd had small offers for content from brands that wanted me to write, create, and shoot the storylines myself. Now, the first offer to come in was offering close to one hundred times more for a single Instagram post that they'd do all the work on. Mary Earps was now seen as somebody who could sell clothes, books, snacks, supplements, event tickets, and most important of all, I could promote goalkeeping and football to international markets.

But I didn't need to rely on my university textbooks to tell me that my next club contract needed to reflect my new worth.

In any other job that would be a given: when you've dedicated years of service and progressed to a point where you bring more value to a company where you want to remain, you might ask for a pay rise when your next review is due. If your boss doesn't offer you one, and someone else does, you'd be a fool not to consider it or ask again.

Seeking your worth is nothing new. In fact, it is the very least that you owe yourself and knowing what your worth is doesn't require permission from others. I was 30. In football terms, that was do or die. Coming off the biggest year of my life or not, I needed to know where and how I was going to see out my career. Without a club, what happens if you get injured, who takes care of you? Can your future still look the same? All these negative scenarios playing out in my head. It was uncomfortable, but most frustratingly, solvable.

But football isn't a normal job and the notion that player power truly exists in the game frustrates me because, while you can voice your opinion, the reality is it is not a job that you resign or even get fired from. You have a contract with a fixed end date and what happens until that point is at your club's discretion, across the entirety of the game

In the women's game particularly it's a job you go into with your whole heart because there had never been a lifestyle or even security attached to it to chase until now. And, just as in the men's, even with all its money to compensate, you are a performer, needed at the drop of a dime, however you feel, rarely with a day off and no matter what family or friend's wedding, birthday or celebration you're giving up to be there.

ALL IN

You have contractual obligations to fulfil and you give your body and your mind, your joints, your ability to run after your future kids or even, as a female athlete, the choice of when and whether to have kids at all, and you hope that through your service you will be treated well because, when you're not, if they fall short, you're kind of trapped. Instead of feeling on top of the world, I felt under tremendous pressure.

Arsenal had come back with a second offer, proving their seriousness and fuelling more anger from United fans and based on the information they had, I understood their frustration.

Meanwhile, I was simply asking for clarity on my future and the future direction.

The result was that I turned up for my first day back at training on a sun-washed morning at the start of September with my heart rate literally racing as more and more anxiety built up the closer I got to the complex.

As I drove up Carrington Spur, the relief road to the complex, I watched the monitor on my watch rise to 111 beats per minute then rocket to 143 once I'd walked through the doors, almost double something resembling normal for a woman my age who was now sitting still.

I'd been told the day earlier that they planned to present the England girls with flowers to congratulate us for making the final and I messaged the club's media guys to explain that I was really struggling with the frenzy that had been whipped up around my future and would really appreciate it if they could keep the cameras at a distance.

I was thrust in front of the waiting photographers and staff when I arrived; I was disappointed that although I had communicated how I was struggling, I couldn't catch a break.

I was also plunged headlong into another sponsor stir, albeit behind the scenes, a few days later, this time with Adidas, because what was one more ball to juggle?

I'd been an Adidas athlete since joining United, initially getting boots from them, then wearing specialist goalkeeping gloves. Adidas had asked me to become a fully Adidas athlete a season in and it had been a dream to be attached to a big sports brand, like Steven Gerrard was when I bought his replica boots as a kid. I took the contract – they gave me my performance gear and I gave them my endorsement and image.

Some time before the World Cup where, as the world now knew I was wearing England's Nike, Adidas had attempted to renegotiate. Commercially the game had come on and across the industry, brand deals weren't keeping up. Yet, they were reportedly paying male Premier League stars up to £20 million a year to wear their boots.

I definitely didn't want to fall out with another sports giant but I was starting to think, *Who is going to stand up to these corporations? When were they going to invest in women's sport and athletes appropriately?*

I did not want to be in a relationship that did not reflect my worth, and that would prohibit me from working with any other brand that sold those kind of products. This meant ruling out an awful lot of lucrative deals that were already coming in from companies that sold lifestyle products rather than sport. There was an opportunity cost. It looked almost certain that we were about to part ways.

This was awkward when we went on a pre-season tour to Germany that included a visit to Adidas headquarters, an arena-style office block named the World of Sports in Bavaria.

It was more awkward still when one of the United staffers came over while I was freshly back to training and sat on the bench, as the girls who'd been in over the summer played a friendly against Bayern Munich.

He explained that the CEO wanted to meet me and insinuated that he was very excited about it. This was becoming quite the thing since the World Cup, people in the business of football were suddenly keen to meet me. It was both wonderful in its capacity to open doors and facilitate the conversations I loved with business minds, and also a bit disappointing as a stark reminder that that's how the world and the sport turned.

'Are you sure?' I asked. 'I'm happy to meet him but just so you're aware, my contract with them is coming to an end and it's looking likely that I'm not going to be an Adidas athlete beyond the end of the month.' I knew the United guy well so the last thing I wanted was for him to look like an idiot in front of his boss. I didn't want to make it awkward for him or anyone else. I understood he needed to look after United's relationships and I wanted to support him. 'Maybe he'd want to meet one of the other Adidas girls instead,' I suggested, hoping that I'd saved my colleague from an embarrassing situation. He thanked me and agreed that was a good idea.

That was that and I didn't think anything of it, until it was reported back to my agent a couple of weeks later that my apparent refusal to shake hands with the CEO was seen to be so rude that Adidas no longer wanted me. I understood the message from Germany was then that I was to be let go.

I was never told exactly what had happened but it felt as though I was losing support.

And I learned a valuable lesson: I'd been honest enough to turn down a conversation that I saw as potentially problematic for someone else, but honesty is a double-edged sword that isn't appreciated in every room. I had no idea what had been said about me without me present but, now, I'd rather be in the room, take my opportunity to connect with a CEO or anyone else, steer change and tell the truth there, even if it's awkward for someone else.

With United, the feeling of being unsupported somehow seemed to creep into the stands back home. In unfortunate timing our first home game was, yep, against Arsenal. Their bid was now long gone, the summer transfer window had closed, further contract discussions were yet to progress, and the anticipated signings never materialised, but when I ran out of the tunnel in front of a full Leigh Sports Village it was to boos from our fans – not the entire ground but a small group big enough to loudly transcend the usual match-day noise.

I was gutted that they felt that way about me, especially as I felt like it was a situation I'd been put in, not by my own choosing. I'd turned up to perform and was doing everything that was expected.

'I have no idea how you played like that,' Safia Middleton-Patel, a young keeper coming through at United, told me after our 2–2 draw. I valued Saf and we shared a wonderful, nurturing relationship.

At Everton away a couple of weeks later, a whole cycle of news headlines blew up from after the game when I made my way around the benches and over to the main stand, signing autographs before a steward asked me to stop. The crowd that had gathered for signatures and selfies was unintentionally blocking the route that a disabled child needed to safely pass through. The family had been patiently waiting but the steward told me it was time for everyone to disperse so that the child could get past and get home. This was, of course, fine, but it meant I couldn't get through the whole queue and a fan later posted an angry comment online because I hadn't been able to sign their autograph. I tried to explain what had happened on Instagram, but I realised I couldn't say anything now without it being picked up and churned up.

It had been a similar story when the manager rested me for the Continental Cup games that started in November, as they had done every year, but the message that made its way around forums this time was 'Mary doesn't want to be part of the team.'

It was constantly booting off with accusations like that on X, and even if I avoided it – because X is a hell of a place to gaze as a footballer – my teammates, who were a particularly brilliant and supportive group, would notice and ask if I was OK after seeing another football fan badmouthing me. I wasn't prepared for how much suddenly being recognised and known about would also lead to others wanting to tarnish my reputation.

I was trying really hard to avoid the chat but my algorithms would serve me all sorts from posts with long threads containing upsetting comments to videos declaring 'Mary Earps is a bitch' with a couple of likes. Combined with the fact that my name was now much more visible, it was becoming almost impossible for me to swerve what was being said about me.

The level of scrutiny was hard. I felt it was unnecessarily and undeservedly cruel.

I'd stop at the supermarket on the way home from training,

or pop out to the local Marks & Spencer food hall and see people following me up and down the aisles before coming up to talk to me and I had no idea if they were going to be kind or tear me apart. It was anxiety-inducing.

Meanwhile, I loved my club; playing for them was an incredible privilege but I felt angry and unprotected as I waited for them to put any real intent to keep me down on paper. Trust was waning.

All of this, I thought, must be what being a public figure is like.

Was this the top? Was this what lay beyond the dream that I'd worked and sacrificed my whole life for?

NINETEEN

CARVE A NEW PATH

On the outside, my life looked like one big celebration. It was beginning to get pretty glamorous and I used the run of parties and awards ceremonies I was invited to as moments of joy to escape the reality of what was happening day to day in football.

In a cultural setting, I was being called a hero and offered endless new opportunities to think about. Burberry wanted to dress me for their London Fashion Week show and brands like Victoria's Secret wanted to work with me to sell their lifestyle offerings with a photoshoot and ad campaign, which was frankly unimaginable for a goalkeeper and thrilling in how far beyond football the influence had now reached: enough to be a poster girl.

I was invited into events and spaces I never even knew existed and was adding to my trophy shelf too. As the year was coming to an end it reminded me of how high I'd soared in that quest for my hard work to be seen and how the majority of people, beyond the angry mob online, viewed me.

I finished fifth in the voting for the 2023 Ballon d'Or Féminin, the highest ever ranking for a goalkeeper in football's most prestigious individual award and I used the opportunity to advocate for an award that would honour female goalkeepers in their own right, in the future. At England, the fans named me Player of the Year, which meant the world, and the Northwest Football Awards, gave me their impact award, named after former footballer Billy Seymour, who had bravely campaigned against child abuse in the game. *GQ* made me one of their Men of the Year honorees and *Vogue* invited me to their annual Forces for Change celebration, photographing me in the pages of the magazine with a host of young grassroots footballers in Manchester that Tina had picked out to appear alongside.

Then, in December, I was nominated for BBC Sports Personality of the Year. SPOTY is the biggest British sporting accolade, transcending all sports. I used to watch it on TV with Grandma when I was growing up and I'd been to the ceremony the year before when the Lionesses won Team of the Year and Beth won the award itself.

There was no way they were going to give it to a Lioness two years on the bounce but I was so honoured to be part of it, nominated alongside big-time names: Katarina Johnson-Thompson, who'd just won her second heptathlon World Champion title; the golfer and Scottish Open winner Rory McIlroy; Stuart Broad, who was retiring from cricket; the jockey Frankie Dettori; and the Paralympian Alfie Hewett, winner of both the singles and doubles Wheelchair Tennis Masters.

The ceremony was on a Tuesday night at Salford's Media

City. I'd had to learn to assemble a team of the stylist, hairdresser and make-up artist, who'd all been helping me to get ready for the starry events I'd been going to and, for a woman who'd never shaken the body-image issues I'd had since my early years of football, I felt lovely in a more daring long, sheer lace cut-out black gown and big blonde waves in my hair.

I arrived at Media City for the ceremony and bumped into Noel Gallagher of Oasis in the lift.

'What are you doing?' he said.

I didn't know if he knew who I was or was just being friendly.

'I'm going to SPOTY tonight. What are you doing here?' I asked.

'Working. Bit of this, bit of that,' Noel replied.

Cool start, I thought.

Since the World Cup, I hadn't spoken much to Dad but we'd discussed a commitment to try to improve our relationship and I wanted him and Mum there, so they came and sat beside me, alongside Kitty, Lewis and Christina.

When the Olympic skaters Torvill and Dean, also from Nottingham, began by paying reference to our shared home city then announced that I had won, the nerves and joy rose inside me. I couldn't believe that this was how I was ending the year, that my name would now be etched on that famous trophy. I hugged the people I loved and walked up to the stage thinking how for a goalkeeper to win an award of this magnitude, and a whole host of other young goalkeepers to see it from home, made me so incredibly proud.

I picked up the enormous iconic trophy and held it up for the cameras and the audience – and for Grandma, who I hoped was waving at the TV.

'I knew you wouldn't drop it,' Gary Lineker joked.

I made another short, unwritten speech, this time expressing how humbled I was to be on the list with other incredible athletes. 'Sport is a fantastic thing, where it brings the world together,' I said.

Standing up there then dancing with my people at the party afterwards following a challenging few months felt like a surreal and beautiful way to end a rollercoaster of a year.

Kitty and I flew to Barbados for Christmas and New Year's Eve. I had never spent Christmas away from my family but after what had happened in Australia, I chose myself and my relationship and I was looking forward to feeling refreshed.

We'd received a letter before leaving with royal markings on it (in fact, the postman had left a note saying he'd left it by the bins) awarding me an MBE in the King's New Year Honours, along with some of the other girls and those who had been recognised the year before. When I got to the desk at Manchester Airport and saw flight upgrades available for £300 I thought, *Brilliant, I've just won SPOTY, I've been given the MBE, that'd be a really nice treat.* But there was only one seat left so we checked in as usual.

When I got on the plane, a stewardess came over and asked: 'Is it Mary?'

'It is, yeah,' I said.

'We've got two seats in business if you'd like.'

The glamour continued and we settled in for the eight-and-a-half-hour flight to the Caribbean, part spent relaxing, part spent up and down, taking photos with people who were excited to see me there, having seen me on their TVs with my award the day before. One guy, oblivious to any of the commotion, was enjoying his flight, reading a copy of his newspaper with me on the front page.

Barbados was like paradise. We were in a delightful family-run hotel for the first part of the trip then moved to a different, bigger resort for the rest. The powdery white sand beaches and crystal-clear sea that I'd only seen in photographs were exactly what the doctor ordered and the food, culture and music all made it an incredible place.

Unfortunately, we had absolutely no privacy.

I loved talking to new people, and hearing fans' stories of how their daughters, sons or grans had enjoyed watching me play made me so happy. I enjoyed what they had to say when it was the right moment for a chat and I wasn't working, trying to nip round the supermarket or just having an off day.

Being in beachwear was an addition to the list so, on holiday, when people came over for pictures with me in a bikini I still really struggled.

I tried out saying 'No, I'm sorry, I'm on holiday' to the first man who asked but when the next person to come over was a child I couldn't possibly turn them down so I self-consciously posed instead.

Later in the week, I went back over to the first guy and explained I'd tried 'no' but couldn't keep it up, so if they still wanted a picture I'd be happy to. I didn't want to be unfair or inconsistent.

I continued to yo-yo up and down from my sun lounger.

It wasn't proving very restful, and the pressure of being 'on' all the time was taking its toll. I was actually feeling incredibly anxious so we tried to manage it by missing breakfast or going for dinner at 10pm when the restaurant had emptied.

On New Year's Eve, we went to a big party on the beach. We'd stayed in our room till 11pm then thought we could head down, have a quiet drink together and listen to the parish bells ring in the new year.

We tried to stay out of the way and keep our heads down while also enjoying what the night had to offer when a guy came over and sat on the arm of my chair, extremely overfamiliar, and asked for a picture.

'I'm really sorry, but I'm not taking photos tonight. I hope you don't mind. It's New Year and I'm having some personal time. I hope you understand,' I said.

The guy went mad, launching into a tirade about how unreasonable I was, how he'd met another player the year before and she'd said yes. I apologised again but he wouldn't stop, and Kitty stepped in to ask him to respect what I'd asked.

It was all so uncomfortable. I shouldn't have let something like that put a damper on my night but it did. I was so grateful to be in the position I was, with the platform I had and on holiday where I was, but fame was delivering another steep learning curve, to accept that in not disappointing yourself, sometimes you will need to disappoint others.

None of this was fun for Kitty either. I'm big on special occasions, I like to be with the people I love and take a moment to appreciate what I have, but I was now stressed about what this man, who was clearly half-cut, would go away and say about me and frustrated that I'd let it ruin her night and mine. We waited for the midnight bells, missed the party and the show that followed on the beach, and went to bed as fireworks went up over the Caribbean Sea and 2024 arrived.

*

I found adjusting to the price of fame extremely difficult.

At home, I'd get stopped every time I went out and I'd grown so worried about looking presentable for the selfies or being in a mood that matched what people needed of me that I would spiral with panic about meeting their expectations and the consequences if I could not. I wanted to handle everything with grace and the appreciation that I felt, often when it required me to put those other feelings of panic aside, but being on a pedestal meant that for all those who wanted to authentically celebrate with you, to feel some part of it too, there were those waiting for you to fail in any way at all. Online, hatred without repercussions is frighteningly normalised and I have never understood the motivation for tearing someone else down. I had incredible support from fans with messages full of kind words, but the reality for anyone on the receiving end of trolling or cyberbullying is that even with hundreds | of those, the few hurtful ones can feel intimidatingly loud.

Meanwhile, at the GQ awards, someone had stood on my dress as he tried to trap me for more time then swore at me in a particularly vile way; when I stayed at hotels for the events I was going to, people would follow me, in the dark, while I was alone.

I've often thought I must be some kind of introverted extrovert – a big personality in the environments I'm comfortable and safe in, training or playing, with friends and teammates or even letting my personality out on TikTok. But I am also content to retreat into myself when I need to. These new situations frightened me, and I'd overthink them for hours before and after. Overthinking had been a strength of mine in many ways for years, it's what made me consider what women's football or goalkeeping needed and use my voice to pursue opportunities or business ventures to fill the space. Now when overthinking happened in this invasive daily way I found it emotionally crippling.

It became easier not to go out and I got into a habit where I rarely did.

I started ordering our groceries online and I stopped going for dinners and brunch with friends, choosing the safety and predictability of my front room instead of encounters outside.

It's kind of dangerous to admit that on a human level I found what came with chasing my dream to the top of football hard to cope with.

And so anything other than saying 'I'm so lucky to do what I do' is risky. But I had crossed over from the reverie now and transcended into a different realm: fame.

Footballers are not considered human, they are thought to be overpaid and living luxurious lifestyles, which make problems less difficult and less meaningful. 'Go cry in your Lamborghini,' seems a reasonable response for anyone carrying the job title because the perception is they are earning six figures a week from an industry based on public fandom. To acknowledge that footballers and other people in the media spotlight have to paper over their personal distress and sadness regularly feels taboo. Because how can you be unhappy when you have so much?

But that was and is not the reality for a female footballer.

I could see that I had a life of great privilege, I played football for a living and my hard work was recognised, which was all I'd ever wished for. As an athlete I had the kind of success I'd yearned for and I was getting the kind of commercial success that I never even dreamed about because it never entered my mind that I could be a brand on this scale.

At the same time, our accessibility and relatability as women was exactly what people admired and what was allowing me to feel approachable as a role model. I was carving a new path, I was trying to maintain that and to pursue the opportunities I needed and had earned for my future. I wanted to generate the change that keepers and players coming into the game now needed to perform at work. I wanted to speak to them and respond to help keep my sanity intact.

I was doing it not from a Lamborghini, and I was still on the same United contract I'd extended on two years earlier and brand deals that were only just coming to fruition were not on a level that provided a life of safety or staff to take the load. Even if they had been, other people's experiences of fame tell you that papering over is only temporary; humans are not well-equipped for attention like this at all and not when it arrives quickly.

I'd spent forever as a nobody obsessed with saving footballs and then crossed over into wide-scale instant recognition. My overnight success had taken 20 years.

I read something that Robbie Williams wrote about his long and incredibly tumultuous experience as a pop star, about how he viewed it as a duty to be of service, to make others happy, how it warmed his heart to meet a fan and hear how he had warmed theirs. But there was a fear that accompanied it and a panic, because if he didn't greet everyone like 'the mayor of the best town ever', the one you let down would probably call you a dickhead and then you'd failed.

If you were dealing with your family, or work stress, or your health, or the health and happiness of someone you loved, or your mental health in the exact same moment someone had their chance for a photo, what were you to do? Was there an acceptable limit to how many people you could have the encounter with as you went about your day without breaking the unspoken rule of public status, which is that you are available to others 24/7 or you are ungrateful?

I wasn't ungrateful but the anxiety of contemplating it each time I left my house was filling me with daily fear of getting it wrong, for me or anyone else.

I was trying to muddle my way through.

Worse still, when I combined these insecurities about placing my reputation in the hands of others with the mixed receptions and the hard work going on behind the scenes at United, it was becoming difficult to retain the consistency I depended upon and my performances had been up and down early in the season.

I had tried different techniques to get the best out of myself in games, first focusing on the details, trying more discipline and then less, or attempting to relax into games. But I was losing my spark and myself there and none of it felt like it worked. The more I looked for a familiar solution, the harder I found it to just do what I knew and focus on football.

When the January transfer window arrived, I was eager for it to pass without fanfare, leaving me to press on with my season till whatever decision I had to face, with a clear head, in summer.

I'd changed football agents and United started getting serious. Matt Hargreaves, a former Adidas guy, had been brought into the club to negotiate transfers and contracts, and we had a meeting. I wanted to discuss the rumblings around my future and understand the situation as it was unfolding.

'You're saying Mary hasn't signed a contract but there's no new contract on the table?' he asked.

We were still looking at the same introductory offer we had discussed before the World Cup, eight months earlier. 'Yes,' we confirmed. 'Nothing else ever came.'

He said he'd try to undo the damage. 'What do you need?' he asked.

'I need this to be a bit more quiet,' I said, indicating the circus that seemed to follow the conversation before, and my strong desire to avoid the rumour mill so I could perform. I had a similar conversation with the manager as I'd had with Matt.

Marc would ask me: 'What can I do to help?'

'Stop talking about me in the press,' I pleaded.

But then my name would come up in a press conference.

At the same time, sensitive information about me was still making its way into the media. My name generated clicks and sold papers, and journalists were calling Tina with specific queries. I was suspicious of where they were coming from.

I was also looking around, wondering who I could trust and who, other than Willco, it was safe to open up to anymore.

If there was a chance that these were going to be my final months there, I didn't want them to feel like that.

I didn't want to feel let down or angry. I wanted to feel football. When you are angry, you can get lost in how upset you are. Anger has always felt counterproductive to me, making it harder to keep my mind open to anything else.

I needed an open mind so I made a conscious effort after

my holiday to take a step back from some of those stressful conversations and give myself as much grace as possible to maximise my experience of what I knew and loved. I'd had a lot to reflect on while on those sandy beaches, some of which was welcome, some less so. I'd employed all I knew and all I'd learned and was determined I wouldn't shrink to survive there. I wanted to make the most of every second in a job I loved, one that had allowed joy back through the door before.

When someone comes to watch you play, I told myself, they need Mary Earps the goalkeeper. They might have saved up to go to just that one game, you can't let them down, or yourself, or the group of girls I played with who shared a togetherness and team spirit that was powerful despite everything going on behind the scenes.

I just needed to focus on football.

TWENTY

AT THE VERY LEAST, EXPECT SUCCESS

I was nominated for FIFA The Best again and had the night off to travel down to London for the ceremony before I was needed back in training the next day.

I left my anxieties and swirling uncertainty in Manchester and set out to enjoy the evening, relishing another opportunity to enjoy my love affair with the game in an environment built to celebrate the work that goes into it, epitomised by the people gathered.

I'd been put up in a sprawling suite at the Grosvenor Hotel in London, where I could bring my own hair and make-up team and someone to style me in a plunging red cut-out dress that did a lot more for my shoulders than the one I'd picked out myself the year before. I was told, on arrival, that I'd made the World Eleven Team of the Year chosen by players worldwide, which felt incredible in itself. Little matched the high of peer recognition. Alessia, Bronzey, Tooney, Alex, Keira and Lauren were also included in the World Eleven, and being there with so many England teammates added to the sense of occasion and community. Their presence and the fact that the ceremony was somewhere familiar, at home in Britain, helped to calm the nerves I'd experienced the year before.

The idea of getting the individual goalkeeper award again was of course tantalising, but I framed my expectations, telling myself walking away with two awards was just too unlikely: last year I'd got the trophy but not made the World Eleven, this time it would surely be the other way around. Australia's Mackenzie Arnold and Spain's World Cup-winning Cata Coll were nominated and more than worthy candidates too.

So when my name was called inside the Hammersmith Apollo and I joined the ranks of Messi, Bonmati and Pep Guardiola as the night's award winners, I didn't know what else to say but 'I'm blown away.'

I thanked my teammates, Darren and Willco, and picked up where I'd left off the year before, with the light that had come out of my darkness before: 'I talk a lot about how it's not been the easiest journey to get here. Some would say I took the scenic route. I've had to wait a long time for this kind of success, but I think, looking back now, it all makes total sense. Everything that I went through. We're all humans, we all have struggles, right, but it just made me feel so much more prepared for the challenges we face today, to be able to enjoy these moments so much more and realise how pretty unbelievable they are, to never take a single day for granted.'

I was thinking of the fans who would be watching again and needed to hear that. And I reminded them: 'If you're struggling and you're going through hell, keep going – it's never too late to be exactly who you are.'

The irony, of course, was that despite another highly visible accolade I needed the reminder too.

I stayed to celebrate at the party afterwards and joined some of the South American legends who had taken over the dance floor. They rolled on well into the early hours but I was in bed by one, with one eye on preparations for the weekend's game against Chelsea.

I became the first back-to-back winner of the award that night; it was an incredible feeling and an incredible accolade not only for me but for goalkeeping. *That* was history, another first, and it would later go into the *Guinness World Records* book. Like the Lionesses' success or what had happened with Nike and my shirts, I was convinced that it would bring with it another opportunity to transcend the game and provide a bigger platform for change, which made me immensely proud and eager to utilise it to that end.

That, to me, was the most rewarding part of accomplishments like this. They earned me a bigger voice to contribute to systemic change that could long outlive anyone's memories, bar mine, of the trophies themselves.

Achieving The Best again, the Golden Glove and SPOTY should have made me feel invincible. And in a way they did; they each bolstered my confidence for a little while at a time when everything looked shiny from the outside but felt dull inside. The recognition made me feel good but I knew I mustn't rely on the transience of an award to feel good about myself. Real contentment can only ever come through intrinsic, internal values, and the things that could deliver sustained happiness.

For me, in football, those were: the capacity to perform in a space that allowed me to be me; exercising the compulsion and constant drive to be better than yesterday; the freedom borne of consistency to meet my potential; and leaving the game in a better place for those who came next.

Awards were valued recognition and I felt great about my career. But I had also done a lot of other work in the couple of years beforehand to remember never to judge myself by other people's opinions of me because those would neither last nor sustain me. Just as I hadn't allowed darkness to fool me, I couldn't allow the bright lights of success and trophies to blind me.

Maybe it is no surprise then that the rapture of those moments could never feel long-lasting, as extraordinarily grateful as I was for what they stood for and as much as I enjoyed the interlude, the buzz, that an award brought each time.

No one could take those accomplishments away from me and they would sit, as they do today, on my shelves, proudly lined up beside one another, as a reminder of where I have taken my body and my mind, of the heights of my potential and the change that I was able to make. But it is a familiar dilemma for those who demand high standards of themselves that what drives them – success – is also the stick they use to beat themselves with.

Picking up another award doesn't become a case of 'no one can touch me now' because I was only ever catching up with myself anyhow, and my assumptions were that I should always be performing at my best.

When that happens, success is the very least you expect of yourself, anything less is, extreme as it may sound, something akin to failure.

ALL IN

Now that I had achieved everything I'd ever wished for over my birthday cake candles and so many things beyond, I was discovering that success could feel both victorious and in some measure vacuous, in that it left a gap. Into that space, a new question always appeared: What's the next dream?

I was in unknown territory; I needed to know what I could dream of for my future in order to hone in on it and fill the void.

With the awards highs, then lows, and the tough spot I was in at United, I looked forward to international weeks with England.

From that very first goalkeeper's meeting I'd had with Sarina when she had called me back into the squad and put her faith in me, I had always felt I could run through brick walls with her support. England was still my safe space. She knew, because you couldn't fail to see, that my life had changed beyond recognition since our first camp together and, because she knew me, she saw that everything that accompanied this success would not feel easy to me. She would often ask how things were going at my club and would reassure me: 'When you move, when you decide what happens next, it'll be better for you.' I appreciated and trusted in her.

Whatever panned out at United, I thought, at least I had England. We were riding high on the back of our World Cup campaign and after everything we'd achieved together and still had ahead of us, I could bank on them being behind me in whatever period of transition I was about to find myself.

When I arrived in Marbella, in southern Spain, for England camp in February, I was looking forward to feeling that familiar sanctuary.

From the first moment, though, I was hit by a creeping, unsettling sense that something had shifted. I couldn't put my finger on it but the energy was off, different.

We had two friendlies that week and there was absolutely no reason to believe I wouldn't play both. I played our second game, against Italy, at the Estadio Nuevo Mirador in Algeciras, but I was unexpectedly benched for the first against Austria and Hannah was chosen instead.

The hangover of what happened before hadn't left the group, there were still ongoing difficulties in the goalkeepers' sessions and I found navigating our relationship challenging, even if I wished that it wasn't. Some people would say that the manager giving a back-up keeper the chance to play in a week of friendlies was fairly standard, but given where we'd just been as a team and the role I'd played in it, which was now a matter of public record with a life of its own, the timing felt odd. My tournament performances for England had been the best of my life and earned such praise that the decision not to play me signalled something was off. It didn't make sense and left me with a feeling that fuelled uncertainties I hadn't expected to follow me to international duty.

The Italy match was a decent one. We won comfortably, 5–1, and I made a breakaway save in the first half. We won comprehensively against Austria too, 7–2, but that whole week started alarm bells sounding that were only about to grow louder.

Something was shifting and the change was rapid.

It became clear, quickly, that Sarina was changing her style of play at the back and when Sarina made a decision, she stuck by it. She got the message to me through goalkeeper sessions that she wanted me to distribute differently, employing new tactics on the backline that didn't match my strengths as a player, but clearly matched my competitor's.

When I boarded the plane home at the end of the week, it turned out a teammate was feeling it too. 'This is pointless, I'm done, I'm retired,' she confided. Then she said, almost in passing, as though it were obvious: 'It'll be you next.'

Her comment knocked me sideways, but I knew better than to ignore it.

Someone explained this kind of shift as the silent discomfort of misalignment. When you have the feeling that 'something's off', it is often the first clue that something you once counted on has now repositioned itself. You could also call it intuition.

TWENTY-ONE

FORGE THE ASCENT, CONTROL THE DESCENT

Back at United I was having panic attacks.

I'd left Adidas and signed with Puma on a better deal, and I'd been relieved when the transfer window had been and gone. It brought welcome respite from the noise around my next move, finally leaving me to get on with my day job till the season was over.

Meanwhile, I was working hard to manage the misalignment that I now felt not just at club but, out of nowhere, at country level too.

I could find my performances at weekends but it was harder than expected to tap into any clarity or peace. I was parking my feelings, and the constant juggle to be the person each situation required me to be was exhausting. When we'd played Arsenal ten days before England camp, I'd taken myself to the showers at half-time, 3–0 down, and stood in my kit and studs, doing breathing exercises away from the eyes of my teammates as a sudden surge of fear threatened to overwhelm me.

But with the added unnerving events happening at England, the emotional pressure got worse. When we played Everton away at the end of March, I staved off a full-on panic attack. I'd conceded a goal ten minutes in and as we walked back into the tunnel I broke out in a cold sweat all over my neck and arms. My breath drew short and I had no idea if I could catch it again. I was back in my childhood bedroom in Nottingham, hiding the anguish I felt when I loved football but it didn't love me back. The sound of my studs was echoing too loudly off the tiles, and I couldn't stop my feet from pacing up and down the cubicle. I did everything I could to stifle the sobs that were threatening to spill out into the changing room, too, making my breath harder still to reach.

My nose started to bleed. I splashed my face with cold water over the sink, again and again, but the blood was down my shirt so I needed a new one from the kitman.

I'd tried to hide myself from my team but there was a commotion now and the girls knew what was going on.

They had never seen me like this. I was the big personality, and you could always rely on me to bring good energy and frankness – not emotion. I don't even think they knew it was possible for me to feel anxiety so acutely. I didn't want them to.

They rallied around. I felt guilty at the prospect of it impacting them or our performance.

'Are you OK to play?' Marc asked me.

I hadn't missed a league game since I'd joined United.

'Yes,' I said.

As long as I could breathe, I needed to set the record straight on the pitch.

I thought of the deep, timed breaths and the guidance I'd so often listened to on my mindfulness app. I returned to my goal and took the game in five-minute blocks to make it more manageable – 50 minutes, 55, 60 . . . 90. We won 4–1.

The darkness couldn't fool me anymore.

When the next England camp came around in early April, with the Euro 2025 qualifiers, February's foreboding hum still hung in the air.

The first game was against Sweden at Wembley, a Friday-night kick-off, and I was starting. I played a decent game, defending the space well, and we drew 1–1. I never like conceding but I felt like the whole team was going through a bit of a difficult time. In the goalkeeper group, Roebuck had suffered a stroke, which was such a frighteningly sad thing to think about, let alone face. She was making a full recovery but she was 24 and had just left Manchester City for Barcelona; if football was fragile, other forces in life were far more so.

Things were changing in the squad. From my perspective, I'd delivered excellent results and consistent performances and the Lionesses, as a team, had soared. Of course, there are always new styles of play and innovation but I was stuck with thinking, *If it ain't broke?*

Before the next game in four days' time against the Republic of Ireland we had the usual pattern of team meetings and training. We were back at the Lensbury, on the banks of the Thames, with all those great memories of the Euros: the prep camp, fancy-dress nights, our celebrations, sitting in the lush grounds reading a book when the sun was shining. It was a really happy place for me.

As we filed out of a team meeting in the hotel's conference room, Sarina called me back: 'Mary, can I have a word?' she said, in front of everyone.

That was unusual and I felt embarrassed being singled out. I didn't know if it was intentional or if it was her way of making an example of me. I hoped it wasn't, but, like at school, when you're asked to stay behind you tend to know exactly what's coming. And you know that the fact you had been called back is going to be the talk of the town. I hated that.

Darren was with Sarina and we arranged three chairs to face each other at the back of the room.

'What have I done?' I asked, genuinely wanting to understand this energy shift.

I felt devastated before anyone else had even uttered a word.

'I want to give someone else experience,' Sarina confirmed. She didn't want me to be upset but she was matter-of-fact about her choice.

I had to respect that, but we could be frank enough with each other that I thought I could explain that I didn't understand or agree with it.

'I don't get it,' I said. 'It's a qualifier match. And bad behaviour is being rewarded.'

'Everything you've said, we're aware and we've taken into consideration,' Darren replied. 'This is still what we want to do.' So they had thought what I was thinking too.

Now this felt unjust. My eyes welled with tears. It was a choice that went against my core values. I couldn't get my head around it because when my values were compromised, the strain always felt heavy enough to keep me up at night. When this kind of a decision compromised my football, I was sleepless.

I was playing week in, week out at United and my performance with England hadn't changed. But the environment around me was changing, again. This time, though, I wasn't trying to get a look in, I'd proved myself and I'd done it over and over at the very highest standard.

Sarina rarely rotated the team like this and no one person's behaviour had ever counted more than the group's wellbeing – that was a culture we all respected. So why the exception, I asked?

'You're changing my position and no one else's,' I hypothesised.

As I tried to process it, with no further clarification, I thought about something I'd learned and logged back in the Phil Neville days: that managers find it far easier to be open when it's good news. This was not good news.

There was more to it and there was, in their minds, a logic to what they were doing, of course there was. Sarina was a professional and a proven, celebrated and seasoned one, too, but I was not going to be made party to her thinking now.

It was abundantly clear to me that while the rest of the world still thought I was on top, and I knew I was still bringing all the same things to the table to keep me there, Sarina had already made a choice about where the number 1 shirt was heading. I just didn't know when or whether it was permanent.

For now, I deduced, she needed to try it out for a while and the best-case scenario for them was to keep me on side and keep me dangling while she tried the new configuration.

In the blink of an eye, the dynamic between us had become unrecognisable, opaque and instantly cold, and it hurt because I had placed such trust in her, in how she cared about me and harnessed how much I cared about England. Her support had helped me scale new heights. That it had all been so significant made the rest harder.

Darren, who I'd worked with so closely and just thanked in all those awards speeches, sat through the conversation without saying another word. The safe space I had in England was disappearing from under me.

The transparency and trust that we'd all thrived on had been replaced with an obscurity and a distancing. I felt totally blindsided.

I went back to my room and messaged one of the girls. She came down the corridor for a chat. In football terms, we both knew what was happening. I was being phased out.

The fans didn't, the press didn't, but she was right – I did, and so did the girls.

I didn't play the game against Ireland. It was a frantic match but a clean sheet nonetheless and a 1–0 win.

Sitting on the bench felt unwarranted and therefore frustrating. Watching someone else in goal, knowing this wasn't a decision based on my own performance, meant that I would be the one to face public scrutiny, and my own, and it hurt.

Factors beyond my own control and nothing to do with my actual performance were already costing me the goodwill of some United fans, and now England commentators and speculators had a free pass to go to town too.

I had known for 20 years that opportunities in football hung on managers' opinions and choices; they were to be respected for the good of the team and the game. But the way this was being handled felt pointedly obtuse, which was something I had suffered many times earlier in my career when I didn't have the voice to speak up. I found it spectacularly hard.

I came home from camp devastated. How was I back here? Why now, after we'd reached the top? None of it made sense and I didn't know where it left me as I tried to press on with my season at United and weigh up whether to take their contract or make a move to Europe.

I wanted desperately to know whether one choice or the other would help or hinder my England career, but my thinking was clouded and that made decisions about my future even more difficult. I knew never to make a big decision when emotion was the dominant driver. I needed it to be co-pilot.

United weren't having a great WSL season so far. I wasn't the only player contending with plenty behind the scenes, and it showed, collectively. But we were a solid group despite, or maybe because of, the off-pitch battles, and we had found a place where it all seemed to click in the FA Cup, where we were putting in mega, resilient performances and enjoying a good run. I'd had a particularly good semi-final, with a series of saves that were described as 'world class' against Chelsea contributing to a 2–1 win.

We had pushed the club hard and were, finally, in the new training facilities after years of fighting. Fans were regularly asking 'What are you going to do?' and wanting to know if my future was there. The booing had subsided when the press died down and, while there was still a group of die-hard haters online, plenty followed the question with 'Please stay'.

As the season ended, we finished fifth in the league – but we made history by winning the FA Cup in a final against Spurs at a packed-out Wembley, claiming the club's first major women's trophy.

I already had such wonderful memories of lifting silverware there – and memories of watching the women play the FA Cup Final as a kid, on TV and back in Nottingham when I'd been a ball girl.

To do it now with my club, to lift a major trophy on English soil, with girls who were friends, all felt full-circle and really special.

Winning at Wembley felt complete and familiar, even patriotic despite being with a club instead of the national side. That day gave something back to those fans who'd been with us, and with me, for so long.

Maybe, looking back, it was the perfect time to say goodbye.

With the work complete on the pitch, the club and I had agreed to talk seriously again.

Paris Saint-Germain had assembled an offer that would reportedly make me the highest-paid goalkeeper in the game. But United's offer was now, finally, on the table and it was the best of the bunch.

Financially, either one would raise the standard of what women keepers were worth, which was the least I wanted to achieve with any new contract I signed, to help push change. Staying in Manchester would have been more financially lucrative, but I didn't just want to stop goals, I was committed to changing the goalposts.

Paris had finished the season in second place in the French Division 1 Féminine (now the Arkema Première Ligue) and had won the French Cup and reached the semi-finals of the

ALL IN

Champions League, as well as qualifying for the tournament next season.

United had set out their vision when I'd joined to be competing to win it by now as well, but we didn't feel anywhere close and I wanted a crack at it.

United laid it all out.

They let me know this was the best they could offer. As for conditions, they didn't shy away from the fact that there would be some rough times ahead, but if I stayed I'd continue building something until I retired; maybe we'd get to the top by the end.

I mulled it all over.

Within 48 hours a message appeared on the team group chat from one of the girls asking 'Is this true?' with a link to an article in the *Athletic* reporting that the United men's team were getting a £50-million refurbishment on their training complex and the women would be moved out of their new building, into portable cabins, allowing the men to take over while it was underway.

No one had bothered to tell me that on the call. What else weren't they telling me?

I thought about all the promises that had been made over the years around infrastructure, about the better player and staff turnover. I thought about the headlines that had swirled around me and questioned, again, the stuff that had made its way into the same press outlets while I'd suffered at home.

Ever since I'd achieved a degree of fame, it had all come back to 'Mary's the problem'. My biggest fear was that I was going to live out the past year over and over again, that if we didn't do well I would be scapegoated because I was a name that got clicks.

My place and my value in football were completely transformed from the day I'd originally signed with United – even when I'd signed my contract extension a couple of years earlier I was on the way out, not England's number one.

I recognised that I needed to rely on the same motivations that had guided every other move I'd made in football, to go to the place that gave me the best chance of both minutes, consistency and betterment. At 31 I had to play wherever I could prolong my career and my potential.

I knew what I needed to do.

Meanwhile, England camp had come back around at the end of May. I'd gone into that season after the World Cup with my heart racing, it had never stopped. I had never before experienced highs and lows in such quick succession, one on top of another with no space to differentiate whether the adrenaline rampaging through my system was the product of being celebrated or denigrated, built up or let down.

The exhilaration of the FA Cup had been banked with other wins of the past, and I was back in the present, plunged into survival mode and extremely apprehensive about going back to England with the lowest reserves I'd had since lockdown.

My fight wasn't gone, though.

In many ways, I thought the hard part was already over. My place was in jeopardy and I'd been told as much. There were two games ahead, and I'd play whatever role was needed.

A couple of days into camp, Sarina brought us into our individual goalkeeper meetings, as usual. 'We're going to review who is going to be England's number one on a camp-by-camp basis,' she told me, frankly.

It turned out the hard bit had not already happened.

This felt worse.

I'd drawn on so much inside myself to get there and now there was another test waiting. Being played off against each other felt more uncertain and excruciating than the last camp. And cruel too. This was how it was in football, this was how England was going to be for me now.

I was told I'd start the first game against France. It was my 50th international cap, a milestone worthy of celebration for any player representing their country. Usually, I'd have been put up to talk to the media, to mark it in the match-day-minus-one press conference, but I was told that wouldn't be necessary. The message wasn't subtle. Was there now a clear move to steer the spotlight away from me off the pitch as well as on it? Whether it was driven by the desire to move the attention onto someone else or simply a fear that I had too much media interest already was as unclear as everything else. I decided to do what I always did – turn up for work and make my performance speak for itself.

During the warm-up, though, I felt something going in my hip, a tiny pull on my right side as I made a pass.

No. Not now.

I got physio treatment and we agreed I was good enough to play. It would be fine, I thought, we played on niggles all the time, and I walked out at St James' Park in Newcastle for my 50th appearance in an England shirt. Eight minutes in, I collapsed in pain.

There's a book by the psychiatrist Bessel van der Kolk called *The Body Keeps The Score* about the impact that stored experiences or trauma have on our mind, body and brain, and how what we endure in life manifests itself in our physical and mental wellbeing. I was mentally and physically fraught: this was my body's way of keeping the score. It had given me the warning signs, the anxiety, the panic attacks, the physical withdrawal into my house to try and protect myself. Now, it was telling me it needed a rest from all this for a while.

I left the pitch on crutches with what was later diagnosed as a tear in the TFL muscle which stabilises the hip and knee.

As my competitor came off the bench, it troubled me to think about what it spelled out for my England future. The team was narrowly defeated 2–1, but the outcome of it all was inevitable. The press were now asking in earnest if Mary Earps was England's number one anymore. The goalkeeper situation had spilled out of camp to become yet another public circus. I tried to avoid reading the speculation: it was unhelpful and I was my own harshest critic anyway.

An injury taking me out of the picture, even just for a short time, felt like the excuse Sarina needed, and I was in no doubt that when it came to my England career this marked the beginning of the end.

What goes up, I knew, must come down: it was the most basic principle of the universe. I wasn't ready for the next chapter, but I'd forged my ascent and now I knew myself and success well enough to control the descent too.

TWENTY-TWO

YOU ARE THE STANDARD YOU ACCEPT

When a flower wilts, you change its environment. You examine the conditions around it, changing the soil that feeds it, the sunlight, its sustenance, its climate, and you replant it in a place where it can bloom.

At the start of the summer, I signed for Paris Saint-Germain and we set to work moving our lives there.

I could have stayed in Manchester where I was comfortable and settled, but that would have been the easy choice, that would have been allowing complacency in.

If I'd chickened out and stayed on commitments that never came to fruition I wasn't sure I could look at myself, today or yesterday, in the mirror.

I felt wanted and valued at Paris. They'd come in for me consistently for years, I could play in the Champions League and there were state-of-the-art facilities that would prolong my football career, which was now a priority.

Women's football is women's football everywhere you go; every club in every country has a budget limited by the money coming in and it's a case of how much of it they're willing to spend at any given time. I wasn't under any illusion that it was all a bed of roses, but playing abroad at Wolfsburg years earlier had given me the space to breathe and grow as a person and an athlete. Now, I felt that same inner nudge to try life outside England again. Moving somewhere no one cared who I was would allow me to focus entirely on my football and my enjoyment of it, and to let more light back in to life and my performance.

My international career was a factor too. I'd called Sarina to consult with her before making a decision and I got the view from her that she thought change would be beneficial.

I felt like I'd been caught off guard during the last couple of camps and the goalkeeper debacle felt detrimental to everyone, including the other players who weren't able to build a reliable rhythm around either one of us. I told Sarina that I didn't feel great about what was happening, that I would accept and respect whatever her decision was, but I'd been thinking about it a lot. I was honest in telling her I didn't agree with it and I was keen to know exactly what the plan was because whatever her choice would be, it would inevitably impact my own decision-making internationally.

I was conscious of it not coming across as 'If you do this, I'll do that,' I just needed the clarity I was once used to in our communication so I had a fuller picture to determine my future. I had already expressed to her in conversation that her decision would naturally have a bearing on my own, and I made sure to vocalise this again.

'The level of competition is really high between the two of you,' she told me over the phone. 'I don't know who my number one is.'

She explained that her plan was to continue alternating us until the new year, when she'd begin forming her team for the 2025 Euros that summer. She was saying I was still in the game. So, I wanted to make a choice about my club that could extend my years as a goalkeeper, including whatever time I had left with England.

I rehabilitated hard and forced myself back to fitness for camps at St George's Park in June and then the Netherlands in July. Technically, I'd been number one last camp, starting for my 50th cap, and, as precarious as my position was, I still had a team to work for. I knew I was still at the top of my game.

The pain in my hip was now minimal, and I told Sarina I was ready.

She had called four keepers into camp this time rather than the usual three: me, Hannah, Manchester City's Khiara Keating, who was a brilliant contender to be the next number one and had won the Golden Glove after taking over from Roebuck at City, and Anna Moorhouse, who was playing in Orlando and was brought in on her first call-up.

Bringing new talent through who do things their way is part of teams' evolution, positions need strength and depth, but I also had enough experience to be honest and realistic with myself about the shape of things to come. I had learned that pragmatism around that was a valuable way to manage my expectations and get the best out of myself.

A behind-closed-doors friendly with the Netherlands seemed like a perfect opportunity to make sure I was fit and practised for the Euros qualifiers we had coming up later that month, which were reverse fixtures against Ireland and Sweden.

But I was getting the impression that Sarina thought differently and I wasn't going to get any minutes.

I asked her for a conversation. 'I've been told I'm not playing and I want you to know I can play. I feel good,' I said.

'We don't want to take any risks,' she replied.

'I'm ready to play, I think it's important I get minutes to get back for next week,' I explained.

'If you play tomorrow, you might not be fit for the qualifiers. This game isn't important, it has no bearing on the decision. We know what you can do already,' she said. Was this another excuse or did she really want me fit for the |bigger games?

It felt like the less information they gave me, the longer they could dangle the thread I was on.

If there had been an energy shift before, there was now suddenly a gulf.

Sitting in the dark, waiting for a straightforward response, was painfully hard.

Darren barely spoke a word to me the whole week and avoided eye contact entirely, including during training, except for the one time we found ourselves in a lift together.

'Are you alright?' I said.

'No, not really,' he replied. 'Are you?'

'No, not really,' I offered back.

It was awkward.

I didn't speak to Kate, the team psychologist who used to come and find me to provide support around training sessions, a priority for all the starting players.

In training sessions, the individual feedback I was used

to from coaches including things to work towards, was now replaced by an attitude that was neutral, passive. There's nothing more effective than being neutral to tell you someone's no longer invested in whether the next thing you do for them is a success or failure, especially when you're part of the same team. It amounts to indifference – a quiet but effective indication that whether you improve or stay stagnant, whether you have a better chance of making that save or not, does not affect their own outcomes. It's another example of misalignment.

'No, we love what you do,' the coaches would say, placidly, even if I felt they didn't mean it.

Maybe they'd already been told to check-out where I was concerned; maybe they'd been told to keep me happy.

I was still being praised as a leader within the group but where Sarina had once solicited my opinions, inviting me to leadership and captains' groups or tactics meetings, I was no longer required and was now kept out.

I felt there was a clear lack of care for me and my welfare because I wasn't a person who needed taking care of anymore.

It all assembled into this odd juxtaposition of superficially being handled with kid gloves, as though needing to keep me on side, while paying me no real heed; of using words as if I was irreplaceable but showing me that I was, very clearly, replaceable.

The rug was slowly being pulled from underneath me and I was fighting between what I felt and what I knew.

No one was saying anything about my future with England but my intuition wouldn't leave me alone: their words and their actions didn't match and I knew that when that happened, it was behaviour not language that spoke the truth.

Every which way I turned it over I couldn't get away from the insight that these ties were being severed in front of me and processing how people treat you differently when they decide they no longer need you, particularly when you are kept in the dark, hurts. It felt like a heartbreak again.

The affinity I had for Sarina and this job – one I'd given every last cell of myself to – was being destroyed, the trust and respect evaporating.

I was trying to hang on but failing. And I couldn't let go either because I was in love with playing for England. Sarina knew how I felt about it, and everyone else did too. But I had to face up to the fact that that now meant doing so in a capacity that no longer existed for me. I was no longer needed to fulfil the role in which I had thrived and where I felt I still had so much to contribute.

All of this time, relationships in the goalkeeper group were dire. What had been a circus was now a bomb waiting to go off.

Heaven knows I'm far from a perfect person, but I know I was conducting myself with professionalism because, if nothing else, people in camp kept telling me so. Meanwhile, they were treading on eggshells and there wasn't a camp that passed without an incident.

That wasn't tolerated in the England I knew and I wasn't the only person who viewed it as a spectacular problem. I tried to wrap my head around the new double standard while the press were having a whale of a time pitting us against each other. It was out of hand and an unwelcome distraction for the entire team.

Kate came to find me to apologise for failing to check up on how I was, and Arjan, the assistant coach, made a point of telling me later that week: 'You've been brilliant this camp, I imagine it's been tough.' But I already felt wrung out. It was hard to bring The Best Mary to lead with experience and TikTok Mary to lighten the load, all while feeling frozen out and watching someone else who brought problems get promoted into my role. My confidence and safe space were shot.

I thought my days of rejections were over, but here I was again at the peak of my career facing another huge blow. I tried to remain positive, to be grateful for all the things I had in my life, all the amazing opportunities, the incredible people, the sport I loved, but I also felt utterly dejected.

And because I knew where that could take me, because I carried the lessons I had learned when I'd moved from darkness into light before, I realised for the first time that year that I didn't have to let anyone else crush my spirit again. I had a choice with England too.

I could stop myself from hitting the kitchen floor again.

I wasn't entitled to keep my place if Sarina didn't want me to but I was entitled to decide what happened next. I could pass the baton on earlier than I had hoped and call time on my England career.

I didn't have to stay in this environment, dangling by a thread and the diminishing hope of another chance to play, if I didn't want to. I could do what other people do if they're no longer enjoying their job: I could leave, I could retire.

I didn't say a word to anyone, but I remember going for a coffee and a cookie on a walk with one of the girls between that week's games. It was a glorious sunny day and we strolled together, catching up on everything but the one thing I was sure she didn't know I was thinking. Except that she did;

she could read the parts I'd left unspoken because she saw it too. A WhatsApp message from her appeared on my phone at 1am that night: 'I know you want to stop. And I get it . . . You might not think it's possible or things are fair . . . But I don't want you to regret the chance of living your dream all over again. You can fight for your spot.'

I sat up questioning why I wanted to leave.

The brutal reality of football, sport and, I can only imagine, countless other pursuits in workplaces and relationships in life, is that when you become surplus to requirements everyone around you changes. Sometimes, you share an experience, a bond, an achievement or overcome obstacles so great that you naively think you're going to share that connection with them forever.

But perception is reality and the reality now was that Sarina saw something in someone else that she preferred and, to her mind, superseded what I brought to the table. Very soon, I would indeed be surplus to requirement.

Being replaced is not easy for anyone. Was my ego bruised by it? Was I hurt by the lack of care for me and my welfare? Was I just embarrassed to experience the transition in front of the world? I was a fierce competitor. My ambition had never been to sit on the bench; I'd only ever chosen my clubs because I was chasing opportunities to play football, to deliver on my potential. There was no denying that it would be hard to take.

Did the goalkeepers need a clear run without me there? If I left and simply hit fast forward on the inevitable would that make the circus leave town and let everyone get on with this new chapter?

I had to let go of the discomfort and frustration that had swirled since February, the denial and deflection that had contributed to those panic attacks. I needed to make space to process what was happening and what I wanted to do next.

I have always believed that you are the standard you are prepared to accept. And those weeks had the cumulative effect of draining me physically and mentally as a connection was severed to an environment that no longer existed. I didn't want to give it up but, equally, I couldn't just sit there yearning for it; nor could I allow it to take any energy from the team. Was I prepared to leave myself in a place that no longer respected or appreciated me or felt like my safe space? Would that serve or take away from the greater good?

Football was my first love and playing for England my greatest romance, but now it was keeping me awake again, filling me with pain and worry. I was torn between knowing what I would tell a loved one to do if their relationship was making them sick and knowing that I'd fought back for every one of my successes before. Could I fight for this one? I honestly didn't know, but I did know that it was in my own hands. All those years of consistency had bought me another freedom, the freedom to see that there was a choice – and at some point soon it would be mine to make.

TWENTY-THREE

KNOW WHAT YOU BRING TO THE TABLE; BE UNAFRAID TO EAT ALONE

I didn't expect to fall in love with Paris the way that I did. In fact, some time after moving there a doctor told me I had too much vitamin D in my system.

I found an apartment to rent in Versailles, a 20-minute drive from the training ground and 20 minutes into the city, meaning we could go in whenever I wanted.

I was only ever approached by people for photos or autographs at the airport or Gare du Nord when I caught the Eurostar back home. And French life was vibrant and right on my doorstep, down to the local boulangerie, which was open for fresh baguettes each morning, and the café culture that I could now enjoy without a spiral of anxiety to accompany leaving the house.

People weren't bothered about time here. When my car got broken into – not such a great start – making me late for training, the club response was, 'Don't worry, it will be sorted. Take your time.'

Things could wait till tomorrow in Paris and it gave me space to emotionally unwind myself and think clearly. I slept on things, I felt freer and, at the same time, I enjoyed the challenge of teaching myself a new language and a new style of football.

At work, I was building something, again, with a team of talented and driven players who were collegiate and friendly too.

Our training set-up was elite, with three or four physios solely for the women's team, a state-of-the-art gym and pitches and parking spaces reserved for the women too.

Parts of my process remained the same (I still don't like training with balls in the back of the net and organise them to either side between drills) but there was a different football philosophy, a different culture and different stimuli. The football was less physical and more technical, the pace was faster and the style of training was new, with different repetitions for me to be consistent in and a coach who kicked with his left foot.

We played matches much later than in the UK, at 9pm at night, and started the day as early as 6:30am to travel the bigger distances for away games, meaning I had to change my entire match-day routine. It was just what I needed – the discomfort of being challenged to learn something new. Diving into this kind of chaos felt exciting, like I could bring another level out of myself there. I felt like I was where I needed to be.

The directorship really backed me and seemed pleased with their signing. I wasn't sure if the manager at the time, Fabrice

Abriel, who had a particularly direct, no-bullshit approach, liked that or me as much but I wasn't afraid of the challenge. My football would do the talking as the season went on.

Of course, things couldn't start smoothly.

No sooner had I arrived with my clear ambition to play Champions League football than we were knocked out in the qualifying stages after Juventus beat us 5–2 over two legs, and I couldn't have been more gutted.

The British press were referring to us as 'Mary Earps' PSG' and their interest was piqued by the fact I'd moved to the previous year's semi-finalists for more silverware only to exit Europe's biggest club competition with it barely underway.

Days later, unbeknownst to me, a journalist came to watch me at work, but the manager was resting me. His more laid-back French approach meant he didn't see it as a big deal at all, an obvious choice against a weaker opposition that gave me chance to rest my body; he didn't know yet that my work ethic meant I didn't want to miss a single game.

The journalist had asked for an interview with me but PSG declined, saying they could schedule it for next time. I think they were concerned about negative press surrounding our competition exit and didn't want to leave me in a vulnerable position by making me the poster girl for the loss. I appreciated that consideration and protection. So instead, they exchanged information with the journalist and he headed into the stands, where he then tried to collar my parents, who'd come out to watch.

Dad had spoken to him briefly, despite me always advising loved ones not to speak to the press, and I then found Mum, Dad and this young reporter who'd hopped on a train from

London stood outside the training complex as I drove out, the reporter was upset because PSG had, appropriately, informed him that trying to go through my family was not best practice and had suggested something on Zoom the week after instead.

'Can I interview you?' he asked me now, through my car window as Mum and Dad climbed in.

'Yes, of course, I'd be happy to. Just go through the club and we can set it up,' I said. If he hadn't been bothering my parents, I'd have appreciated his perseverance. But I knew that not everyone had straightforward intentions and going through club media channels was standard practice for a reason. I was also conscious of the manager's perception of me and didn't want to be seen as someone who'd go rogue and give football interviews whenever I felt like it. I was still trying to get my head down and settle in.

The next day, on a break in training, I went on my phone and saw an article that was a complete hatchet job: a 'how the mighty have fallen' type takedown that revealed that without the interview he'd come out to get he'd been dispatched to the club shop, where you had to ask for my name and number on the back of a shirt, like pretty much all the other players, and couldn't buy a pre-printed one. This apparently spelled my demise.

Sarina called me: 'Why didn't you play?' she asked.

Great.

Six weeks later, I made a dash back to London, where my waxwork was being unveiled at Madame Tussauds, the first female footballer to feature in the world-famous lookalikes museum. I had attended sittings for them to take my measurements and get the exact colour of my eyes, skin and hair. And I donated one of the famously sought-after green kits that had been made for the World Cup Final for my waxwork to wear.

Not only had they done an incredible job in capturing my likeness, which was utterly surreal, they did a great job of creating a wonderful moment for me too.

My family, including Grandma this time, were there and girls from West Bridgford Colts had been given VIP passes for a first look and were surprised to find the real me waiting to see them too.

You could see representation in their eyes when they beamed back at me. A waxwork was fun but a real-life footballer from the same place as them to reach out and touch was far better. The day was packed with press, photographs and formalities but the museum ordered pizza into the Hollywood room where the unveiling had taken place and I was able to sit there afterwards when the exhibition was closed with people I cherished and the faces of movie stars, and me, staring down at us.

From the surreal back to the persistently unsure.

By the time England camp had arrived a month earlier, in October, I was honestly no longer certain I'd still get the email that arrived at 11am the Tuesday before to call you into the squad, despite Sarina's guarantee that she would alternate us into the new year.

It came, though, and we had a series of friendlies to play. I sat on the bench at Wembley, where we lost 4–3 against Germany. The cameras kept panning to me to capture my reactions and when I looked at my phone that night I had a stream of people tagging me on social media, questioning why I wasn't number one anymore.

I wasn't chosen for Switzerland at the end of the year then started the next game against South Africa and made some important saves. Our 2–1 victory boosted me. Then, I was chosen to play the showpiece USA game at Wembley which, despite the 0–0 score, felt like a solid, reliable England performance. We'd been struggling to find momentum since the World Cup and this was the first time we'd defended resolutely in some time. It left us all buzzing, like it was coming back together again. I'd done what I and everyone else knew I was capable of on the pitch and I headed into 2025 with my confidence at England higher than it had been for almost a year since that Spain camp when everything had begun to misalign. With Paris, I'd played a brilliant game against Lyon, who were the perennial Division 1 champions, keeping us in the game with a run of saves including two particularly strong goal-line blocks that showed my mettle. *If I'm not picked for England now*, I thought, *then it really is never*.

When the first Lionesses camp of 2025 came around in February I felt better about my chances and more assured mentally than I had been for some time.

I was eager now for the clarity that Sarina had promised around her own decision: that she would choose her number one in the new year. She was a woman of her word and that's what she'd promised, a decision to close what had now been 12 months of turmoil and uncertainty bubbling through camp and through me.

It didn't arrive.

A couple of days in, I sat down for my goalkeeper

meeting with her in the dining area of the sprawling and picturesque Pine Cliffs hotel complex in Portugal's Algarve, where pine trees twisted over the coast below. And she told me: still no decision.

I felt exasperated.

I attempted to reason: 'I don't feel this serves anyone – me, her or the team.'

It was, I said, mentally draining.

Much like when I was young and people mistook my self-belief as a sign that I didn't also need their care, it has been my experience that those who handle what is thrown at them without fuss, people who bear it with broad shoulders, are then expected to carry more and more again.

As if unknowingly making the point, Darren said: 'But look how you've responded. Look at your performance against the USA.'

'Football's hard sometimes,' said Sarina.

That much was true.

My inner monologue was screaming: *You've made your mind up – please just say it*. But it wasn't going to happen. I was being left alone to decipher and agonise over it all and search for clarity myself on what was causing my pain.

My journey in football had covered enough ground to know that no matter what you put in or what you want the outcome to be, you must face the brutal reality that the time will arrive when it comes to an end. A person who once saw your potential, invested in your success and shared it alongside you no longer will. No one is going to take care of you for ever, not the way you take care of yourself.

I felt like a frog that had been placed in tepid water with

the heat gradually turned up. It was an environment I couldn't survive in.

I was either going to boil to death or jump before it killed me.

This would be my England end-game and it was as though someone had pierced my insides.

When my competitor played against Spain at Wembley, another showpiece against the world champions, I knew my England career was over before the match had kicked off. Even when I outperformed her, it was never going to be good enough.

'I'll never understand why you did this,' I said to Darren.

'I know you won't,' he said.

People think that being forced out is being told at some point that you're no longer needed, but a pattern of behaviour can achieve the same outcome.

From the bench I soaked in the entirety of Wembley. I knew it was the last time I would put on an England shirt there or wear it to stand between those famous posts.

When the final whistle blew and we walked back in through the tunnel I quietly took a photograph of my place in the dressing room. To remember. When I got back to my room the tears came, and they didn't stop.

As soon as camp was done I told a small select group who loved me: 'It's over.'

'You've hung on this long, don't go before she's made a decision,' one told me. 'Don't have a question mark in your mind, don't wonder *What if I went to one more camp?*'

It was draining the life out of me. It was also turning me into someone I'm not. My performance level was still really high but I'd just spent night after night crying in my room. I wasn't going to do it this way. Not after everything I'd achieved and for everything I still had to give to football at club level, at the very least, if my country was now ready for me to pass on the baton.

The parts of football that are played off the pitch, the way the business of it is taken care of, had threatened to steal my love for the game and take me with it before, and now I knew enough to spot the signs, the patterns of behaviour, in others and in myself. I didn't have to sit and wait for the monster to arrive.

Pain, great and small, is a mechanism that helps all of us to survive; it sends nerve signals to our brains as warning signs that we need to change something to prevent future damage. I was so used to using pain and discomfort for growth – but I had also learned to tell the difference between that and the kind that will become self-destructive. This was the latter.

I would be able to manage it, one day its purpose would make sense, but I didn't want to grow bitter and resentful, upset or frustrated because I knew that staying on the team to sit on the bench, in that atmosphere, would have brought those negative feelings out in me. I understood what a healthy goalkeeper group, where everyone felt able to perform their role, looked like. And I knew what an unhealthy one looked like because I had been in both and stayed resolute in my pursuit of the first, both for me and whoever came next. I wasn't going to stand in the way of someone else the way others had to me. The cost of staying was too high to me and to the team.

Sarina may not have been willing to say it but I knew she had decided I didn't have any more years under her as number one. I had more club years in me, though, at the high level I demanded of myself. If that's where I was going to get minutes now then future-proofing and extracting myself from a situation that was mentally grinding me down would have to be my priority.

The way the past year had been handled meant I no longer felt connected to the national team in the way that I had when it was a place that made me feel I could run on water.

I realised I could pass the baton on, on terms that worked for my successors, my teammates, myself and the legacy I had created there.

Letting go of something you love is one of the hardest things to do – even when you know it's right, especially when it hurts. But life is too short to forfeit your peace of mind. You have to remember what you bring to the table and be unafraid to eat alone.

It was time to stop. I knew some people would consider it selfish. For me, though, it was self-preservation. I'd loved every minute of playing for my country, with these girls, but I knew that loving every minute was over. If I didn't walk away from this I would stay in a place that was already hurting me. I'd risk the mental fortitude I needed now to sustain my career and I owed myself, future goalkeeping and England far more than that.

I had to go out on a high. I had to be able to look in the mirror and see myself looking back. I'd had an unbelievable England career and I had to return one more time and give every ounce I had, be the best goalkeeper in training for my own self, for my past and future self, for my team.

This was my end-game but the least I'd earned was the right to play it my way, with my teammates and with a smile on my face.

TWENTY-FOUR

FALL IF YOU HAVE TO FALL – YOU WILL CATCH YOU

In April I was called back to St George's Park and went with my head up, even if I was working extra hard to keep it that way, not knowing exactly how things were going to play out but at peace with the fact that it would most certainly be my last.

A day in, earlier than usual, I had a message to meet: 'Mary, Sarina wants to talk to you.'

I went to room 206, a bedroom that had been converted into meeting space where our conversations usually took place, at the allocated time.

I felt sick and anxious as I took my seat with her and Darren.

Then came the words I'd waited over 12 months to hear: 'I've decided Hannah's the number one for now.'

I felt the weight of my heart sink to the floor and the relief that I had finally had clarity lift from my shoulders all at once.

'She's a little bit ahead of you,' Sarina continued. 'It's nothing you've done or done wrong.'

'I expected this,' I said. I had 30 seconds to say my piece. I told her I wasn't surprised by what she'd just said, that it had been a long time coming, but I felt extremely disappointed, nonetheless.

Then I said: 'I just think you could have been more direct and honest from the jump.' She wasn't happy with that.

'No, I don't think that's fair. I always communicate openly. We've only just made this decision,' she cut in.

That sounded like bullshit to me.

Darren didn't look up from the floor the whole time.

'Respectfully,' I said, 'we're going to have to agree to disagree. You've made your decision. I've had to make one too. This will be my last camp, I'm internationally retiring.'

Sarina wasn't at all shocked – we'd already discussed the fact I needed to consider my future. She said she could see I'd been thinking about it for some time and now asked me why. 'It doesn't align with my morals and values to continue,' I said. 'I'd like to graciously step aside. I'd rather Khiara get the experience. I've had my time in the sun.'

I continued with honesty but my voice broke as I said: 'I used to feel invincible here but I don't feel that way anymore.' That saddened me the most of all.

I told her that playing for my country had been the greatest privilege of my life but I couldn't bear to look back on it as a place where I cried in my room, where I didn't recognise myself. I said I no longer felt supported there and that the goalkeeper dynamic had been too unhealthy for too long.

'I know it's hard but you have so much more to give and your level is so high,' she said.

'I know my level is high, that's not the question,' I said,

defiant in the truth. The reality, I told her, was that none of it made sense anymore: 'It's better for the team if I move on.'

I was choked up, visibly holding off a flood of emotion I didn't have space to swim in. I knew that no matter how much I said, they wouldn't understand because it wouldn't fit their agenda. From where they stood it looked better for me to be there, in the background, during the Euros that summer and to be dropped entirely afterwards.

She talked about all the external noise around my position, referring to the press, as though that was a contributing factor in this decision, but I was so tired of being told how misguided my own inferences were about what had been happening to me that I just needed to fight for what I knew to be the right choice now.

'Do you want to sleep on it?' Sarina asked. 'I want you to reconsider. You have so much more to give,' she said again. 'This isn't the end of your England career.'

The words and actions didn't match.

'I don't want to sleep on it,' I said. I'd been sleeping on it for so long. I wanted to make the most of my last camp.

'It's been a good run,' I added with a slight smile. They half-laughed at the pragmatism.

We'd been sat there now for 20 minutes. To my surprise, they both thanked me for my honesty.

'That took incredible bravery,' Darren said, looking up for the first time. It felt like the most frank thing he'd said to me in over a year.

They asked if I'd spoken to any of the girls about it.

'Not yet,' I said. There were two important games that week and I felt the bare minimum professional conduct was not to burden them. I walked away, and didn't start either game, but later that week I had another text, this time directly from Sarina: 'Mary, could I have ten minutes?' I headed back to room 206.

'I was thinking about what you said and I don't accept your retirement,' she said. 'I don't want you to go.'

I had told her in the earlier meeting that I knew it was time for younger keepers like Khiara to step up. Now she told me: 'She will have her time. This is your time now.'

I was stunned. It was a 180-degree turn – she had changed my role for over a year and put me on the bench, my brain had done a mental Olympics trying to figure out what to do for the best, for everyone, now I was being told it was my time?

Then, she added: 'I also don't think it's the right thing for you to go.'

'What do you mean?' I asked.

'I just worry what people will say. I think it's better that you stay for the tournament, win a trophy then go.'

For a long time, I had been told to block out the external noise, and I tried to take that advice on board. In later conversations, though, it was raised as a reason to reconsider retiring. It struck me as a shift in the message, and it left me quietly reflecting on the contrast.

The team was packed with talent and the girls had a brilliant shot at winning the Euros with me as they did without me. I could recognise that if Sarina was implementing another set-up it was because that could work and win. If it was just about sticking around and collecting a tournament bonus and a medal this would have all been far easier, but it was about much more than that.

I'd been clear that I wanted to get off at the next stop, now I felt like I was being manipulated into staying.

As we parted for the week they lavished me with praise: Kate commented on how professional I had been. Darren spoke up: 'You've been brilliant this week, absolutely fantastic.' And Sarina now told me: 'Your standards have been unbelievable, what you have given this team.'

I agreed to think on it just a little longer if they needed me to. I had an important end of season with PSG, where we were fighting for the title and automatic promotion to the Champions League. We said we would speak in a few weeks' time when it was over, before she announced her tournament squad; I had to clear all of that if I was going to have any headspace to authentically and meaningfully reconsider my decision – and decide if they actually meant what they now said.

My head was spinning.

Then, out of the blue, two days before my league semi-final play-off in May and two weeks before the next England camp, Sarina texted me asking for my decision. I was totally focused on not derailing my PSG season and wasn't expecting it yet. Besides, mentally, I wasn't at all convinced I wanted to change this enormous decision I'd thought so long and hard about.

If I was really being asked to reconsider, I asked her for a definitive reason as to why I'd lost my spot. 'There has to be a reason beyond just the high level of competition between us,' I said.

'Distribution and defending the space,' she answered.

I thanked her for the clarity of response. The PSG game was at 9pm on Sunday. She said she needed an answer by 1pm on Monday. I felt pressured but I agreed.

The way this next bit played out is the only part of my retirement that I wish I had done differently, where I wish, more than anything, that I had stayed true to myself, that I'd stuck to my intuition.

It was 11am and I was in my Paris apartment when Sarina and I spoke. We'd won our match the night before, and a place in the final. I'd barely slept, fuelled by adrenaline, thinking about that and the conversation I had to have.

I felt completely up against it and I couldn't shake her words of warning from camp about it being better for me that I stay.

The timing was now terrible – I still had a club final to play, and if I was going to be forced into a choice, in this very moment, I knew it wasn't the right time for anyone to announce a retirement.

I also finally had the information I'd been after for so long and so, I thought, if it was just those two things costing me my spot – distribution and defending the space – I had what I needed to do something about it. Maybe she meant it. Maybe she did believe it wasn't time to pass the baton.

Dubiously, I told her: 'OK, I'll continue.' She was pleased. Then, before we left the call she offered up, in passing: 'Well done, I saw you won last night.' I was glad she'd noticed, as it reinforced what she'd said. Then she said she hadn't watched it.

With that, I knew instantly that I'd made the wrong choice; I immediately wished I hadn't uttered the words. I had committed to something and someone who didn't seem committed to me; whose words, where I was concerned, still didn't match their actions, and I'd known it all along. Backtracking was entirely the wrong choice from me and for everyone involved and I felt my body fill with immediate regret. Now I had to either live with it or fix it. I felt trapped.

We lost Friday's game, finishing second in the league, but qualified for next season's Champions League. I dived into a week of back-to-back commercial work with day after day full of shooting adverts and social media campaigns in London.

Then, Kitty texted: 'I need to tell you something.'

If there were ever an example of the universe putting me where I needed to be it was in the call we had next.

Christina had been diagnosed with lung cancer, she said.

News like that stops your world.

Christina was my best friend, like family; I constantly joked with her that she was my fit-spiration, always up at 6am on the Peloton or doing yoga. How could she be so ill?

I picked up the phone to her, thinking back to a visit she'd made to Paris in February; we'd jogged across the train station and she wasn't breathing well, puffing away on her inhaler. We'd laughed about it but later had queried if it was something that she should get tested. Now this.

'What's the treatment plan?' I asked.

They didn't know.

'How bad is it?' They didn't know that either. They didn't even know if it was curable.

She was about to face an almighty battle.

The thought of losing her and the reminder of how temporary it really all is petrified me.

It also reaffirmed my decision: life was too short to be anywhere where you're not supposed to be.

I needed to talk to Sarina. My head had been in a hole that I needed to dig myself out of, quickly. How could I ring the manager back and say, 'I know I said I'll continue but it was a mistake'?

I was going to the Champions League final at Wembley that weekend to watch my England teammates play for Arsenal. Maybe I could meet Sarina there and talk to her face to face. I messaged to ask if she was going, telling her I needed to talk. She replied saying she wasn't. Camp was due to start two days later on the Monday; she suggested we speak at lunchtime then.

This couldn't wait. I arrived back in Paris late on the Sunday night and hit her number on my phone.

'I can't do it,' I said.

'Wow,' came the reply. Her only word shook me. 'I can't believe it,' she said. 'I'm so disappointed. What made you change your mind?'

'I don't think I ever really did,' I replied.

I couldn't have been more honest.

I had been all along.

They say that life puts you in the same situation over and over again and if you approach it in the same way it will deliver you the same lessons too. Sarina had given me the confidence to fulfil the potential I always believed I had inside myself and now our journey together was ending with me having the confidence to say no to her.

Walking away from this wasn't for the weak and I wasn't doing it to teach anyone else their lesson, but because I had learned mine and because I took all that life had already shown me, I put it to use. I did something differently. I saw what had once been good for me was now bad – my loved ones saw it in me too – and I said I don't want that.

In many ways, as much as I had finally taken things into my own hands, really I had just played the hand that I was dealt and I'd used all that had gone before to do it. I could let myself fall if I had to fall because the person I had become would catch me.

Maybe I had been put in that situation at the last possible moment deliberately but I knew I had given everything for the girls and for my country. I had fulfilled my responsibility to both and now I had to fulfil it to myself because, while change is hard, staying where you no longer belong can destroy you. My decision stood.

I take full accountability for my flaws during those two weeks. My intuition had been right the entire time and I slipped, I went against what I knew and ignored it. In the drawn-out course of retiring I let my judgement be clouded by others, maybe once more by a glimmer of hope that being at England could feel different, and for those final few days I sat with the wrong decision. That's how it goes sometimes, even when the stakes are so high, but afterwards it's only you who's left to examine your actions each day; others will do so too, they are entitled to, but their interest will dissipate while yours will stay with you forever if you don't address the misalignment. As you grow, misalignment has to make way for realignment: positive change looks like letting go of what no longer fits and what's no longer yours. There would be consequences, I knew, to making this right but the consequences of not doing so were worse. I was certain of that.

If it's not OK, I told myself, it's not the end.

I didn't sleep.

The next morning, I messaged Sarina, asking if she'd allow

me to tell the girls in person. I said I didn't want to get in the way but hoped that would be more personal, going there with my best foot forwards and my heart in the right place, my last act of international duty and my final responsibility to the team and job I loved. I waited for a response and booked myself a flight before it came. There were only a few hours to get there; I'd take the financial hit if she said no.

She replied, setting out how the day would work. She would talk to them first in the welcome meeting, then I would be allowed on site for one hour between 7 and 8pm to join them and have dinner.

I made my way to Paris Charles de Gaulle Airport. I quietly cried for the entire flight into Birmingham and took a taxi to my parents' house before borrowing Mum's car to drive on to St George's Park. (Mum was pleased to have insured me on it for six quid.) I rang a couple of the girls I was closest to and gave them a heads-up about what was coming. I still hadn't spoken to any of them about retirement and knew it was a long time till they'd get the full story of the last year, or even the last few weeks. I wanted to be as open with them as I could now that they were about to find out.

I headed up the drive of St George's Park a final time, a place where I'd arrived so many times before to live out my dream. Now I was there to do the hardest thing, to say goodbye.

Darren was one of the first people I saw. 'I'm gutted. I just really worry for you now, about what people will say,' he told me, that warning again.

Then I saw Sarina.

'Hello, are we friends?' I asked, as we paused to speak outside The Drum

She replied, 'We've been through a lot, we're like family. Of course we are. I'm just angry.'

I stood against the glass balustrade, my elbows rested on top, as I tried to hide my face and the tears filling my eyes from anyone passing by.

She told me how frustrated she felt by my decision and I explained again that it was the way it had all happened, the circumstances in camp, the constant search for clarity and how I had been treated that had led me there.

'I only had reasons from you the other day,' I said, referring back to our phone call.

She found it hard to believe no one had mentioned it previously. They hadn't. 'I wouldn't have been asking all that time if they had,' I told her.

'We're never going to see this the same,' I continued. 'You don't see it the way I see it and I don't see it the way you do.' It didn't need to be a sour ending, I suggested.

I'd been told how she'd expressed to the team how disappointed she was in me when she'd spoken to them earlier in the day. That felt saddening but I had to accept and respect the fact that we were two people on different ends of the same situation. We would always have different versions and separate feelings about what had happened. But now, she offered me the chance to say something to them all during dinner.

It was barbecue night and the chef was cooking on the grill outside. The girls all sat around the long dining tables with their food, as they always did, and I got to my feet. 'I'll keep it short,' I told them, through tears. I thanked each of them, my teammates and the staff, for an incredible few years.

'I'm so proud of everything we've achieved,' I said. 'Winning the Euros was the best day of my life and I really hope you go and do it again. I can't wait to watch.' It was extraordinarily tough. I meant it all.

They clapped, I cried, then it went silent.

I went around the room, hugging each person who'd been part of my England journey. I felt their support in the meaningful ways they put their arms around me or the words they whispered. 'This has been coming for so long,' one told me.

'I'd have done the same,' another said into my ear.

Others put into text messages later that night what they couldn't say in person: 'Not only have you become an absolute legend here, you've been written off multiple times and it's amazing to see you work your ass off to achieve what you've achieved . . . People on the outside don't know how difficult this environment can be and being true to yourself is so admirable.'

As dinner finished, Bronzey suggested that Sarina say something. She did, placing her hand on my shoulder and uttering a few words before conceding: 'I'm not handling this very well.' She didn't say thank you and maybe it was naive of me to hope for a moment of celebration among it all. Keira stepped in to speak instead, offering up kind words about me being an incredible teammate who'd done so much for goalkeeping. It meant a great deal, from the girls I cared for so deeply.

I made my way back to my parents' house as dusk set during the 50-minute drive home. I had one more thing to do before I closed that chapter of my life: tell the world.

TWENTY-FIVE

PEACE IS SOMETHING YOU CHOOSE, NOT SOMETHING YOU FIND

The reality was that I had started writing my retirement announcement almost a year earlier than when it went live on 27th May, an entirely unplanned but, as the universe would have it, fortuitous parallel with my initials, shirt number and business: MAE 27.

I'd met with the England PR team while I was at St George's Park and agreed a 10:45am embargo for press, meaning nothing could run beforehand.

They showed me the England announcement which was, I thought, cold, not least because it expressed Sarina's disappointment in me. I had wanted to retain positivity; the decision-making and the time and conversations that had passed had been arduous and painful but now the decision was here I hoped we could pass the baton on together, celebrate something that had been great and look ahead to the good that could follow for the team and for me.

I sat up late, putting my own words into a design app, adding photos of career highs to match, for a series of social media slides talking to fans:

'I have taken the difficult decision to retire internationally,' I wrote. 'It has been the greatest honour and privilege of my life to wear this badge, represent my country and play alongside such an incredible group of players . . . I wish I could do it forever – but sadly, all good things must come to an end. My journey has never been the simplest, and so in true Mary fashion, this isn't a simple goodbye – right before a major tournament. Nonetheless, I know this is the right decision.'

I continued: 'This is a new era and a new England team, and I'm looking forward to watching them this summer. In the end, all you have is all you are – your character. And I know that while this won't make sense to some who are reading this, you can trust that I would not be doing this unless I thought it was absolutely the right thing to do, as much as it hurts.' I signed off, 'Lioness 198 over and out', and felt the tears flow again as I stored it, ready to go the next morning.

Around 10am, Tina received a call from the *Telegraph*. They already had the story and I didn't feel good about it. It hadn't come from me and I felt my retirement was my news to break. I spoke to the England PR again to gauge if the journalist was going to break the embargo. I wanted us to stay coordinated but it was proving hard. He just kept saying, 'Let's stay close on it,' which I thought we already were.

Tina called again: 'It's out,' she said. I hit post on my TikTok and Instagram but the narrative from England, their

ALL IN

disappointment in my decision, was already all over that first piece: MARY EARPS QUITS ENGLAND AFTER LOSING STARTING PLACE, they published as an exclusive. Maybe this is how far too many business breakups end, with petrol poured on the flames instead of sand to make it easier for one party to pull away from the other.

Downstairs, my dad had Sky Sports News on and I could hear the sound of my announcement carrying up the stairs. I closed the door to quieten the noise. I wanted to leave gracefully and none of this felt graceful.

One paper wrote a scathing piece about my ego being out of control that was targeted and deliberate, and another paper went to town on my character after trying and failing to barter an exclusive out of Tina in order not to run the piece.

It generated clicks to simplify the situation to, 'She's not number one anymore so she's out', but that wasn't the story by a long shot.

Regardless, in certain corners of the press and internet I was written and spoken about as a brat who had thrown my toys out of the pram at the eleventh hour with a tournament right around the corner. On TV, some of the pundits who were the first to talk about players' mental health now offered visceral points of view about me, without heed, it seemed, for the human being at the centre of the story or an understanding of any of the factors behind it.

Women's football needs the media to grow and the media needs access to us for content, but this felt hateful and the reactions to it were contagious. Other people's opinions were fine, they were welcome and an entirely expected part of football chatter, but this approach felt reckless and speaking or posting words online without care for the consequences they bring to another individual could never sit OK with me.

I never felt entitled to be liked for my decision, but I didn't think I deserved the daggers. It was like they were piling into an open wound with the influx of comments on social media.

I knew that my England career would have ended that summer whatever I did, and I knew there would be greater scrutiny to face as the Euros edged closer. It was completely obvious that I was putting my name on the line.

I could have gone ahead and joined the squad. I could have listened to those who suggested: 'Go, it will put her under more pressure,' knowing what I had experienced, but that wasn't me, I didn't want to be disruptive, and I didn't need anybody else to do badly because my biggest competitor is and always has been myself. I wanted the team to succeed.

And I wanted a retirement, not a public hanging. Public perception may be 'reality' but this was such a long way from my experience of the past year or all the years before that had given me the capacity and courage to make my choice, to draw a line and bet on myself, to know that you can disappoint others and still be good.

As I scrolled through my phone, reading what was being written, those words of warning around what people would say about me if I went through with retirement rang in my ears.

I felt sure there had been another unseen layer of betrayal to the way my news broke. They had pushed me away then acted like I'd given up on them, and I was left taking the flack publicly for things that should never have weighed on my shoulders. I felt I hadn't been considered as a person but they wanted my consideration in return. I felt they didn't treat me with respect and wanted respect back; you can't treat people like that because their dreams once hung on you. It was not my responsibility to prepare the next generation of keepers, that had to be the manager's task, but it didn't stop me taking the blame that it would be my fault if things went wrong in Switzerland. Heaven knows I had taken it upon myself to leave the shirt and the gloves in a better place for those who followed. This was the flip side, the exposure, of earning the spotlight then moving it on while others had their own agendas to serve in its shadows.

We talk about loyalty in football but I wonder if it really exists within the hierarchy, the institution. It is not a game that has space for players to come up against their employers – nine times out of ten, the club or organisation will win. You don't have to play the game, or even be in the public spotlight to know that at some point, inevitably, your actions will disappoint others and you will be the villain in someone else's story.

Even if you communicate clearly, even if you are fair, even if you do everything with the best intentions, someone won't like the truth you shared or the boundary you held.

But it is only you that has to look yourself in the mirror forever more and square your actions with your own conscience. People loved me for doing it with the goalkeeper shirts but hated me for having the same morals with my England career. But I am who I am: love me or hate me, at least I could be respected for being consistent in character, for being true to myself so that I could see my reflection looking back. Everything that had spanned my time in England, until that point, had led me to be able to advocate for and make a decision myself. But the guilt piled on for setting boundaries, for outgrowing the younger version of yourself who was pushed around at every turn, is only a sign of how you were trained to abandon yourself.

The distorted, incomplete views hurt but they were not the only voices. Fans rushed into my messages and comments, thousands of them thanking me for what I'd done, sharing disbelief and sadness that they wouldn't see me do it again in an England shirt. They celebrated my legacy, in football and in goalkeeping, and the inspiration they'd gained from the things I'd said, the victories I'd won and the battles I'd shared. They remembered the Euros and the World Cup, the speeches, the TikTok videos, the fun, the football, the saves that we'd all shared and celebrated together.

Public support came from my teammates, too – they knew more than most how it was to stand where I had.

When you're in the eye of a media storm, players' safest path is to stay out of controversy. They'd had plenty of unwanted practise dodging questions about the goalkeepers' situation in the preceding 12 months, and I had never wanted them to be drawn into it. In the regular press conferences that followed, as the media raked over the possible reasons behind my retirement, my teammates didn't deflect: they chose to comment.

Leah, as captain, told reporters: 'I'm devastated just because I love her. I love being her teammate. I think the way that she wears an England shirt is an example to us all . . . I'm very sad that those memories aren't going to continue in an England shirt, but for her, if she thinks this is the best thing, I'll always support her.'

Jess described what I'd done as 'really brave' and said: 'The way she helped raise the women's game is unbelievable.'

Others messaged publicly and privately too. I would never have asked for that and will forever be grateful that they stood by me.

I held tight to the words of those who knew and cared for me as I read through multiple character assassinations. I chose to stay quiet, knowing that to say more, then, would have been to detract from the team and the tournament to feed the dying throes of a beast that had roared too loud, too long. It was not the appropriate time for my truth, it would be selfish, so I let the media run its course knowing that one day I'd get to tell it.

I took myself off social media and hastily arranged a holiday, stopping in Chicago to visit Ella and Babett and my godsons, then to Aruba and Curaçao in the Caribbean. We spent two weeks away, the longest I'd ever had off in football and the first, instant rebalance I bought myself with my decision.

At first, I fizzed, day and night, preoccupied with the worry that staying quiet about my decision didn't measure up to my standards: being true to my unapologetic self.

I wanted to tell everyone who had asked me about it what had really motivated me. I wanted them to understand how I'd agonised and had conversations for months and months, and how I had hung on in there almost to the detriment of my self-esteem. I wanted them to know how hard I had tried, seeking clarity and asking questions and how I'd thought about the team non-stop and how I hoped that I'd cultivated my England legacy to a point where I could leave it behind.

But I couldn't sit there waiting for closure; if you are waiting for it, it is not closure you are looking for but a different ending, and that comes from someone else.

Closure comes from within.

Like peace, it is something you choose, not something you find.

Even with everything racing through my mind, there was not one part of me that didn't believe I'd made the right decision.

The only thing that stays the same is change; the Lionesses were moving on to a new chapter and I had to move on to mine. I had to spend my time being a good person, not wasting it trying to prove that I was.

I dampened the noise inside my mind as the sun sank into the horizon, painting the skies purple and pink.

TWENTY-SIX

BE THE BLUEPRINT

What leaves makes space for what is meant to stay; I had known that since I was a teenager choosing which of my many after-school activities to give up to allow me to follow the one thing I wanted to pursue the most.

I went into that summer processing the loss of a great love, a part of football that had kept me grounded and given me purpose, and moving on from something you love so much is hard to do. Now, though, it was time for me to reframe reality again and I packed my days with work, friends and spending time with the people I cared about the most.

Without the tournament, the closest people in my life depended on me for things they would otherwise have kept from me, fearful it would impact me at England: I was with Christina as she started cancer treatment and I went home to my family in Nottingham.

I also spent 14 days in paradise with Kitty. To be seen in

totality by another human being is truly special and that's what I have in her. The love we share has been fundamental in me being able to stand up for myself in all parts of my life, and to know that I have someone who fights for me, advocates for me and makes me a better person is to know all of me.

I was grateful to be somewhere so beautiful and made the most of having the luxury of travel days, when I had been used to trading off time zones and distance to allow myself as much rest and recovery as possible before I needed to hit the ground running again. Then I plunged head first into work, writing this book, fulfilling brand obligations and appearing on podcasts and TV. I attended the King's French state banquet at Windsor Castle, went to Wimbledon and Silverstone for the F1 and I did something for me, for my future, too.

As a footballer, the question of whether and when your body and the game will allow you to have children is one that demands thorough consideration, the answer usually a fine-tuned balance dictated by schedules, career milestones or choosing to abandon the idea entirely.

I have always wanted to be a mum. I knew players internationally who had timed their pregnancies and births between tournaments so they could be back for big moments, returning their bodies to peak athletic fitness, which I thought was an incredible feat for any woman who has already achieved the triumph of growing a baby and giving birth. When you've focused on keeping your body in goalkeeping condition your whole life, there is no way of knowing whether you would be able to achieve it until the time comes, so attempting it while still playing would always be a risk.

Around March, I'd had medical investigations for a

prolapsed disc in my back, which I'd been managing with pain medication and supplements for a while. During their explorations, doctors had found a cyst near my ovaries. After the Wembley game in April I'd been to see an expert in London.

'Would it affect IVF?' I asked, knowing that in a few years' time whenever I hung up my boots for good, not just internationally, that was the first thing I planned to do.

I had some extra scans that concluded it was nothing sinister but the conversation expanded and we began to discuss fertility options in more depth, including the possibility of freezing my eggs and creating embryos now while I was still in my early 30s so that I had an option to start my journey to motherhood when I was ready.

After retiring from England and as soon as I had the dates I was needed back in Paris for pre-season training, I messaged her again.

'I've got three weeks. Do you think I could fit in an egg-freezing cycle in that time?' I asked. She referred me to a fertility specialist who could do it that week and I booked in to start the process of hormone injections, four days later, to begin the preparations for a surgical egg retrieval procedure.

'See you on Friday,' I said and added 'egg freezing' to the list of things I could do with a summer.

Investing time in myself like this was brand new. I didn't know what it would look or feel like to navigate my time or play football without an international driver in the background, and working it out was part of the task I now had on my hands to reassess and redefine what was going to make me happy.

It was in equal measures liberating and frightening to change what I had known for so long.

I found that I craved routine and my club schedule, so getting back to Paris after seven weeks away couldn't come quick enough and I enthusiastically launched head first into the busiest pre-season schedule I'd ever experienced.

It didn't take long, though, for the emotion of not being at the tournament to hit.

I couldn't have predicted how I would feel, even though I'd spent a year thinking through all the facets of leaving. And it was strange: I knew I had made a decision that gave the team their chance of winning and gave me my best chance of happiness. I went out to Switzerland for the group stage game against Wales and I felt a lot of pride seeing them play and then win the tournament from afar.

But I was putting on a brave face publicly, and among those close to me too, to sidestep the difficult part of watching. The group stages were a joy, but the high-stakes, high-pressure knockout stages felt more tricky. I watched on with great pride but equally, of course, I thought about where my personality or experience or attributes as a player could have been a perfect fit too. I sat on the sofa and willed the girls to win like a every other fan; after all, that's what I was now. I much preferred playing to watching: it's nerve-wracking from the sofa.

Truth be told, it felt quite lonely. The whole experience made me question if what I'd achieved was that special after all. Had I robbed a living all this time?

The questions I asked myself and knew others would ask felt heavy and there were days where it didn't matter what people said, the question of whether my success had all been an illusion hung over me. The hurt and the circumstances that I needed to make sense of it all were far from simple.

ALL IN

You should never compare yourself with others and I try hard not to. It's true that comparison is the thief of joy but sometimes I find myself caught up.

I wondered why my journey in football had so often been paved with challenges while some had access to the quicker, more scenic route?

I put some of it down to being within a generation of women's football that was still making change and who bore the double-edged sword of creating space and leaving a legacy that I hoped would serve so many girls and young goalkeepers for years to come.

There was so much beauty in seeing my friends win the Euros, in seeing England lift another trophy, not least for the good that it could continue to create in the game and fulfilling the commitment we made to leave it in a better place. But, on the most personal level, there was an ugly truth to it as well: the end justified the means, and everything else that had passed would be of no consequence. Dwelling on the negatives, though, wasn't where peace would come from. To play victim serves no positive purpose. And difficulties for me had become stepping stones on which I'd learned to tread, they were something to use and not fear, to prepare you for what comes next.

The answer to the questions I was asking myself was that I had a difficult path precisely because I could carry it, because I could walk that way and carve out a future that looked different for others.

In football, as in anything else, everything was temporary. You spend your whole career at the mercy of other people's changing beliefs about you, and you accept that they have the right to change their mind at any time. You can never lose sight of the inevitable truth that when the tide turns it was never all within your control to start with. Football is magnificent and intoxicating but it is not life and death, as much as it can fool you into feeling it is when you play.

When success arrives, even when it looks like shelves full of trophies, you celebrate for five minutes and it feels amazing. Then the work starts all over again. You go back to doing what you've always done and the world keeps on spinning.

Nothing lasts forever.

The achievements can mean a place in the history books, though, and with it they can spark long-lasting change. That is what people remember: the resilience it took to get there. It is you who remembers the day-to-day.

And each morning now, as I drive through Paris on my way to the training ground, I see the opportunity in every day.

I listen to my playlist or to a podcast that's helping me learn French (because I always want to be better at it than I was yesterday) and I find beauty in the small things, a call with my grandma or my cup of coffee, and I'm grateful for them all.

Each day, I pass a junction where I can look across to the Eiffel Tower. As I travel home, on an afternoon without clouds in the sky, the view is clear and then, or when I go into the city at night and see it sparkle for the umpteenth time, I can't believe that football has taken me to such a beautiful city. It gives me a sense of purpose and gratitude for the lust for life, the energy, the health, positivity and thirst to keep learning that allows me to do what I love.

I'm here to tell you that I am far from finished. I still have years left in the game and I will play until my body gives up.

I will never win best keeper in the world again – I ruled myself out of those races when I ended my international career – but that is OK. I am grateful to have got to the top at all. That loud, gleaming version of success that the world can see is very satisfying; it is an antidote to delayed gratification but it is also a high and the chase can feel addictive. Without it, my obsession lies now, as it always has, in the process and I feel content, relishing the challenge of what the next season might bring, the role I can play and how I can help the team compete, seeing where it can take us and me.

I am proud that my achievements created new dreams for people to emulate and I will continue to use all that I do to push for and ask what more I can do for the game and how collectively we can make change to better women's football. How we can create a place for a new generation of goalkeepers and young girls to play and achieve on a global stage, so the spotlight never leaves them or their hard work again.

I hope I created a blueprint for how it can be done, committing wholeheartedly and pursuing with confidence what feels right, going all-in to grasp the opportunities that came when the world saw me for who I was and seizing the moments that followed.

Each time I use my voice I remind myself of how life has so often aligned with where I needed to be or given me the tools to place myself there. I think back to moving schools and moving clubs, to Wolfsburg and that match against Bayern, to the call-ups and the kitchen floor, the tournaments, the saves and the trophies. I think of the hard work, graft, resilience, self-discipline, consistency and authenticity that I relied on then and still do today. Often it doesn't happen in a straight line, you don't know in the moment what it is that's arranging itself around you but you have a hand in it all.

People have often spoken of football as a representation of life and I believe that to be the case. In both we have to remember what it is all for, for being happy and doing good, for telling our children or those who come next that you did something valuable with your time.

My journey didn't look how I imagined it would when I wrote those storybooks as a little girl. My story wasn't the kind you'd see in films or written in the stars. Sometimes the road felt lonely. Sometimes it was hard for people to understand my mentality and motivations.

At other times this game has lifted me higher than the moon, and I did things that no one had done before. Even with all the bumps and struggle, I wouldn't change any of it.

Everyone has a story and this one is mine – it's what made me who I am. The only way to live it is by not wasting a second. And being exactly who I was meant to be. My self.

TWENTY-SEVEN

A LETTER TO YOU

Thank you for reading my story.

To be unapologetic in who you are and relentless in your pursuit of a dream or vision of success takes courage and strength.

I told you that my story of reaching the top was about much more than just one save. And I hope that the honesty and fearlessness with which I have shared my account of all that came before and after has given you insight into the principles of personality and performance by which I live my life.

It brings me joy and gratitude to imagine that the lessons that I have learned through my journey can influence and help you in yours too.

To goalkeepers, young footballers and fans of the game. The women's game has been on a tremendous journey since it was banned by the FA at the height of its popularity the first time, around a century ago. The battles for parity, visibility and investment continue, and to represent my country in a resurgent era of Lionesses who have been able not only to win but to use success to fight those battles has been my greatest privilege. More than anything, it fills me with immense pride to have played a part in putting goalkeeping in the game on a global footing, to have helped change attitudes and culture, raise standards and pave the way for the next generation of goalkeepers coming through, knowing that they will now benefit from opportunities that I wanted to smash the door down for. I would rather put my body and myself on the line than let a shot at anything pass me by. My work is not done and my hope is that anyone who chooses to follow will join me and continue in the same vein, sharing in my legacy for good.

To women. Too often the world still believes we are not meant to have confidence, we are not meant to pursue things with the audacity, relentlessness or ruthlessness of men.

There are arenas and workplaces that still expect women to be fragile, apparently too emotional to lead or too apologetic to state that they want to be or that they are the best at what they do, while offering commendations and platitudes to men when they do the same.

I never wanted to be pushed into that box. I only ever wanted to be free, even when parts of me spilled over that others didn't know what to do with or like. That unnerves people. I am not without insecurities; I have many, but I have fierce self-belief too. Every woman and anyone who has experienced life on the margins should feel free to have the same. Remember that you are the standard you accept –

imposter syndrome is an illusion. Your pursuit is yours alone, so reach out and grab it with both hands.

To those in pursuit of success, of any kind. I only ever gave myself one option: to make it. Success, the way I have experienced it, is not for the weak but the uncharted path brings the greatest rewards. I was single-minded in my ambition – to play to my high potential and become the world number one. People move jobs for money or status but, in mine, I only ever followed opportunities to play to that end, chasing my own betterment across countries over financial stability and comfort.

They say the price of progress is pain and elite performance has many lessons to share. I benefitted from a team but I also experienced singularity – my position was the first thing to see to that. The loneliness made the road harder but it made the personal success sweeter, too, because of what I'd overcome to achieve it.

Not everyone will share your standards and not everything will serve you; knowing where the conditions you need to thrive do or do not exist and being OK with walking away or needing to change your environment is a strength.

Remember those who helped to put you there, consider those who will follow you and know that you have no obligation to those who gave you a hard time when you were already facing a battle.

Never let complacency in – that is the moment you cease to improve. The fear of being average, not maxing out on everything I have, still terrifies me.

And when your pursuit feels in vain or you have to make choices you don't want but need, remember that self-discipline is your greatest form of self-love. Not taking any risks is the biggest risk of all and through your hard graft, the work will reveal itself.

Finally, to those who have been in a dark place, know that there is always light and know, too, that you are not alone.

Everything you ever wanted is on the other side of fear.

You can wait a long time for 'a win' but the little wins are there all along. Don't miss them – your next one is just around the corner.

The difficulties and fears that you encounter are more universal than you can sometimes see. Hard work doesn't always pay off the way you believe it will but it pays off eventually, sometimes in ways you didn't expect or imagine, maybe even for the better, because everything you thought was drowning you was, in fact, teaching you how to swim. Not everyone will always like you but that is OK: you can be the juiciest peach in the whole world but some people just don't like peaches. Don't count yourself out or allow other people's opinions to limit you. None of it means you are not worthy and cannot reach your dreams.

For almost 30 years my work often went unrewarded, but I arrived somewhere pretty great in the end.

If one person can read this story and know that I achieved my career highs after sitting in my darkest place, then I hope you can see the change that is waiting for you and that the best is yet to come. Don't stop, don't give in, don't let the darkness fool you. Without rain, there are no rainbows.

One of the things I love most about goalkeeping is that we all do it differently, just as we all approach life differently.

It can feel easy at times to lose yourself or become a version of you that other people want or need you to be. My plea to you is: never abandon yourself. Believing in yourself doesn't have to be loud, it exists in the quietness of your discipline and your consistent actions, but whichever you choose, believe in you more than anyone else ever will.

Do not change the things that you know will get you to where you want to be.

My saves, my mentality, my passion, the composure – they had lived inside me all along, I just had to wait for the world to see them, for my work to be seen, to matter.

Repetition, consistency. Consistency in performance, consistency in character: rely on them even when it is tough because together, they breed freedom.

Do not compromise your authenticity, speak your truth, even when your voice shakes, stand up for what's right, even if you have to stand alone.

Sometimes you will have 100 per cent in the tank, sometimes it will be 10 per cent; the volume doesn't matter, only that you can look yourself in the mirror and know that you gave all that you have.

Be unafraid of the hard work that allows you to learn exactly who you are. When I understood that, everything else fell into place; it became my greatest strength and my greatest tool for unlocking success.

There's only one of you in the world, and that's more than good enough.

Be unapologetically yourself,

Mary Earps
MAE 27

ACKNOWLEDGEMENTS

Every relationship in my story has helped to shape who I have become, some above all deserve my endless thanks.

To Kitty, my ride or die. For advocating for me and being on my side, for telling me the most unadulterated truths and showing me the deepest version of love. Words are not enough. I am grateful everyday that we share the same lifetime in this universe.

To Mum and Dad, for the love that you have given me, for my childhood and for the sacrifices that you made. I would never have had a shot at making it without you and I will always be grateful for what you have done for me. To Joel and Annabelle, you have been in my corner since day one and I will always be in yours. Thank you for understanding and accepting my dream and for every family dinner time that was dominated by my football.

To Grandma, my best friend, for your love and for all of

our conversations over tea and biscuits or FaceTime, you're the very best.

Lewis, my oldest friend, I treasure how our conversations go beyond the surface. Thank you for your patience, for seeing things before I did and for being there and understanding me in every chapter of my story.

Christina, you are a constant source of inspiration, love and light, even at the darkest times and your friendship means the world to me.

Willco, for believing in the human before the player and for your unending and generous commitment to nurturing me as a goalkeeper. Thank you for being my coach and also my friend, for knowing when to kick me up the arse and when to give me a cuddle.

To Babs, for a friendship that defies language and culture, thank you for your candour in football and in life. And to Ella and the boys, Zykane and Tayo, my family across The Pond, you'll always have my love and support.

Tina, you understand me. You saw the vision before anyone else and you helped to make it a reality. You get my delusion, my business brain, you advocate for me and you brought out my creative side. We're bad for each other and we're brilliant for each other and I wouldn't have it any other way. I'm grateful for everything you do and for your friendship.

To my teammates, past and present. Playing this beautiful game is my absolute joy. Growing up and feeling alone or different, playing in goal, I never thought I would feel the deep connections that I did playing alongside you in football. You taught me the power of friendship and of teamwork. You accepted me and showed me how beautiful it is to be part of a team. I saw some of you more than I saw my own family and, along with the coaches and staff who believed in me and supported me, we have memories to last a lifetime. You have each been part of my journey and taught me so much about myself as a player and a person. I will forever be grateful to have shared the pitch with such talented women who are game-changers in their own right. Thank you for all of it. And thank you to all the players who went before us, whose sacrifices and work paved the way.

For the creation of this book. To Deborah Linton, for allowing me to speak my truth and putting my story into words. You have matched my energy, worked tirelessly and cared about my story as if it were your own and I'm grateful for your time, patience and effort to go All In and make this book as open as it could be.

To Kate Evans at Peters Fraser and Dunlop, to Madeleine Penfold for your beautiful photography, and to Carole Tonkinson and all of the team at LEAP and Bonnier Books UK – Lucy Tirahan, Natalia Cacciatore, Holly Milnes, Lucy Richardson, Beth Whitelaw, Florence Philip, Alice Dovey, Charlotte Brown, Emily Peyton – thank you for all of the work that you put into bringing this book to life.